Contents

Entrepreneur
MAGAZINE'S

ULTIMATE
GUIDE TO

YouTube
FOR BUSINESS
Second Edition

- Spotlight your business with low-cost, high-impact videos
- Master the art of storyselling to **more than a billion active users**
- Learn the monetizing secrets of today's successful YouTubers

Entrepreneur
PRESS

JASON R. RICH

Entrepreneur Press, Publisher
Cover Design: Andrew Welyczko
Production and Composition: Eliot House Productions

This publication is designed to provide accurate and authoritative information in regard to the
subject matter covered. It is sold with the understanding that the publisher is not engaged in
rendering legal, accounting or other professional services. If legal advice or other expert assistance is
required, the services of a competent professional person should be sought.

Library of Congress Cataloging-in-Publication Data
  Names: Rich, Jason, author.
  Title: Ultimate guide to YouTube for business / by Jason R. Rich.
  Description: Second Edition. | Irvine, Calif. : Entrepreneur Media, Inc., [2018] |
      Series: Entrepreneur Magazine's ultimate | Revised edition of the author's
      Ultimate guide to YouTube for business, [2013]
  Identifiers: LCCN 2017052344| ISBN 978-1-59918-619-1 (alk. paper) | ISBN 1-59918-619-5 (alk.
      paper)
  Subjects: LCSH: Internet marketing. | Webcasting. | YouTube (Firm)
  Classification: LCC HF5415.1265 .R518 2018 | DDC 658.8/72—dc23
  LC record available at https://lccn.loc.gov/2017052344

Printed in the United States of America

22 21 20 19 18   10 9 8 7 6 5 4 3 2 1

On YouTube, You or Your Business Is the Star

Are you an entrepreneur launching a new business and need to build product awareness among a highly targeted audience using limited resources? Perhaps you're a small-business operator looking for creative ways to grow your business, find and reach new customers or clients, retain your existing customers, and keep costs down, but at the same time discover innovative ways to outmaneuver your competition—all on a tight budget. Well, you're not alone!

In today's business world, traditional advertising and many real-world marketing and promotional strategies no longer work because the shopping and media consumption habits of consumers have changed. More and more consumers are researching what they want or need using the internet and then shopping online to find the lowest prices. Plus, beyond just using desktop computers, consumers are relying on their internet-connected mobile devices and smart television sets when doing their shopping-related activities, even if they're still making some purchases from local retail stores.

As a business operator, you've probably already discovered that the internet can be a powerful and cost-effective sales, marketing, advertising, and promotional tool, and that online social networking services, such as Facebook, Twitter, Instagram, LinkedIn, Snapchat, Yelp!, Pinterest, and

WHO WATCHES ON-DEMAND STREAMING VIDEOS VIA YOUTUBE?

As of mid-2017, YouTube had more than 1.3 billion active users (which is equivalent to about one-third of all internet users). With the media habits of consumers changing so rapidly, when it comes to reaching the core 18- to 34- and 18- to 49-year-old consumer groups, YouTube reaches more of these important demographics than any cable television network in the United States.

However, as a YouTube channel operator and content creator, you can also reach a global audience. YouTube operates local versions of its service in 88 countries, and users can navigate the service in more than 76 different languages in order to watch the video content they want, when and where they want to watch it.

YouTube is owned and operated by Google, which is the world's most popular internet search engine. When it comes to consumers finding information they want online, YouTube has become the world's second most popular search engine. When you publish a video on YouTube, not only can you attract viewers who are looking for content like what you're offering, but a search result for each of your videos will also be added to Google (often within minutes of the video being published online), which can improve your company's overall search engine optimization (SEO) and help you drive traffic and highly targeted customers to your company's website and/or YouTube channel.

many others, allow you to easily and informally reach existing and potential customers using text, photos, and other multimedia-based content.

In fact, to be competitive, your business must have an online presence. This means having a company website, as well as a Facebook page and Twitter account, for example. However, there's yet another resource you can inexpensively use. It's called YouTube, and it's the world's leading on-demand, streaming video service.

Virtually anyone with a high-definition video camera, webcam, smartphone, or tablet, for example, can easily record, edit, and publish videos online—about any topic whatsoever—then share them with the world, or in this case, with the target or niche audience for your company's products or services.

Millions of small businesses, entrepreneurs, and organizations have discovered innovative ways to create original YouTube video-based content as a low-cost tool for building their brand, reputation, and image. It's a way to attract new customers, share information, showcase products and services, compare your products with your competition's, offer video-based tutorials about how to assemble or use your products, and share testimonials.

YouTube can also be used as a highly targeted but low-cost advertising vehicle that allows you to reach potential customers at the exact time they're looking for information about what your company offers. Plus, if you don't want to invest the time and expense to produce your own videos, you can pay for product placements in the videos produced by high-profile YouTubers (online personalities), some of whom have millions of dedicated subscribers to their YouTube channels. You can also arrange to have your product(s) reviewed by influential YouTubers who target the same niche audience as your business.

The Ultimate Guide to YouTube for Business, Second Edition, will introduce you to just some of the ways small businesses are using YouTube as a business tool. You'll soon discover proven strategies that can help you promote your company, brand, products, or services, using high-definition video, without spending a fortune. You'll learn the best approaches to planning, creating, editing, promoting, and sharing your videos with the public, as well as how to leverage YouTube's tools to help achieve your objectives.

This book also explores ways to identify your target audience and keep them top-of-mind as you create your video content, then populate what will become your company's branded YouTube channel. You'll learn how to incorporate YouTube with your overall virtual and real-world marketing efforts so your YouTube content can complement and enhance what you may already be doing with a website, blog, electronically distributed newsletter, Facebook page, or other business-related social media presence, for example.

As you'll discover, there are a handful of steps related to creating and producing the best possible video content that's targeted to your audience. From this book, you'll learn about the most important pre-production, production, post-production, and promotional tasks required to create successful YouTube videos, then learn how to use free online-based tools to help you measure and track the reach and traction your videos have when it comes to people viewing your content. For example, you'll discover easy ways to enhance each viewer's quality of engagement as they watch your YouTube content.

Since YouTube has become the virtual home to countless high-profile YouTubers, many of whom have built audiences that reach into the millions, this book will also explore how your business can work with appropriate online personalities to help you promote your products in a highly targeted and cost-effective way using paid product placement and by getting highly influential YouTubers to review or endorse your product(s) within their videos.

LIKE EVERYTHING ON THE WEB, YOUTUBE IS EVOLVING

In addition to becoming the world's most popular destination for computer and mobile device users to select and watch free, unlimited, on-demand streaming video content created by individuals and companies, YouTube offers other video-based services. For example, any company or individual can broadcast live on YouTube, as opposed to pre-recording and publishing videos. The focus of Chapter 16, "Go Live with Your Broadcasts," discusses how and why a small business can use live broadcasts to communicate with a targeted audience.

YouTube is also expanding the original programming and content it offers through services like YouTube Red, which is a subscription-based (paid) platform for watching premium video content and programming produced by YouTube and its partners. In 2017, YouTube also began streaming live and on-demand television programming (from popular television networks), as well as movies from top Hollywood studios and other premium content providers through a separate service, called YouTube TV.

As YouTube evolves as a service, the video-watching habits of viewers are also changing, which as a result, is creating new opportunities for small businesses to reach highly targeted or niche audiences in cost-effective ways.

Plus, you'll also learn from the experiences of successful YouTube and online marketing experts who share their advice in exclusive interviews that can be found throughout this book. You'll soon discover that YouTube has dramatically changed how people worldwide, and from all walks of life, experience on-demand video content. Now, you can begin tapping this vast and ever-expanding audience to grow your business, even if you are not technologically savvy.

Don't worry; it's not too late to jump on the YouTube bandwagon. Even if you're on a shoestring budget, you can quickly begin using YouTube without expensive video production equipment or Hollywood cinematography skills. Beyond what this book offers, all you'll need to be successful is creativity and a strong understanding of your target audience.

Keep in mind, while you can use low-end video production equipment (or even a smartphone) to create, edit, and publish YouTube content on a tight budget, the actual videos you publish on what will become your company's branded YouTube channel all need to be well-written and shot so the content is crystal-clear when viewed on each viewer's screen. Your videos should also showcase excellent lighting and high-quality sound so the content can be clearly seen and heard on any computer or mobile device the viewer is using to access YouTube. In other words, what you publish online can't look or sound amateurish, and it must appeal to, and attract the attention of, your target audience while meeting or exceeding their expectations.

Before you start planning your videos and making plans to create and populate a YouTube channel for your business, let's take a closer look at what YouTube is and focus more closely on some of the ways small businesses, entrepreneurs, and organizations working in virtually any industry are already using YouTube. That's the focus of Chapter 1, "Using YouTube as a Promotional and Marketing Tool."

Using YouTube as a Promotional and Marketing Tool

IN THIS CHAPTER

- An introduction to YouTube and how businesses can leverage it
- Developing a YouTube strategy and integrating it into your overall online marketing strategy
- Identifying your audience and its needs
- Developing realistic expectations and goals
- What you need to get started

To be competitive, it's virtually mandatory for a business in almost any industry to tap the power of the internet and online social media. YouTube, the popular video-streaming service and world's second most frequently used search engine, can and should be a powerful part of your overall marketing and promotional strategy. It can be accessed from almost any computer or internet-enabled device, from almost anywhere, 24 hours per day, seven days per week, 365 days per year. YouTube launched in April 2005 and has since become the third most visited website in the world.

As of mid-2017, more than 300 hours of video are uploaded to YouTube every minute of every day, and almost 5 billion videos are watched by YouTube's more than 30 million daily visitors. During a typical month, this translates to more than 3.25 billion hours worth of video content being viewed. More than 1 billion video views per day (about half of all YouTube video views) are conducted using an internet-connected smartphone or tablet. Based on this last statistic alone, as a content producer, this means your videos need to cater to the smaller sized mobile devices. For example, if you're using text-based titles and captions within your videos, you must ensure that the size, color, and font selection for the text is easily readable, even when viewed on a smartphone-sized screen.

Approximately 38 percent of YouTube's users are female, while 62 percent are male. When broken down by age, 11 percent of viewers are between the ages of 18 and 24, 23 percent between the ages of 25 and 34, 26 percent between 34 and 44, 16 percent between 45 and 54, 8 percent between 50 and 64, 3 percent age 65 and older, and the age is not known for about 13 percent of viewers.

Based on research conducted from 2015 by MWP (My Web Presenters, https://mwpdigitalmedia.com/blog/10-statistics-that-show-video-is-the-future-of-marketing), among business executives who are given the choice to read a text-based article about a topic online or watch a video about the same topic, 59 percent would opt to watch the video. In addition, 54 percent of senior executives repeatedly share work-related videos with colleagues on a weekly basis.

Meanwhile, according to a 2016 survey conducted by Think with Google (www.thinkwithgoogle.com/consumer-insights/video-trends-where-audience-watching), almost 50 percent of all internet users look for videos related to a major product or service purchase before visiting a store to do their shopping. Research published in 2015 by Animoto (https://animoto.com/blog/business/video-marketing-cheat-sheet-infographic) reported that four out of five consumers believe that demo videos are helpful and that online shoppers who opt to view a product- or service-related demo video are much more likely to make a purchase. Based on these statistics alone, hopefully a lightbulb has switched on in your head, and you're already thinking about ways your business can incorporate demo videos of your products and services into your online-based sales, marketing, and promotional activities.

As you're about to discover, businesses use YouTube in a myriad of ways, including simply buying ads—from text-based and display ads that link to websites, to video messages that resemble 10-, 15-, 30-, and 60-second TV commercials. In many instances, paid advertising on YouTube is one of the most affordable and effective advertising options available on the internet.

Many businesses also produce and publish their own YouTube videos as part of their overall online marketing and promotional strategy, either by hiring a video production company or doing it themselves.

As a YouTube content creator, your business will need to create and maintain its own branded YouTube channel, which can give you the opportunity to share in advertising revenue that's generated when optional ads are shown in conjunction with your original video content on your YouTube channel. In fact, many people have actually developed a highly lucrative career producing original videos for YouTube, which then generate revenue by attracting large audiences. These people are often referred to as "online personalities" or "YouTubers." When it comes to producing YouTube content, take an extremely creative approach in order to set yourself apart from your competition, capture your target audience's attention, and build their loyalty. Using original video to do this is the focus of the *Ultimate Guide to YouTube for Business, 2nd Edition*.

FIRST, LET'S GET ACQUAINTED WITH YOUTUBE

YouTube's launch in early 2005 changed forever how people use the internet. YouTube allows everyday people, entertainers, business operators, and entrepreneurs—from all walks of life—to produce, upload, and share original videos, for free, and build a potentially global audience for them. YouTube can also be used effectively to target a regional audience, or attract a highly target (niche) audience, based on demographic criteria you define.

Thanks to advancements in high-definition (HD) camera technologies that have occurred over the past few years, today anyone with even the most basic video camera can participate as a content producer. YouTube makes it extremely easy for non-technologically savvy web surfers to use their computer (or most other internet-enabled devices) to quickly find and watch videos.

When you visit YouTube (www.youtube.com) or use the official YouTube app on your smartphone, tablet, or smart TV (or related video-streaming device, such as an Apple TV, Amazon Fire TV, or Google Chromecast device that connects to a television set), you'll discover content that's as diverse as the people who create it. Virtually every topic imaginable is covered. When people want to find information on the web, they often use YouTube's search feature, as opposed to a search engine, such as Yahoo! or Google, to find what they're looking for.

MAKING YOUTUBE WORK FOR YOUR BUSINESS

As a small-business operator, you have vast opportunities with YouTube, limited only by your ingenuity, creativity, the time you invest, and to a much lesser extent, your video production and promotional budget. Later in this book, we'll explore just some of the ways small-business operators are using YouTube as a cost-effective sales, marketing, promotions, and advertising tool. Just about any entrepreneur or business can benefit from using YouTube as a cost-effective way to entertain, inform, educate, or rally your audience/customers (or potential customers) to action. To use this online-based marketing and promotional tool to its utmost potential, however, you need to determine:

- What YouTube is capable of and how it can be used
- Your core message and how YouTube videos can be used with your other online marketing and promotional efforts
- Your target audience and what it's interested in
- The best ways to use video to present your core message

Once you have discovered what the YouTube video-streaming platform offers, the next decisions involve determining how you'll use this resource for your business. For example, you can opt to produce and publish your own content on your company's branded YouTube channel. You can use paid advertising on YouTube to drive traffic to your website, or you can use paid product placements, for example, to get well-established YouTubers (with audiences in the millions) to talk about and showcase your products or services within their videos. All these options and others will be discussed throughout this book.

Exploring YouTube

Before you begin developing, shooting, editing, and uploading videos, start by establishing a YouTube account for yourself or your business—it's free. At the same time, you should also begin exploring the service and seeing firsthand what's possible.

When you begin exploring YouTube, seek out videos that are of interest to you and relate to your business or industry. Beyond just watching free videos, invest the time to become an active part of the YouTube community by "liking" videos, posting comments, and sharing videos with your online friends. Find videos already available on YouTube that cater to your target audience, then consider ways you can create content that will further benefit your audience (your potential or existing customers).

All the videos published on YouTube are easily searchable using keywords and search phrases. You can also seek out videos by category, the channel on which they're offered, and by using the popularity charts and "trending topics" that are continuously updated and published on YouTube. It's also possible to link your Facebook and other social media accounts to your YouTube account, as well as discover what your online friends are watching on YouTube.

As you begin to consider who your target audience will be for your YouTube videos, consider that more than 50 percent of the people who access YouTube to watch videos now do it from some type of wireless mobile device. So when you start producing and sharing your own videos, avoid production elements (such as a lot of text) that will be hard to read on a small screen. Download the official YouTube app for your tablet and smartphone to experience small-screen viewing.

Then, when you're ready, follow the directions offered within Chapter 5, "How to Start Your Own YouTube Channel," in order to establish a YouTube channel for you or your business. This is the online-based forum you'll use to upload, showcase, and share your own video productions via YouTube.

DEVELOPING YOUR STRATEGY

If you're an entrepreneur or business operator, as you explore the YouTube service and check out how your competition is already tapping the power and capabilities of this service, you'll discover it's possible to create, produce, and publish videos that can help to:

- Boost your company's brand awareness and enhance its credibility
- Introduce details about a new product or service
- Advertise an existing product or service
- Share details about your company and what it offers with a local, regional, national, or international audience
- Generate new leads for your sales team
- Teach potential customers about the benefits of your product(s) or service(s), and explain how to best use them through demonstrations, thus helping to remove buyer objections
- Share customer endorsements or testimonials from existing customers with potential customers
- Compare your product/service with what the competition offers
- Tell your company's story—its history, philosophy, and goals
- Provide support for real-world or online-based retail promotions or contests
- Broadcast and stream an event live over YouTube, or share recorded highlights of an event with customers/clients or others who couldn't attend in person
- Increase direct sales for whatever your business sells. Someone could watch a video, click on an embedded link, and then place an order from your company's website, or call a toll-free order line, for example
- Expand and enhance your company's product or customer support
- Use a live broadcast so viewers can experience an event in real-time (such as a press conference or product launch), without being there in person
- Enhance your company's internal employee training

As you consider how other businesses like your own are already using YouTube, consider some of the ways you can begin using this service to share original video content with your audience. Remember, you'll want to study what's already offered on YouTube carefully, pinpoint a niche, and then figure out who your target audience will be. Only then can you begin writing, producing, and publishing videos that have the potential to gain the popularity you'll need to generate the online audience you desire.

Develop Your Core Message

With a specific goal or set of goals in mind, the next step is to draft a core message that you want to consistently convey through your videos to your audience. This message should be consistent with the existing marketing and advertising messages you've already developed for other forms of media.

The message you develop should be carefully crafted for your audience and be short, memorable, and easily understandable. Once you have brainstormed your core message and the goal(s) for your YouTube online presence, start thinking about all the ways you can present that message via your YouTube videos, again focusing on originality, memorability, and consistency. Depending on the approach you take with your videos, you'll want to keep them short (between one and six minutes in length) and stay on-point with your messaging. YouTube viewers have very short attention spans, so it's important to capture someone's attention quickly and expect to hold it only for a short period of time.

Determine how you want your audience to react as they watch your video(s) or after watching them. For example, do you want viewers to visit your company's website and place an order, or do you want them to share your message with their own online friends? Perhaps you want your viewers to "like" the video by clicking on the thumbs-up icon or leave a public comment about the video. Think about how you'll rally your viewers to do whatever it is you'd like them to do. This will be your *call to action*.

Always remember, however, that your videos should help convey your core message, be synergistic with your company's other online activity, and be aimed at achieving your overall goals or objectives.

MAKING YOUTUBE A PART OF YOUR ONLINE MARKETING STRATEGY

When it comes to your online activity as a business operator or entrepreneur, everything you do in cyberspace should be synergistic, be focused on the same core message, and fully integrated. In other words, use your company's Facebook page and Twitter feed, for example, to promote your YouTube videos, while using your YouTube videos to drive traffic to your website, blog, Facebook page, and/or Twitter feed. At the same time, your videos should drive home your core message and call to action.

How you approach this online synergy can be blatant and in your face, or you can take an extremely subtle approach, based on your audience makeup and overall objectives. We'll explore this concept in greater detail within Chapter 14, "Promoting Your YouTube Videos."

For now, however, as you learn more about what's possible using YouTube, consider what you're already doing in cyberspace and in the real world, and also figure out what you could be doing using services like Facebook, Twitter, Instagram, LinkedIn, Google+, Pinterest, Snapchat, and others, in conjunction with what you plan to do on YouTube. Think synergy!

Synergy also refers to how you communicate your message. Fonts, color schemes, specific wording, music, sound effects, logos, the use of slogans, and other elements that appear within your YouTube videos should all be consistent with what your audience will see on your website, within your blog, on your Facebook page, by reading your Twitter feed, and as they explore your online presence on other social networking platforms.

Figure Out What You'll Need to Get Started

Based on your objectives, it's possible to begin producing quality YouTube videos on a tight budget, then, over time, upgrade your equipment and tools to achieve more professional-quality production results. However, step one is to create a YouTube Channel for your company, customize the look of the channel's page (which is referred to as branding your YouTube channel), then populate the channel with original video content. It all starts by visiting www.YouTube.com, clicking on the "Sign In" button, then clicking on the "Create an Account" button.

In later chapters, you'll learn how to pinpoint some of the key video production equipment you'll need, which will include a video camera that's capable of shooting HD resolution video. You'll also need to contend with lighting and sound quality considerations to ensure good enough production quality that will satisfy your audience's expectations and maintain the professional image of your company.

What you'll need to consider during the pre-production (brainstorming and preparation), production (filming), and post-production (editing) phases of the process will all be covered in Chapter 8, "Filming YouTube Videos." Once again, the key to success during each of these phases is to stay on message as you cater to the wants, needs, and expectations of your audience, while also staying within your budgetary limitations.

Specialized Skills That May Be Required

As you read each chapter of *Ultimate Guide to YouTube for Business, 2nd Edition*, the focus will be on one or more aspects relating to the pre-production, production, post-production, publishing, and promotional phases of creating YouTube videos (or otherwise using YouTube as a powerful and highly targeted marketing, sales, and promotional tool). While you'll no doubt face many challenges as you embark on this project, you also have the opportunity to be creative and have fun as you discover cutting-edge and innovative ways of growing and/or promoting your business.

Like so many things, producing semi-professional or professional-quality videos requires that you learn a handful of skills, all of which will ultimately be used together during the pre-production, production, post-production, and publishing phases. For starters, you'll need to become proficient at brainstorming unique ideas for videos, then figuring out how you'll take your raw ideas and transform them into video productions that achieve your goals. To do this, you'll need to master skills such as:

- Storyboarding and scripting (writing the scripts) for your productions
- Video camera operation
- Set design or location scouting
- Lighting
- Sound recording and mixing
- Managing a "cast" (people who will appear in your videos) and crew (people who will help shoot and edit your videos)
- Dealing with hair, makeup, and wardrobe considerations for your cast, if applicable
- Video editing
- Managing production resources and budgets
- Creating and incorporating special effects and titles into your videos
- Incorporating music and sound effects in your videos during post-production
- Using YouTube's tools for uploading and publishing your videos, then managing your YouTube channel
- Promoting your videos in the real world and cyberspace to build an audience for your videos
- Interacting with your audience on an ongoing basis

At least initially, you probably won't have all of the skills, knowledge, and experience needed to juggle all the responsibilities that will be required of you as a YouTube content producer. Thus, you have several options. First, seek out friends, co-workers, employees, or relatives who might be able to contribute to your productions and lend their expertise. Another option is to hire freelance professionals to help you.

Professional writers, camera operators, production crew, hair stylists, makeup artists, lighting experts, sound engineers, musicians, animators, illustrators, video editors, and people who are experts when it comes to using online social networking sites for marketing and promotional purposes, for example, can all be hired on a freelance, per-hour, or per-project basis.

Use a service like UpWork (www.upwork.com) to help you find people with the experience and skill set you need to round out your production crew. If you need specialized on-camera or voice-over talent for your productions, contact local talent or modeling agencies, or hold an open casting call by publishing an audition notice on social media or a show-business-related website that caters to your geographic area.

The following are a few popular websites for posting show-business-related casting notices:

- *Backstage:* www.backstage.com/casting
- *Model Mayham:* www.modelmayhem.com/casting/search_casting
- *Production Hub:* www.productionhub.com/casting-notices
- *SAG-AFTRA:* www.sagaftra.org/casting-notices

Another excellent and low-cost (sometimes free) resource when it comes to putting together a video production crew that has specialized skills is to seek out college interns from a local college or university. College students who are majoring in video production, writing, video editing, computer animation, lighting, sound engineering, fashion, cosmetology, or marketing, for example, will jump at the opportunity to intern for your company and get real-world, hands-on experience working on a project that they can later showcase on a resume, within a portfolio, or as part of a demo reel.

What's great about using college interns with specialized majors is that they're typically very familiar with the latest trends, technologies, and tools for producing semi-professional or professional-quality videos, and they're willing to work for little or no money. To find college interns, contact the career counselor or internship coordinator at a local college or university to discuss your needs. With permission, you can also post "help wanted" fliers on bulletin boards on college campuses, or publish internship opportunities online (on Monster, http://hiring.monster.com, for example).

To achieve the best results from the start, don't try to cut corners and just "wing it" when it comes to producing your videos, especially if your productions will represent your company and/or its products/services and will have the ability to enhance or tarnish your company's overall image and reputation. Instead, gather a production crew that together has the skills, knowledge, experience, and creative talent you and your company will need to achieve your overall objectives.

DEFINING YOUR GOALS FOR YOUTUBE

After you've spent at least a few hours exploring YouTube firsthand and seeing the different ways content producers create videos designed to appeal to their respective audiences, start defining what your own goals will be for using YouTube. Chapter 2, "Defining Your Goals for YouTube," further explores ways your business can use this popular video-streaming platform and help you devise appropriate ways to use it in order to share content with your audience.

One thing you should understand from the start is that for a small- to medium-sized business, one of the biggest keys to success when using YouTube is to create and promote content for a highly targeted (niche) audience. This should be the same audience you've identified as being your target customer base. If you attempt to create videos that will appeal to everyone on a global scale, with the goal of each video going viral and being seen by millions of people, chances are you'll fail and wind up wasting a lot of time, money, and resources. You could also tarnish the reputation of your company.

A video on YouTube does not have to go viral for it to be successful. The best way to leverage YouTube as a powerful sales, marketing, advertising, and promotional tool is to first identify your target audience, then cater to that audience. Defining your audience is the focus of Chapter 3, "Identifying and Catering to Your Audience."

Chapter 2

Defining Your Goals for YouTube

IN THIS CHAPTER

- Developing realistic goals and expectations
- Learning from popular videos
- What it costs to get started
- 12 ways businesses use YouTube

Yes, publishing videos on YouTube is free, but it will require a financial investment to produce them, whether you do it yourself or hire someone else to do it. And even if you produce an absolutely amazing video that's worthy of an Academy Award, simply putting it on YouTube won't guarantee you an audience. If all you do is publish your videos on YouTube, then let them sit there, nobody is going to see your productions. You need to heavily promote them.

Keep in mind, having your video go viral and be seen by millions of people would be nice, but to realistically achieve your company's online goals, this probably isn't necessary. Instead, if you carefully target your videos to a niche audience—your potential or current customers—you can achieve the desired results even if your videos receive just a few hundred or a few thousand views.

With more than 2.9 billion views since July 15, 2012, the official "Gangnam Style" music video by Psy is an example of a video that's gone truly viral—with no paid advertising support. It's an example of a quirky and original video that has captured the attention of a grass-roots audience. For a video to ultimately go viral, it must begin to get traction online via word-of-mouth, then somehow pique the interest of major traditional media outlets so it gets mainstream attention. This attention then drives more traffic to the video, fueling its popularity until it ultimately skyrockets.

If you have visions of producing videos that go viral or at least attract vast audiences, this will require you to make a significant time and financial investment to promote your videos and your YouTube channel on an ongoing basis, after the videos are produced and published online. What you'll soon discover is that videos that have gone viral are often a result of an accident, pure luck, or a fluke, not careful planning. In fact, large companies have tried investing hundreds of thousands, or even millions, of dollars trying to force their videos to go viral, but these efforts typically fail miserably.

Realistically, for videos produced and published by mainstream companies, the popularity of these videos is typically driven by extensive promotional efforts by the company, using both online and real-world resources. With this in mind, it's important to develop very realistic expectations. Whatever time, money, and resources you invest in the production of your videos, this is only the beginning.

To gain viewers for your videos and generate a consistently growing audience, you will need to invest time, effort, and potentially money to promote your productions and your YouTube channel on an ongoing basis. Only if you achieve your objectives within the content of the videos themselves, then promote them properly and consistently to the right target audience will you achieve your overall goals related to using YouTube for yourself, your company, and/or its products or services.

This chapter offers a general overview of ways your business or organization can use YouTube as a sales, marketing, and/or promotional tool. One important concept to understand from the start is that there are millions of videos already posted on YouTube, with many more being added every day. Making your video(s) stand out and get attention will probably be the biggest challenge.

Just because you post a video on YouTube does not guarantee it will quickly go viral and be seen by millions of viewers. It's important to have realistic expectations, but know that there is a wide range of things you can do, either for free or inexpensively, to promote your videos and build an audience for them. You'll learn about several of these techniques within Chapter 13, "Interacting with Viewers and Subscribers"; Chapter 14, "Promoting Your YouTube Videos"; and Chapter 15, "Using Social Media to Build and Interact with Your Audience."

While some YouTubers (online personalities) have established a large audience on YouTube and are able to generate a respectable and ongoing income as a YouTube

Partner—by displaying other company's ads in conjunction with their videos—many traditional businesses, entrepreneurs, and online business operators, for example, have discovered other ways to use YouTube as a powerful and low-cost marketing, advertising, sales, and promotional tool that can generate new customers and sales in other direct and indirect ways.

YouTube videos can also be used effectively to demonstrate products, provide how-to or educational information pertaining to a product or service, showcase customer testimonials, and/or to help establish and build a company's brand and online reputation. One way small businesses use YouTube videos very effectively is to "personalize" their business by introducing key personnel and to share the company's story and philosophy in a way that captures the attention of their potential and existing customers.

Regardless of how you decide to use YouTube, make sure the videos you create are well produced, short, to the point, and highly engaging. The content needs to be easy to understand and well organized.

SEE WHAT'S POPULAR ON YOUTUBE

YouTube constantly monitors what videos people are watching and maintains ever-changing charts of top videos in various categories. As you prepare to create your own videos for YouTube, invest some time watching other videos to see what works and what's popular. To view YouTube's current most-watched videos, visit www.youtube.com/feed/trending.

From this listing, you can view what's popular today, this week, or this month, plus see a listing of the all-time most popular videos based on a variety of criteria. To sort and view videos by category, visit: https://www.youtube.com/channels.

Google also keeps its pulse on what's trending on YouTube. The YouTube "Trends" blog focuses on what videos are the most popular. To read this insightful blog, visit http://youtube-trends.blogspot.com.

Many of the all-time most viewed videos on YouTube are music videos from well-known recording artists and bands, such as Lady Gaga, Justin Bieber, Katy Perry, Beyoncé, and One Direction. Some of these videos have received more than 1 billion views each. However, there are many other types of popular videos that use humor, or some type of other original content, to capture the attention of viewers.

Depending on what your goals are for using YouTube and the type(s) of videos you plan to produce, focus on watching similar videos that have already become popular to discover what works well and what YouTube audiences are responding favorably to. In addition to studying the content in other videos, focus on their production quality, use of music or sound, as well as how special effects are being used in a positive or creative way.

Simply studying other popular YouTube videos can be highly educational and useful when it comes to creating your own videos. You can also discover how other people, bands, artists, performers, entrepreneurs, traditional business operators, and online business operators, for example, are using YouTube to their advantage and how they're integrating YouTube content into their overall online presence and marketing strategy.

As you're brainstorming concepts for your own videos, planning, and then producing them, keep in mind your audience's short attention span. Most people do not access YouTube to watch long-form programming. Even if your video is highly entertaining and engaging, keep it short (between 30 seconds and 6 minutes) and to the point. If you believe your video concept needs to be longer, consider breaking it into a series of short videos that appear on the same YouTube channel, linking them together, and presenting them as a YouTube playlist.

Keep in mind, producing multiple short videos, as opposed to one long one, will also work to your advantage when it comes to search engine optimization (SEO), because each video will be listed separately when someone uses YouTube's search feature or Google.

Remember, simply producing and publishing a video on your custom YouTube channel is only the first step. If you want your video to achieve its objectives, attract an audience, and be seen by the masses, you'll need to invest considerable time and resources to promote your videos and your YouTube channel. While you'll learn more about promoting your videos later, as you're brainstorming ideas for your videos, consider what your target audience will want and appreciate, then stay focused.

Also, as you're brainstorming ideas for your own YouTube videos, especially if you're a small-business operator, focus on three primary objectives: *entertain*, *educate*, and/or *inform*.

THE COSTS ASSOCIATED WITH USING YOUTUBE

YouTube is a free service, but depending on the production quality you're striving for, there are costs associated with producing and editing professional-quality videos, as well as with marketing and promoting your videos—both online and in the real world. If you opt to use YouTube as an advertising tool or have your products or services featured within a YouTuber's videos, there are also costs associated with that.

Chapter 6, "The Equipment You'll Need," and Chapter 7, "Selecting the Right Video Camera," both explore some of the costs associated with producing and editing professional-quality videos. Chapter 14, "Promoting Your YouTube Videos," discusses some of the potential costs you may encounter when promoting your videos and building an audience for them. Chapter 17, "Using Product Placement in Videos as a Promotional Tool," focuses on your options for paying YouTubers to feature your products or services within their videos, as well as opportunities that exist when it comes to sponsoring YouTuber videos or hiring an established YouTuber as a spokesperson for your business.

When it comes to producing great video content on a budget, plenty of individuals have used nothing more than the camera that's built into their computer or smartphone to film HD videos that they upload to YouTube, and some of these videos have become as popular as, if not more, popular as videos that cost hundreds or even tens of thousands of dollars to produce.

The quality of your videos—both from a content and production-quality standpoint—should cater to your target audience's expectations and demands. For example, if your business is using YouTube to promote a product, your audience will expect a professional-quality video that's in focus, shot in HD, well lit, and features high-quality (stereo) sound. Achieving these results may mean investing in higher-end equipment and editing tools.

So, while using YouTube will cost you nothing, to achieve professional-quality results, you will most likely need to pay for video equipment, lighting, sound equipment, editing tools, props, sets (backgrounds), licensed music and/or sound effects, and acquire other necessary equipment related to the production and editing of your videos. How to develop a realistic budget, based on your unique needs, will be covered in Chapter 6, "The Equipment You'll Need," and in Chapter 8, "Filming YouTube Videos."

12 WAYS YOU CAN USE YOUTUBE TO REACH YOUR AUDIENCE

Everyone who uses YouTube to promote themselves, their company, a band, product, service, or organization; to share information; or to just provide entertainment to their audience, has their own goals. The following is information about 12 popular ways YouTube can be used as part of your overall online strategy to achieve your company's goals.

Based on your own creativity, as well as the new features and functionality that are constantly being added to YouTube, and the ever-more advanced tools available for shooting and editing video, you'll probably come up with many ways YouTube can help you reach your audience in a cost-effective way.

Promote Yourself as an Online Personality and Entertain Your Audience

YouTube offers the ultimate platform that allows you to turn a video camera or webcam onto yourself and say or do just about anything that you believe will capture an audience's attention. While there are a few limits, few topics are taboo. You'll find these limitations by reading the YouTube Community Guidelines (www.youtube.com/t/community_guidelines).

One strategy small businesses use effectively to personalize their brand and build a rapport with the audience is to use YouTube videos to introduce their company's leaders and position these people as spokespeople who appear in videos.

That said, millions of people, while sitting in the comfort of their own bedrooms, basements, backyards, or offices, have used YouTube as a platform (a virtual soapbox) to communicate with whoever will listen and watch. Out of all the people who post their rants and exploits online, some stand out and ultimately break out as online personalities, and wind up with thousands or even millions of dedicated viewers (and subscribers). This is sometimes a result of one or more of their videos going viral or the result of months or years of regularly publishing content on YouTube and slowly building an audience.

Without the backing of a TV network, movie studio, record label, publicists, tabloid coverage, or red-carpet appearances, many YouTubers have become vastly popular online celebrities—and for a few, this has escalated them into mainstream stardom. Meanwhile, some company spokespeople have achieved celebrity status from starring in YouTube videos to promote themselves, their products, and/or their companies.

Whether you have something to say, a song to sing, a poem to recite, a joke to tell, a dance to perform, information to convey, knowledge or wisdom to share, or simply want to rant about absolutely nothing important, YouTube offers a forum, as well as a potential global audience. Often, the people being featured in these types of videos wind up becoming popular not necessarily because of the content within their videos but because of their over-the-top or outgoing personalities. So, if you're a small-business owner with a big personality, consider starring in your own YouTube videos to help build your company's brand, tell its story, and promote its message.

If your videos capture attention, strike a nerve, inform, or entertain, you have a personality that stands out, and you're not afraid to share it with the world via YouTube, you too can become an online personality. Featuring actual leaders of your company can help personalize your business and build its credibility. Your spokesperson can demonstrate products, speak authoritatively, and boost your company's brand recognition and reputation.

Just like a Hollywood celebrity, professional athlete, or major recording artist, an online personality or a company that's featuring itself, its spokespeople, and/or its products on YouTube is doing so to build a recognizable brand that they can cultivate on a grass-roots level using YouTube and other online social networking sites, including Facebook, Twitter, Instagram, Google+, Tumbler, and Snapchat. Gaining online popularity on YouTube can lead to a vast and dedicated base of loyal subscribers to your YouTube channel.

While there are many YouTubers (who become YouTube Partners) who earn a respectable income from their exploits online, a growing number of them are now crossing over and achieving mainstream fame and fortune in the real world's entertainment industry. In recent years, many well-known YouTubers have gone on to star in network television shows and mainstream movies, release chart-topping records, and become bestselling authors, for example. Many others earn high incomes by making public appearances, participating in meet and greets with their fans, and selling their subscribers branded merchandise.

Several companies produce national and international tours that allow fans to meet and interact with their favorite YouTubers in person. VidCon (http://vidcon.com), DigiTour (www.thedigitour.com), and MAGCON (www.magcontour.com) are examples of tour promoters and event producers that work with some of the most popular YouTubers.

You may discover that YouTube offers the perfect platform to share your talent with your followers and help you build an audience, whether you're an up-and-coming singer, comedian, artist, or dancer, for example. Many up-and-coming performers make a name for themselves on YouTube before being "discovered" by a record label, casting director, or major studio.

Meanwhile, many small-business operators have also found success using YouTube to feature themselves in their own videos, to tell their story, build their brand, educate and inform people about their products, or to demonstrate their products. When business operators appear in their videos, they are able to build a virtual relationship with their customers or potential customers in a way that's never before been possible.

Share Your Knowledge, Commentary, or How-to Information

One reason why YouTube has become so popular is that in addition to watching countless hours of entertaining videos, as a consumer, you can quickly find informative and easy-to-understand how-to videos about any topic imaginable.

If you have questions about how to do something, enter it into YouTube's "Search" field, and chances are, you'll find at least a handful of experts providing free answers that you need—day or night. In addition to well-known experts sharing their know-how and advice in the form of YouTube videos, you'll find everyday people sharing their own knowledge, expertise, and personal passion about a wide range of topics.

At the same time, you'll discover many people on YouTube sharing their own opinions and commentary about just about anything and everything, from politics to the weather. If you're a business operator, chances are you have expertise that other people could easily benefit from. One way to share this knowledge is to present it in the form of videos on YouTube and, in the process, build your own personal brand as well as your company or product's brand.

YouTube offers an informal yet powerful way to communicate directly with your customers, in your own words, in a forum that gives you absolute control over the content. Using a bit of creativity, chances are you'll come up with a handful of ideas about how your business could benefit from communicating directly with its customers (or potential customers) using YouTube. For example, you could create a product demonstration or product comparison video. Other options might be to showcase customer testimonials in a video or to create how-to videos that explain how to assemble, operate, or use your products/services.

One popular trend on YouTube is for companies or individuals to produce "unboxing" videos. Basically, someone takes a new (still packaged) product, then films themselves opening and using the product for the first time, as they share their initial impressions. You'll find unboxing videos related to all sorts of consumer-oriented products. These videos are watched by people interested in the product, but who haven't yet purchased it.

For example, in March 2017, Nintendo released a new home gaming system called the Nintendo Switch. Within hours after its release, dozens of "unboxing" videos were published by gamers, YouTubers, and businesses that sell video game products. Many of these videos quickly racked up tens of thousands, or in a few cases, millions of views each. To see unboxing videos related to a product you're interested in, simply type "[Insert Product Name] Unboxing Video" in YouTube's Search field and click on one or more of the search results. Watching some of these videos might give you ideas on how to create similar content related to your own company's products.

In addition, many companies have dramatically cut costs associated with offering telephone technical support by supplementing printed product manuals and product assembly instructions (which people hate to read and find difficult to understand) with informative how-to videos that are highly engaging.

Introduce a New Product or Service and Direct People to Your Online Store

Especially if you're operating an online-based business, or there's an online component to your traditional retail business, showcasing products on YouTube is a low-cost yet highly effective way to demonstrate products to your customers, showcase features, and explain how to best use a product. In addition to showcasing a product's features or functions, you can use YouTube videos to answer commonly asked questions.

If you opt to use YouTube to showcase your products, be sure that the production quality of your videos is professional and what your (potential) customers see will help boost your company's brand, credibility, and reputation. Trying to demonstrate a top-quality product using a poorly produced or blurry video with bad lighting and inferior sound is counterproductive and will hurt how a (potential) customer perceives your business. As you'll discover later, it's possible to produce professional-quality videos on a low budget that will allow you to showcase your products in a way that will capture the attention of (potential) customers in a positive way, while enhancing your overall brand.

Keep in mind, people who use YouTube do not want to watch blatant commercials for your products or services. Consumers are already bombarded with advertising in their everyday lives. While your videos can certainly promote a product or service, and build awareness or demand for it, take a soft-sell approach that's entertaining as well as informative.

Especially if you're operating an online store or can take orders for your product online, posting product demonstration videos on YouTube and on your actual website is a lot more compelling than even the best product photography. Ideally, consider offering a variety of professionally shot product photos on your website, plus a short product demonstration video that offers top-notch production value and an opportunity for your (potential) customers to see the product in action. These videos can be embedded in your website and linked from your YouTube channel (where the videos are hosted).

Teach People How to Use a Product or Service

Many businesses have discovered that producing YouTube videos as an instructional tool can help improve customer loyalty, reduce returns, and allow a business to enhance its customer service efforts without putting a strain on resources.

How-to videos for a product offer a different approach than a product demo, yet both approaches can benefit businesses looking to promote and sell products. While a how-to video is designed to teach someone how to do something, a product demo simply showcases a product's features or functions, and gives the viewer a chance to see a product in action. Either type of video can be used as part of a business-to-consumer or business-to-business sales and marketing strategy.

Instructional videos can help to reduce incoming customer service (and tech support) calls. You can produce instructional videos to teach people how to assemble and/or use a product, for example, plus help customers easily discover the true potential of a product, while eliminating their potential frustration.

Use this type of video as an opportunity to share simple solutions to common problems people have that relate to your product or communicate ways people can avoid pitfalls or problems using what you sell.

Of course, you always want to put a positive spin on these videos in terms of the content and the approach you take. For example, instead of "overcoming problems," you want to stress "how to fully use" a product or its features.

Whether someone has already purchased your company's product or they're on the cusp of making that all-important purchase decision, offering informative, insightful, easy-to-understand, and entertaining videos about your products is a viable way to share information, as well as assembly, installation, and/or how-to tips that your customers will perceive as valuable. Your videos can also be used to highlight lesser-known features of or uses for a product that your customers might not otherwise consider.

Many consumers are intimidated by difficult-to-read printed manuals or instruction booklets. Offering free YouTube videos that help people best use your product also demonstrates a loyalty to your customers. These videos can be promoted on your company's website, within its blog or Facebook page, using Twitter, on the product's packaging, and/or within the product's manual.

Through your YouTube videos, you can also encourage customers to post comments and interact with each other to create a close-knit virtual community comprised of people who use and love your products. Encouraging customers to support each other in a moderated online environment (your branded and customized YouTube channel) can help to reduce incoming customer service and technical support calls, as well as product returns.

When posting videos on your YouTube channel, be sure to select the option that allows you, the channel's operator, to approve all viewer comments before they're publicly posted. Then, encourage your customers to share their own ideas and testimonials.

Share Video Footage of Business Presentations You've Given

As a business leader or expert in your field, if you've presented a lecture, workshop, or some type of presentation, consider uploading the edited video footage of it to YouTube for your customers, clients, and the public to see. This will help establish you as an expert or authority, allow you to convey valuable information to potential customers and clients, plus help you build awareness of you and your company.

This information can be supplemented with an animated and narrated digital slide (PowerPoint) presentation that you post on your YouTube channel, and/or include a recorded one-on-one interview with you talking about something in which your (potential) customers or clients would be interested.

Provide Background Information about Your Company and Tell Its Story

Every company has a story to tell, as do the founders or current leaders of that business. By telling your story, chances are you'll be able to enhance your customer loyalty and brand awareness, while also educating the public about what your company does and its core philosophies.

Any type of behind-the-scenes videos can also be useful. For example, you can produce and publish a video that focuses on how your product(s) are made, provide a tour of your company, and introduce some of the people who work at your company within the video(s). If you have invented a product, as the inventor, you can explain in a video where the inspiration for the product came from, and why you're personally passionate about the product.

Showcase Customer Testimonials

If you have been in business for a while and have earned the respect of many loyal customers or clients, using a YouTube video to showcase some of these people or companies providing real testimonials for your products/service can be a highly effective and low-cost promotional and sales tool.

Present a Call to Action

Because YouTube allows you to speak directly to your audience, you can use your videos as a platform to raise awareness about an issue or encourage your viewers to take a specific action after watching your video. A video's *call to action* is a request for the people watching your videos to take an immediate action—such as to visit your website, "like" the video, subscribe to your YouTube channel, call a toll-free phone number, send someone an email, share the video's link with their friends, make a donation, or make a purchase.

One way many companies use the call-to-action approach is to create some type of contest that encourages people to reply to the video or take a specific action to participate, with the hope of winning a prize. Keep in mind, there may be legal guidelines you'll need to adhere to based on the type of contest you want to host, so do your research first.

For a business selling a product, one potential call to action is to embed a link within your video to a website that offers a money-saving coupon or special offer for what you're selling. This might be 20 percent off the purchase price (for a limited time), free shipping, a buy-one-get-one-free offer, or some other incentive to encourage someone to make an immediate purchase. Make it clear within the video that it's an exclusive offer for people watching the video, and make the "special offer" available immediately at the end of the video.

Incorporating a call to action within a video is one of the key ingredients for producing a successful video when it comes to communicating with your audience and getting them to take action. When using a call-to-action approach within a video, follow these basic strategies:

- Include the call to action multiple times within the video, not just at the end.
- Start by describing the reward, then tell people exactly what they should do. For example, "To receive $50 off of your first order, visit our website right now by clicking on the link below."
- Make sure your call to action appeals to your target audience and that it's easy to understand. Be specific and succinct.

You can also use YouTube to conduct unofficial focus groups or research. In your video, showcase a product, for example, then solicit feedback from your (potential) customers by asking specific questions and using a call-to-action approach to encourage viewers to post comments with their honest feedback, criticism, or ideas.

Create Mindless Entertainment, but Use Product Placement

Many people turn to YouTube for entertainment because the service is chock full of funny, whimsical, and outrageous videos. You or your company can jump on this bandwagon and produce videos that offer mindless entertainment but, at the same time, offer subtle product placements or marketing messages about your company or its products within the videos.

For this type of video, creativity is essential, as what you post needs to be unique, engaging, funny, and entertaining. Again, taking a soft-sell approach is key.

Promote or Share Highlights from an Event

By default, any type of event in the real world that you or your organization participates in is held at some geographic location and will draw crowds from the surrounding area. However, by sharing videos shot at recently held events, you have the opportunity to share it with the world. Showcasing edited-down (shortened) footage or highlights from a previous event can also generate interest in and help boost attendance for future events.

Once you publish your videos on YouTube, be sure to take full advantage of the YouTube Analytics tools to help you discover who the audience is for your videos and other useful details about when, how, and by whom your videos are being watched. Use this information to help you better promote your existing videos and improve the focus of the content of future videos.

As you develop ideas for your company's videos, think beyond simply producing a video that replicates a TV commercial or infomercial. Instead, consider ways you can use video to communicate effectively with your audience, to build and expand your company's online reputation, educate the audience about your products/services, separate yourself from your competition, address the wants and needs of your (potential) customers, share information, or entertain your audience in a way that will help you and your business achieve its goals.

Broadcast (Stream) a Live Event via YouTube

In addition to filming an event, editing and shortening the video, and then publishing it on YouTube via your company's branded YouTube channel, it's possible to broadcast live via YouTube Live (www.youtube.com/live_dashboard_splash) or on other social media platforms like Facebook (www.facebook.com), YouNow (www.younow.com), Twitch.TV (www.twitch.tv), or Instagram Live (www.instagram.com/instagramlive).

When you broadcast live, your video feed steams directly to your audience in real time. In other words, there's no editing, no retakes, and no margin for error. As events happen, your audience sees it live.

Businesses can use live steaming to broadcast a special event, product launch, or press conference, for example. However, as you'll learn from Chapter 16, "Go Live with Your Broadcasts," this strategy has some pros and cons that you should be aware of before turning on YouTube's live streaming feature for the first time.

Pay to Have Your Product(s) Featured in Videos Produced by Popular YouTubers

Instead of producing your own video content, promoting that content, and using the time, manpower, and financial resources required to promote your videos and build an audience, one option that's becoming increasingly popular is to pay an established YouTuber to incorporate product placements (for your products/services) into their video content. Your company can also sponsor a well-established YouTuber's video(s).

An established YouTuber already has a massive following, which can be in the tens of thousands, hundreds of thousands, or even in the millions. Some well-known YouTubers have between 10 and 15 million loyal subscribers (which are a larger viewership than most network television shows), so each of their videos is virtually guaranteed to have many views within just hours after its put online.

What you'll discover is that in addition to having a large audience, the subscribers to popular YouTubers are extremely loyal. So, when one of these YouTubers endorses a product, their subscribers are often very willing to try it out.

Most YouTubers appeal to a specific demographic. For example, there are countless beauty gurus that millions of young women turn to on a weekly basis for beauty tips, makeup tutorials, and reviews of makeup, and cosmetic or skin-care products. If you're about to launch a new line of lipstick or nail polish, for example, paying an established YouTuber, who is a beauty guru with a large following, for a product placement is a quick and easy way to promote your product and have it seen by many targeted viewers.

As you'll learn in Chapter 17, if you think your company's products or services could benefit by being featured in the videos of established YouTubers, you can either do your own research to determine which specific YouTubers you want to approach with a product placement or sponsorship offer, or you can work with an established agency that matches companies with appropriate YouTubers for product placements and video sponsorships. These agencies can also help match your company with the perfect YouTuber to hire as a paid spokesperson. One such agency, which was recently acquired by YouTube, is called FameBit (https://famebit.com).

Become a Paid Advertiser on YouTube to Promote Your Message

If you want to avoid producing videos and hosting your own YouTube channel, but still want to tap directly into YouTube's vast and growing audience in a way that allows you to reach your target market, one option is to become a paid YouTube advertiser.

As a paid advertiser, your video-based or display ad will appear in conjunction with video content created and published by other producers (YouTube channel operators). A paid advertising campaign on YouTube can be created and launched within hours. You have full control over your daily spending for ads and can see real-time statistics about who's seeing your ad(s) and the actions the viewers are taking as a result.

Like other forms of paid advertising, as the advertiser, you have 100 percent control over your message, as well as when and where people will see your ads within YouTube. One potential drawback to YouTube advertising is that some tech-savvy computer users (consumers) install web browser plug-ins that keep them from having to view ad content when accessing YouTube from their computer. Plus, any YouTube user can pay an optional monthly fee of about $10 for a YouTube Red subscription, which removes all ads from the regular YouTube videos they watch.

Chapter 14, "Promoting Your YouTube Videos," covers how to create, launch, and manage a successful ad campaign on YouTube. However, for more information about YouTube advertising, you can also visit: www.youtube.com/yt/advertise.

START THINKING ABOUT WHAT APPROACH YOU WANT TO TAKE

Now that you're familiar with some of the ways companies are using YouTube, go online and discover firsthand how your competition is using YouTube and what types of content that's related to your company, or its products or services, is already available.

Then, start thinking about the various approaches you'd like to take with the content you create based on the audience you want to reach and the core message you want to communicate. As you'll discover, there are many ways to convey information in YouTube videos. One of your initial goals should be to identify which options offer the best opportunities for your business.

Identifying and Catering to Your Audience

When it comes to creating a branded YouTube channel, then populating it with fresh content on a regular basis, one of the most important factors to consider when making each creative decision is your target audience. Not only must you have a clear understanding of who comprises your target audience, but as the content creator, it's necessary to put yourself in their shoes, think like them, and make creative choices based on what you believe will cater to the wants, needs, and tastes of your viewers.

Before creating your channel or brainstorming ideas for content, it's necessary to define and get to know your audience, then determine the best ways to develop content for those people. Do not take a shortcut and state that your target audience is "everyone," because when you sit down and think about who will be buying your company's products or services, you'll likely determine that you can identify specific characteristics that make up your target customer. For example, you may determine that your product or service appeals mainly to college-educated women between the ages of 24 and 36 who live in a major city and are employed full time. They're married, earn more than $55,000 per year, and have at least one pet.

As a business operator, the more you know about your primary customers, the easier it will be to reach this audience with highly targeted marketing, advertising, and promotional content. This is also true when it comes to managing a YouTube channel that will feature your original content. To build an audience for your content, you must have a clear understanding about who you're trying to appeal to, then develop content that caters to that niche audience.

IDENTIFY YOUR AUDIENCE AND DISCOVER WHAT IT WANTS OR NEEDS

Using YouTube requires that you take a dual approach when writing, developing, producing, editing, publishing, and promoting your videos. First, focus on your own wants, needs, and objectives. Figure out how to use your YouTube Channel, your individual videos, and your overall online activity to achieve those objectives.

Then, put yourself in your audience's shoes as you consider every aspect of your video productions and how you brand your YouTube channel. From the perspective of someone who perfectly fits into your target audience, ask yourself:

- Is the YouTube channel branded appropriately? Does its appearance, description, and listing of content (your individual videos) appeal directly to the audience?
- Why should they watch your video(s)?
- What is it within your video(s) that will appeal directly to your intended viewers?
- What will people get out of watching your videos?
- How will watching your videos address their wants and/or needs?
- How will your videos solve their problems, help them overcome their challenges, save them time and money, and/or provide them with information that they deem valuable or important?
- Why should someone watch your videos, as opposed to any of the countless others on YouTube that cover the same material? How is your approach different and more beneficial to your audience?
- What will inspire the viewer to respond to each video's call to action?

Only by truly defining your audience, then understanding the people who make up this audience, can you answer these questions. Do your market research. Understand your product/service. Learn as much as you can about your audience, then use your videos to reach these people by communicating what you deem to be the perfect message targeted specifically to them.

How to Define Your Target Audience

What your business does, the products it sells, the services it offers, the company's philosophy, and a wide range of other factors that are unique to your organization defines exactly how you'd describe your target customers. This should be based on a combination of demographic criteria, such as their:

- Age
- Club or association memberships
- Education level
- Gender
- Geographic region
- Hobbies and special interests
- Housing
- Marital status
- Occupation
- Physical attributes
- Race
- Religion
- Sexual orientation
- Social media habits
- Spending habits

The target audience for your YouTube channel and individual videos should be the same as the target customer/client for your business. If you have not already done so when creating the business plan for your organization, or when developing previous sales, marketing, advertising, and/or promotional campaigns, take a moment to pinpoint and write down a detailed description of your target audience, using some of the demographic criteria previously listed.

Then, once you've clearly defined who this audience is made up of, consider if you also have a secondary audience that you'd like to reach. This group of people may also have a strong interest in your company's products/services and the content you'll be offering through YouTube.

Now that you've defined your target audience for your YouTube channel and the videos you'll soon be creating, ask yourself one simple question: Do the people who make up this audience already watch YouTube videos? If so, when and how do they typically access YouTube? This is information that will help you develop your content.

If you determine that your target audience is over the age of 65, you may recall that only 3 percent of YouTube's entire audience of 1.3 billion people is within this age range.

Thus, unless you know you'll be able to reach people in the over-65 crowd who are tech-savvy and comfortable enough to access YouTube, your company may be better off using other, more traditional platforms to promote your business and disseminate your core message to this audience.

However, if your target audience comprises people between the ages of 18 and 44, for example, this represents more than 60 percent of YouTube's overall audience. Chances are you'll have a much easier time attracting viewers to your videos and subscribers to your YouTube channel.

Next, consider how and when your audience already uses YouTube and other forms of social media. If most of your audience is extremely active on Facebook and typically accesses their Facebook account from their mobile device, you now know that one of the best ways to attract viewers to your videos may be to promote them and your YouTube channel via Facebook. You also know that when producing your videos, it's particularly important to ensure they're easily viewed on the small screen of a smartphone or tablet.

Meanwhile, if you're looking to attract new potential customers to your YouTube channel, it will be helpful to know whether members of your target audience already use YouTube as their go-to search engine when seeking information. If so, every time you upload new content to your channel, it becomes important to focus on including the best possible video title, description, and keywords/tags, so people who are performing a search on YouTube (or Google) will more easily be able to find your videos. You may also determine that using paid advertising on YouTube will help to quickly drive new viewers to your channel.

Another thing to consider, once you've identified your target audience, is whether these people typically seek out YouTube videos before making a purchase. If so, at least some of the content you publish on YouTube should cater directly to these people, in terms of providing an introduction/overview of your product, product demonstrations, product comparisons, customer testimonials, and perhaps an unboxing video. Knowing that you're able to reach potential customers before they make a buying decision, you can use your content to help sell your company and your product(s) to those people (using a soft-sell approach).

Depending on the goal of your YouTube channel and the content you publish, it's your responsibility to determine who you're trying to reach, then develop content that caters directly to what this audience wants. If instead of attracting new customers, the goal of your YouTube channel and content is to enhance a customer's experience *after* they've purchased your product, instead of creating videos that focus on the buying experience, you may opt to focus your content on teaching your customers how to assemble and use the product, and to showcase innovative ways your existing customers can save time and money, or enhance their lives by owning your product. In this case, the target audience is the same, but the content, approach, and core messaging within your videos will be dramatically different.

Choose the Best Type of Video Content to Appeal to Your Audience

There are very few limitations when it comes to producing and presenting original video content on YouTube. It's your job to tap your creativity and present your message and call to action in a way that achieves your goals, using the resources at your disposal. As you brainstorm the concepts for your videos, keep in mind you can use:

- Live-action video (video of people, places, or things)
- Graphic titles (text) that can be stationary on the screen or animated
- Voice-overs (a voice from someone who isn't seen, but who can be heard speaking)
- Music and sound effects
- Animated graphic sequences
- Animated or still charts and graphs
- Visual special effects
- Text within the video's description to provide more details, contact information, and related website links, for example
- Interactive "cards" to incorporate hyperlinks into videos (learn more by visiting https://creatoracademy.youtube.com/page/lesson/cards)

With this in mind, what is the best way to present your message to your target audience? What approach will they understand and relate to the best? Remember, your YouTube audience's attention span is short. It's essential that you capture someone's attention very quickly (within the first few seconds of your video), then present your video and your message in the shortest time possible (within just a few minutes).

In addition to competing with all the other videos on YouTube, which for your audience are always just a mouse click or screen tap away, the content and quality of your videos need to meet or exceed your audience's expectations from a production standpoint. Thus, if you're planning to produce your own videos in-house, but don't have the resources and know-how to produce a slick, animated sequence that you envision including in your videos, don't settle and use an amateurish or cheesy-looking animated sequence. Instead, choose an alternative way to communicate your message that will look professional and help you build, protect, and maintain your company's online image and reputation.

There is a wide range of software and online-based tools that can help you create and produce extremely professional-looking graphics, animations, and other production elements that can then be incorporated into your videos. Most of these tools, however, require some level of knowledge and skill to properly use.

You'll learn about just some of these tools, such as Apple's iMovie (www.apple.com/ilife/imovie), Apple's Final Cut Pro X (www.apple.com/finalcutpro), Adobe's Premier Pro CC (www.adobe.com/products/premiere.html), Camtasia (www.techsmith.com/video-editor.html), and Microsoft PowerPoint (http://office.microsoft.com/en-us/powerpoint), in Chapter 8, "Filming YouTube Videos," and Chapter 9, "Editing Your YouTube Videos."

To discover other cutting-edge video editing applications for Windows PCs, Macs, iOS mobile devices, or Android-based mobile devices, visit the app store for your computer or device. Then, within the app store's search field, enter "video editing." Read the descriptions of apps that are available, and focus on the post-production features and functions you want or need to achieve the objectives of your videos.

However, it's up to you to invest the time needed to learn how to effectively use these and other tools and not simply clutter your videos with an overload of eye candy or bells and whistles that will wind up distracting or annoying your target audience.

It's very rare that your content will be so compelling or perceived as so important or valuable to your audience that they'll forgive amateurish production quality and sit through a poorly produced video. Instead, they'll simply watch another video, or exit out of YouTube altogether, and seek out the information they are looking for elsewhere—from your competition's website or Facebook page, for example.

As a content creator, YouTube offers a vast assortment of online tutorials, tools, and resources that will help you learn the basics of content creation and video production. Above and beyond the knowledge you acquire from this book, the YouTube Creator hub (www.youtube.com/yt/creators) can teach you the skills needed to produce compelling, attention-grabbing, and well-produced content, regardless of your budget. This information will prove even more useful, however, once you've developed your company's overall objective for using YouTube, you've clearly defined your target audience, and you've given some thought about the approach you want to take within your videos to appeal to your target audience and at the same time achieve your company's objectives.

At least initially, as your company begins to develop its online marketing and promotional strategy—especially if you want to include video in that plan—consider hiring an independent video production company that can help you write, produce, edit, and promote YouTube videos that will cater to your audience and achieve your goals. Hiring professionals can help you avoid costly and potentially embarrassing mistakes, plus help you generate the desired results much faster and with the least amount of confusion or frustration.

YouTube offers a vast database of approved production companies and content creators that your company can hire to help you develop, launch, and maintain your

YouTube presence. The YouTube Creator Services Directory can be found at: https://servicesdirectory.withyoutube.com.

A Video Does Not Have to Go Viral to Be a Success

Every YouTube channel will have its own unique set of objectives. As a small-business operator or entrepreneur, for example, your sole objective should not be to create videos that will go viral and be seen by millions of people. Unless you're trying to generate revenue by becoming a YouTube Partner and having people see ads in conjunction with your video views, reaching millions of viewers won't necessarily be beneficial, unless every one of those viewers fits within your target audience.

Instead, if you're trying to reach new customers and sell your products to a niche audience, you'll likely discover that it's much more beneficial for one of your YouTube videos to reach a few hundred or a few thousand people who perfectly fit within your target audience. These people are more apt to watch your entire video, respond to your call to action, then visit your company's website to place an online order for your product, for example. If one of your sales-oriented videos ultimately receives 1,000 YouTube views, and just 1 percent of those people visits your website and places an order, you just obtained 10 new paying customers and sold at least 10 of your products.

Now consider what would happen if you fine-tuned your future videos and improved the call-to-action response rate to 3, 4, or 5 percent? At the same time, what would happen if you use some of the video promotion strategies outlined in Chapter 14, "Promoting Your YouTube Videos," and you're able to attract 5,000 or 10,000 (or more) views per video? Then, over a period of a few weeks or months, you create and publish five to ten separate videos on your YouTube channel, and each takes a slightly different sales approach but targets the same core audience. What you'll likely discover is that, over time, your YouTube channel will become a powerful sales tool that allows you to reach many new customers in a cost-effective way.

Remember, however, establishing a YouTube presence, then earning lots of video views, will likely take time and resources, so you need to be patient and have realistic expectations. This is particularly important if you're using YouTube on a shoestring budget and will be relying on grass-roots efforts to build the popularity of your channel. Unless you hire professional content creators, spend whatever is necessary to produce a highly professional-looking video, then invest a lot of money to advertise and promote your video content. Don't expect to publish your first video, have it generate 100,000 or more views, then immediately achieve hundreds of new sales.

Early on, focus on defining the overall objective of your YouTube channel, choosing the best core message to communicate to your viewers, then adopting an approach within your videos that will cater to your target audience. Planning videos that will capture your viewers' attention is the focus of the next chapter.

MEET BRITTNEY CASTRO, HOST OF FINANCIALLY WISE WOMEN

YouTube Channel URL: www.youtube.com/user/brittneycastro

Brittney Castro is the founder and CEO of Financially Wise Women, a Los Angeles-based financial planning firm that focuses on helping women and couples better manage their money. She's a Certified Financial Planner, Chartered Retirement Planning Counselor, and an Accredited Asset Management Specialist who also hosts her own YouTube channel.

The Financially Wise Women YouTube channel is populated with dozens of short videos featuring Brittney Castro offering tips and answering financial questions in an easy-to-understand way. Most of the videos featured on the channel are shorter than five minutes, and each addresses one finance-related topic.

"I started my channel in April 2011 with the goal of building my credibility as a female financial planner. I wanted to help other women improve their financial knowledge," says Castro. "At the time, I saw a lot of women who were launching YouTube channels focusing on beauty and fashion. I wanted to talk about money in a fun and entertaining way by sharing personal finance tips and inspiring women. I looked at YouTube primarily as a low-cost brand-building tool.

"Right now, my YouTube channel really helps with organic search engine optimization for my website," she adds. "Because I post videos on a regular basis, if someone searches for a female financial planner, they're apt to discover my videos and website. I would not say, however, that I get a lot of new clients as a direct result of people stumbling on my videos and watching them. I look at YouTube as a part of my overall online marketing plan."

What Castro does use her YouTube channel for that's very impactful is to nurture her existing clients. "Every week, I publish a new video, and I email a link for that video directly to all my existing clients. The YouTube channel has also helped me obtain a lot of media opportunities, because the TV producers find my YouTube channel and see that I am knowledgeable and look good on camera."

Early on, Castro wrote, starred in, filmed, and edited all her own videos. As she's become more successful, however, she has since hired a professional video production company. "Every quarter, I create ideas for 12 videos, and then write the scripts and plan them. I then schedule a video shoot and film all 12 videos back to back in a single day. The video production company edits the videos and prepares them to be uploaded onto YouTube on a once-per-week basis," explains Castro.

"Once I write the outline and a script for each video, because I know the topics so well, when it comes time to film, I don't actually read the script word-for-word. I just speak freely. This allows the videos to come across as more conversational. Most of my video ideas come directly from questions and concerns expressed by my clients," says Castro. "For additional ideas, I search for personal finance-related videos already on YouTube and look for keywords and topics that are currently trending and getting a lot of views. I then develop my own approach to those topics."

According to Castro, if you're trying to portray a professional image within your videos, and build your credibility and brand, good lighting and sound are as important as the actual content. "People are bombarded by content. If you want your videos to stand out, they need to be engaging, plus produced and edited in a professional way. The videos also need to be short and focus on a specific idea or topic. Based on my experience, shorter videos are always better. My aim is to keep videos between three and five minutes in length," says Castro.

In terms of the call to action incorporated into each of Castro's videos, in the past, she encouraged people to visit her website and subscribe to her blog. More recently, she's been trying to build her YouTube's channel's subscriber base, so she reminds people to subscribe to the channel. She's also discovered that by grouping together videos that focus on related topics into playlists, she's able to retain and engage viewers for longer periods of time. This also makes it easier to convince her viewers to subscribe to her channel, since after sampling several videos, she entices them to want to see more related content.

Castro has discovered the importance of getting directly into the topic within the first few seconds of the video. "Two of the biggest mistakes I made early on were that I took too long to get into the topic, and I dragged out the video for too long. My advice is to get right to the point, and keep the video itself short and on-point. As for the video's title, it too needs to be very specific and compelling," she says. "Again, determine what keywords are trending on YouTube and work those keywords into your own video titles."

Chapter 4

Planning Videos That Will Capture Your Viewers' Attention

IN THIS CHAPTER
- Defining an overall objective for your company's YouTube channel
- Focusing on current YouTube trends
- Identifying your audience's wants and needs
- Choosing the approach(es) your videos will take

Before you start brainstorming, storyboarding, and filming your first YouTube videos, it's essential that you seriously consider the overall goal for your videos, as well as for your YouTube channel. Chapter 2, "Defining Your Goals for YouTube," outlined some of the ways YouTube videos can effectively become part of your overall online marketing and promotions strategy. Hopefully, you will now begin kicking around some video ideas in your head or writing them down so you don't forget them.

Next, clearly define the overall message that you want to convey within your videos, what the video's call to action will be, and who your videos will target. As you engage in these pre-production steps, it's important to focus on what information about yourself, your company, and/or your products/services you want to convey, and how you ultimately want to share this information.

Once again, it's important that the message(s) and call to action you incorporate into your videos be consistent with your company's overall image and reputation, and be synergistic to your other branding and online activities (on Facebook, Twitter, Instagram, etc.).

THREE REASONS TO HAVE YOUTUBE HOST YOUR VIDEOS

As for why you'll probably want to use YouTube to host your videos, there are several reasons. First, YouTube offers the world's largest streaming-video library, and it's the world's second most popular internet search engine. More than 1.3 billion people visit YouTube on a consistent basis when they're looking for specific types of content to watch in video form. Thus, with very little additional work on your part, people will be able to find your videos when they're seeking related content.

A second compelling reason to have YouTube host your video content is that within minutes after publishing each of your videos, they become searchable on both YouTube and Google. So, if within the video's title, description, and keywords, for example, you include the name of your company and product(s), this will improve your company's search engine rankings and help potential customers easily find your video content (and potentially your website) when they're performing a relevant search. How to best create and use video titles, descriptions, and keywords is covered in Chapter 11, "Uploading Your Videos to YouTube."

The third reason why it's a good strategy to host your video content on YouTube and then, if you choose, embed links to that content directly within your company's website, Facebook page, blog, or other social media presence is the price. Creating a YouTube channel and then populating it with as much content as you desire is free. There are no monthly hosting fees, no bandwidth considerations, and no online storage space restrictions. Plus, YouTube is virtually guaranteed to stay online because it's operated using a vast network of state-of-the-art servers that's supported by a global IT infrastructure that has many redundant backups.

DEFINE THE OBJECTIVE OF YOUR COMPANY'S YOUTUBE CHANNEL

Before your company can begin publishing video content on YouTube, two important things need to happen. First, your company needs to create a free YouTube channel, then properly brand it with its logo and other related graphics (referred to as Channel Art), along with a channel description. Your YouTube channel is a unique area of YouTube that has its own website URL, where you can publish and display your video content, making it easier for people to find.

As you move forward, fans of your videos can subscribe to your channel. By doing this, they can automatically be alerted every time you publish a new video, plus see the videos you've published to date, all in one place. If you've created playlists (groups of related videos) for your viewers to watch back-to-back, these also become readily accessible from your channel's page.

The focus of Chapter 5, "How to Start Your Own YouTube Channel," is on how to create, brand, and fully customize your YouTube channel, then organize and populate it with content that will appeal to your target audience.

However, before you complete the steps required to create a YouTube channel and obtain a unique URL for it, take the time to really focus on what the objective of your company's YouTube channel will be.

Why do you want to create video-based content in the first place? In other words, what do you want your company to get out of it? Possible answers might be:

- Introduce new products/services to new and existing customers
- Attract new customers and drive them to your company's website
- Better educate potential customers about your company and its products, by offering video-based product demonstrations, comparisons, and unboxing-type videos
- Help existing customers better use your products by showcasing ways to use them that customers might not have thought of, and by sharing ways your customers can save time and money, and simplify their lives by using your product
- Help customers assemble your products and reduce the amount of time and resources required to offer telephone or email-based technical assistance and customer support
- Answer common customer questions related to your products using a video format that will reduce the number of customer service-related calls or emails your company receives
- Offer a "behind-the-scenes" look at your company, allowing you to tell your company's story, "humanize" your company, share your company philosophy, and discuss ways your company is superior to your competition
- Build customer loyalty and better define your brand by sharing information, then allowing people to share comments about your videos, as well as your products/services, plus interact with each other through video-related comments and replies
- With your target audience in mind, will your videos entertain, educate, and/or provide information or insight into your company and its products that your audience will find valuable?
- What will initially attract potential viewers to your YouTube channel and your videos? What will be included within your videos that will be perceived as valuable, so demanding viewers with a short attention span will watch each video in its entirety? How will you present your call to action and encourage viewers to respond and react favorably to it?

- What types of content do you want to create and publish? As you answer this question, focus on your target audience, then think about what approaches you'll take within your videos to convey the most information possible, in a succinct but attention-grabbing way.
- How will the YouTube channel and the individual videos you publish help your target audience? In other words, what will your audience get out of the time they invest to watch your content?

Once you know what the benefits of your YouTube channel and content will be for your company, focus carefully on the benefits your content will offer to your audience. To make your YouTube channel (and your individual videos) a success, you'll need to create content that caters to your company's own wants and needs, but that simultaneously appeals to your target audience in a way that will keep their attention.

After all, your company's goal may be to showcase and sell a product by driving traffic to your website. Your viewer's objective may be to learn more about the type of product you're selling and save money when buying that type of product. However, the potential customer has a lot on their mind, has a short attention span, must stay within their budget, and does not want to waste time on YouTube watching videos that resemble TV commercials or infomercials.

Always be thinking about how the content you create will offer a balance between what your company wants and needs vs. what will appeal to your viewers so they'll respond favorably to your videos, watch each video in its entirety, and follow through on the call to action that's presented to them. Learning to achieve this perfect balance will require some experimentation and creativity on your part. Once you figure out an approach that works for your company and its target audience, that's when you'll start generating the most favorable results from your video content.

Be Sure to Organize Your YouTube Channel

It's very common for a company's YouTube channel to have multiple objectives, then over time, for that company to populate its channel with groups of videos related to each objective. For example, you have created videos to help sell your products to new customers. These might include product demonstration and comparison videos, along with customer testimonial videos, for example. The focus of these videos is to get viewers to purchase your product and become a customer.

Another goal for your YouTube channel might be to provide valuable information to new and existing customers. These videos might include tutorials for assembling or using the product, or showcase the product being used in a variety of different ways.

You might opt to produce "lifestyle videos" that show your product being used by actual customers in real-world situations.

When your YouTube channel will be populated by videos that have vastly different objectives, be sure to properly organize your content into playlists and/or categories. This way, when someone visits your channel, they can quickly locate and watch only the videos that pertain to them, and you won't waste their time by making them watch videos they're not interested in or that are not relevant.

Chapter 11, "Uploading Your Videos to YouTube," explains how to organize your individual videos and present them in a way that's straightforward and inviting to your viewers and subscribers. In addition to creating highly descriptive and accurate titles for your videos, as well as short but informative video descriptions, you can group videos together into related categories that should also be clearly labeled.

Even if you're able to produce a series of incredible videos with valuable, informative, and compelling content, if your audience is misdirected into watching videos they don't feel are relevant, you'll quickly lose their attention. As a result, organizing your content and presenting it in the most appealing and straightforward way within your channel is as important as the content itself.

YOUR VIDEOS CAN ADOPT MANY DIFFERENT TYPES OF APPROACHES

You want all content offered by your YouTube channel to be synergistic and cohesive so it appeals to the same core target audience; however, each video can adopt a vastly different approach. Once again, as the content creator, it's your job to determine what approaches your viewers will respond to best and simultaneously allow you to convey the information you need to achieve your company's objectives. Oh, and all this must be done in the shortest amount of time possible. If your videos run too long, a viewer's attention will start to wonder, their retention and interest level will decrease, or worse yet, they'll get bored and click away to watch something else.

Each YouTube video can showcase and use content in vastly different ways. As you now know, some of your options for presenting information include using:

- Live action video footage
- Text (titles, captions, etc.)
- Graphics
- Animations
- Charts and diagrams
- Music
- Sound effects

- Voice-overs (a person's voice is heard, but the person is not seen)
- Other multimedia elements, such as PowerPoint slides, digital photos, etc.

Any, all, or a combination of these can throw some extra sauce on your videos to make them stand out for both marketing and monetization.

Many Live Action Video Options Exist

As YouTube and camera technology continue to evolve, new types of video content can now be created in a very affordable way, then presented on YouTube. At this point, all video you produce should be created in a 1080p high-definition format, at the very least. Depending on your target audience and how tech-savvy they are, and what devise they'll be using to watch your videos, you may opt to capture and publish your video content in 4K HD resolution, which is quickly being adopted by consumers.

Beyond just considering video resolution (which is covered more in Chapter 6, "The Equipment You'll Need," and Chapter 7, "Selecting the Right Video Camera") based on current trends and consumer demand, other types of video can now be showcased and shared via YouTube. Some of your newer, more cutting-edge options include:

- *360-degree video*. Using a specialized camera, you can create compelling 360-degree video content that can be viewed on any standard TV, monitor, or mobile device screen. This type of content allows viewers to scroll upward, downward, or side-to-side to see all areas of a location. Real estate agents, for example, are using this type of footage when creating immersive, video-based property tours, although musicians and other types of content creators have also found creative ways to use this type of content.
- *Virtual reality (VR)*. In recent years, the cost of VR equipment for home computers and mobile devices has dropped considerably, making it affordable to consumers. As a result, what consumers now seek is compelling VR content that allows them to immerse themselves in virtual worlds. The cost to produce VR content is also dropping quickly, as the necessary equipment is becoming more powerful, yet more affordable to content creators.
- *Augmented reality*. This type of content combines real-world video with computer-generated graphics to create new types of experiences for viewers that blur the line between real and artificially created content and locations.
- *Drone footage*. The cost of a remote-controlled drone with a built-in HD video camera has also dropped considerably, and thanks to technology, these drones are now much easier to pilot than ever before. As a result, videographers can use drone-based cameras to capture visually stunning aerial content that can be interspersed with traditionally produced video content. The result is that

content creators can capture aerial views and perspectives, with equipment that costs less than $1,000. In the past, this same imagery would have required using a helicopter or a high-end aerial videography solution that would have cost thousands of dollars. The GoPro Karma (https://shop.gopro.com/karma) is just one example of a relatively low-cost drone that uses an HD video camera capable of producing broadcast-quality content. By visiting the GoPro website, you can see demo footage created using the Karma drone and see how this type of aerial videography can be used to capture the attention of an audience with visually breathtaking content.

- *Live broadcasting.* Instead of recording a video, editing it, and publishing it on your YouTube channel, one of YouTube's newer features, called YouTube Live, allows channel hosts to broadcast live via their YouTube channel so viewers can watch events happen in real-time. Companies are using this technology to share time-sensitive product launches and press conferences with consumers and media representatives alike in an affordable way. Refer to Chapter 16, "Go Live with Your Broadcasts," to learn more about this option for populating your YouTube channel with live content that then gets recorded and becomes available any time, on an on-demand basis, to viewers.

Select the Best Approach Based on Your Target Audience

Using some or all of these video production elements, it's possible to adopt a serious, comedic, lighthearted, or dramatic approach to presenting information. The approach you use should be based on what you perceive will work best for your target audience. In the "Develop Your Strategy" section of Chapter 1, a listing of ways companies often use YouTube videos was presented. As you move forward, think about what you want the goal of your videos to be, then consider creative ways you'll present the information using the resources that are at your disposal. For example, do you want to use live-action video to showcase a company spokesperson demonstrating a product, or include video shot at an event, but have someone providing a voice-over to share information while the viewer is watching specific content?

Based on the information you're trying to convey, would it be faster, easier to understand, more entertaining, more visually interesting, and more attention-getting to include a colorful (or potentially animated) chart or graphic as opposed to having a person in the video (a talking head) spewing out lots of numbers or statistics?

Without overwhelming your audience with too much "eye candy" or animated content that will distract or confuse them, figure out the fastest and best way to convey the information you plan to present. You may discover that to improve viewer retention, it makes sense to present the same information in several different formats simultaneously. For example, showcasing a colorful graph or chart as someone explains what the viewer is seeing in an easy-to-understand way.

Develop an Ongoing Production Schedule for Content

There are two main approaches a company can take with its YouTube channel. The first is to create a channel, then immediately populate it with a collection of individual videos designed to help the company achieve its goals. From day one, once your YouTube channel goes live, it will offer all the video-based content your customers need, all pre-organized and ready to be viewed.

This approach requires weeks or months of preparation, and potentially a large upfront cost to produce a comprehensive selection of videos that will be made available all at the same time you launch the channel. Moving forward, you always have the option to update videos or add new content as your company releases new products, for example.

The benefit to this approach is that your viewers will have access to all the information and content that you deem they need, all at once, if they're willing to invest the time to watch all your videos. The drawback to this approach is there is no incentive for the viewer to subscribe to your YouTube channel or come back on an ongoing and regular basis to view new content.

A second, more common approach is to launch a new YouTube channel with just a few videos, then promise your viewers and subscribers that new content will be published on a pre-set schedule moving forward. For example, you can promote that new videos will be published every Monday at noon (EST) and that by subscribing to your channel and clicking on the "Alert" icon, they can immediately be notified each time a new video becomes available. This approach allows you to spread out your production schedule and amortize the cost to produce your content over time. It also encourages viewers to subscribe to your channel, which means that you can potentially communicate with them (via your videos) on a regular and ongoing basis. Thus, when you have a new product to promote or a new promotion to launch, you can quickly share this information within a new video that your subscribers are apt to watch immediately.

Again, based on your objectives and the relationship you want to create with your viewers/subscribers, as well as what you believe will best benefit your audience, choose an approach that makes the most sense for your company. However, once you commit to a production schedule and promise a new video every week or every month, it's essential that you stick to this schedule so you adhere to the expectations you've now created among your audience. If a viewer visits your channel on Monday afternoon, expecting to see a new video, but it's not there, you'll quickly lose credibility.

Also, by taking the approach of publishing new content every week or month (following whatever schedule you choose), you're able to promote what's coming in future videos and build anticipation and demand for your content. You're also able to solicit ideas for future content from your audience and more easily adapt to their wants and needs as your YouTube channel becomes more established.

A FEW COMMON TRAITS OF SUCCESSFUL YOUTUBE VIDEOS

No perfect formula exists for creating a successful YouTube video. What works for one company to reach a specific audience will not necessarily work for another. However, if you analyze other successful videos on YouTube, particularly videos produced by your competitors or that target the same audience as you're striving to reach, you'll probably discover some common elements.

Many popular videos produced by small businesses and entrepreneurs typically have some or all the following traits and production elements:

- The video is short and to the point. Keep your videos under six minutes in length.
- Within the first few seconds of the video, what the video is about and what it offers are quickly and clearly explained to the viewer.
- The video's call to action is incorporated into the video near the beginning, then repeated several times within the video, including near the end. The call to action begins by stating what reward the viewer receives for following through and completing the call to action.
- The video incorporates contact information for the person or organization that created it. This can be done using voice-overs, statements by the people featured within your video, titles/captions, and/or annotations or links embedded within the video itself. This information should also appear within the video's description.
- The video is targeted to a specific audience and has a specific goal or objective.
- The content of the video is unique and sets itself apart from the other videos on YouTube.
- The video offers information that the viewer perceives as useful, informative, entertaining, highly engaging, educational, or directly relevant to what they're looking for, wanting, or needing.
- In terms of production quality, the video is professional looking and offers good-quality sound.
- The video uses some type of background music.
- The video offers clearly defined and easy-to-understand information that the viewer doesn't have to wait long to receive. The information is not buried in clutter or hidden by eye candy or audio that can be distracting or confusing to the

viewer. For example, animated shots or scene transitions are not overused, and the background music is set at a proper level and is appropriate to the content.

■ The look and messaging within the video is consistent with the company's brand and reputation.

■ The title of the video is appropriate, descriptive, and to the point. When someone sees the video's title, they immediately have a good idea what the video is about and what they can expect from it. This is supported by a carefully worded description and accompanied by a carefully selected group of relevant tags and keywords.

With these common traits in mind, as you explore YouTube for yourself, you'll easily discover very popular videos that follow none of these suggestions and that offer a truly unique or vastly different approach. There are no hard-core rules to follow because video production is a highly creative endeavor. Focus on originality and ways you can communicate your core message as quickly and easily as possible to your audience.

REASONS WHY MOST VIDEOS NEVER BECOME POPULAR

Out of all the videos uploaded to YouTube every day, a very small percentage generate more than a few hundred views, and only an elite few of those manage to go viral and attract thousands, millions, or in a few rare cases, billions of views. Instead of focusing on trying to create viral videos, dedicate your efforts to catering to your target audience when writing, producing, shooting, and editing videos.

The results you'll then receive in terms of the percentage of appropriate and interested people watching your videos and following through on your video's call to action will be significantly higher. These days, when it comes to measuring a successful video on YouTube, it is not just about the number of views. What's more important is the quality of the engagement the viewer of your video has.

Quality of engagement can be measured based on:

■ How much of your video someone watches before clicking out of it

■ The percentage of people who watch your entire video vs. how many people click out of it before it's over

■ The number of people who "like" your video vs. how many "dislike" it or take no action after watching it

■ The number of comments a video receives

■ The percentage of people who follow through with the video's call to action

Even if your video has top-notch production value and costs you a fortune to produce, this does not guarantee an audience. Later, in Chapter 14, "Promoting Your YouTube Videos," you'll learn more about how to effectively promote your videos once they're published online. However, you first need to develop ideas for your videos and then produce them, which is the focus of this chapter, as well as Chapter 8, "Filming YouTube Videos."

ADDITIONAL REASONS WHY YOUTUBE VIDEOS SOMETIMES FAIL

There are many reasons why videos fail to attract an audience. Some of the more common reasons include:

- They're poorly produced and boring to watch.
- The content of the video is unoriginal and doesn't stand out from the competition.
- It fails to cater to its target audience.
- The content is not entertaining, informative, or perceived as containing any type of valuable information—it does not address any type of work or need.
- It's too long and fails to hold the viewer's attention.
- The content doesn't properly take advantage of the visual aspect of multimedia, so it fails to keep the viewer's attention. If the viewer wants to just listen to content that doesn't use visuals, he/she could download or stream a podcast or audiobook, or simply turn on the radio. Consider ways to make your videos visually compelling.
- The video is given a nondescriptive title and has poorly chosen tags associated with it, which makes it hard or impossible to find using YouTube's Search feature or a search engine.
- The video isn't properly promoted after it's published on YouTube.
- Early on, the video receives "dislikes," low ratings, and negative comments, which indicates to those who stumble on it later that it's not worth watching.
- The producer or "star" of the video has a negative reputation online, which turns potential viewers off to what the video has to say.

Now that you know some of the more common reasons why many videos published on YouTube fail to attract an audience, you can more easily avoid these pitfalls by taking a different approach when presenting your unique content to your target audience.

Remember, creating videos with top-notch production value and appealing content requires creativity, skill, and experience that you'll probably develop over time. It's not realistic to expect everything to fall into place perfectly as you're creating and producing your first few videos. Right from the start, however, make sure your videos will help establish or boost your company's image or reputation. If you're not able to achieve a good enough production value to showcase a professional image, seek the help of a professional video production company or upgrade your production equipment.

As you publish your first few videos, take advantage of YouTube Analytics and the comments, likes, ratings, and other feedback you receive from your initial viewers. This information can all be extremely useful as you're getting to know your audience and discovering the types of videos and approaches within your videos that work best.

For a video to become successful on YouTube, it has to offer the right content and approach that's targeted to the right audience within an appropriate time frame, then it needs to be promoted properly. Thus, many different pre-production, production, post-production, and promotional elements need to come together.

GET TO THE POINT—FAST

Whatever approach you take with your videos, remember that it's your job to capture your audience's attention very quickly, then keep the content of your videos succinct so their running time is kept short.

You're much better off producing a few short three- to six-minute videos that can be daisy-chained together as a YouTube playlist than you are trying to hold your audience's attention for 10 to 15 minutes or longer with a single video.

The attention span of most people who use YouTube is extremely short. The moment people get bored, they'll simply click to the next video. If someone decides that they want to watch your video and it's just a few minutes in length, chances are they'll watch it as soon as they stumble on it. Most people aren't too concerned about investing two to six minutes out of their already busy day.

However, if that same person sees that watching your video will require a commitment of 10, 15, or 20 minutes, they're going to be much more reserved about clicking the play button. If a viewer notices a video's long play length, that alone can be a huge deterrent, especially if the viewer doesn't know who you are and doesn't already subscribe to your YouTube channel.

There is no optimal length for a YouTube video. How long someone will commit to watching a single video depends on the subject matter, the production quality of the video, how the content is presented, and a wide range of other factors. That being said, the chances of someone choosing to watch your video, then sticking with it until the end, are much greater if the video is short, engaging, and to the point. On average, most YouTube users prefer videos three minutes or shorter in length regardless of the topic or content. If the content is of interest to them and presented well, you may be able to keep their attention longer, but don't push your luck.

As you're managing your YouTube channel, you can group videos together as a playlist for your viewers, so one video automatically plays after the next, in the order that you preset. Of course, a viewer can pause or exit out of the playlist at any time, but if one of your videos holds the viewer's attention until the end, having another relevant video begin automatically is an excellent strategy for retaining viewers as they watch multiple videos. This is a great way to build your audience and YouTube channel subscriber base.

HOW TO GENERATE IDEAS FOR YOUR VIDEOS

Ideas for new videos can come from anywhere. Look for inspiration in your daily life, and be sure to seek out ideas from friends, co-workers, employees, customers, and clients. You'll also want to invest time to explore YouTube and watch plenty of different types of videos that other companies and individuals have produced.

The core concepts for videos that you generate should stand out and excite you (as well as your audience). They need to be original, creative, interesting, thought-provoking, entertaining, and/or informative, and at the same time, be of interest to your audience. One way to begin your search for ideas is to determine what your competition is already doing, then figure out how you can do that better or differently within your videos.

With so much content already available from YouTube, coming up with truly unique ideas is going to be extremely difficult. Instead, focus on ways to set your ideas apart from what's already out there. Don't be afraid to jump on the bandwagon and use currently popular videos as your inspiration, as long as you're able and willing to add a unique, original, or compelling twist to your videos. If you opt to use other videos as inspiration, make sure you're not violating anyone's copyrights, intellectual properties, or trademarks when you produce your own videos.

Once you have a general idea about what your overall goals are for YouTube, have defined your audience, and have outlined your primary message, it's time to brainstorm ideas for individual videos. Start by determining what you want to say. Then, based on your video production skills, equipment, and capabilities, consider the very best way to present that content.

For each potential idea you come up with, ask yourself these questions:

- Is my idea consistent with what I'm trying to accomplish on YouTube?
- What is the best approach to take with my idea within the video?
- Will my idea and my intended approach appeal to my audience?
- Do I have the skill, knowledge, and proper equipment to produce the video I'm envisioning and do it well?
- Can the video be produced within my budget without compromising production quality?

- How do I want the audience to react to the video? What will be the call to action?
- How do I anticipate the audience will react to the video?
- Will watching this video entice the viewer to watch other videos on my YouTube channel, to contact me or my company, and/or place an order for my product/ service, if applicable?
- While someone is watching the video, or immediately after it's over, will they be motivated to click on the "like" button, give it a good rating, write and post a favorable comment, and/or share the video (or a link to it) with their online friends (via Facebook, Google+, or Twitter, for example)?
- Does the video, its message, call to action, and overall approach fit with what I'm already doing for myself or my company elsewhere in cyberspace, using Facebook, Google+, and/or Twitter, for example?

During the entire pre-production phase, and then later when engaged in post-production for your videos, go back and ask yourself these questions again and again to make sure you're remaining on target.

As you answer each of these questions, you'll often discover the need to fine-tune or tweak your original ideas to transform them into something that's more viable or on target with your message, call to action, and overall goals. At the same time you're evaluating your ideas, however, think about creative, off-beat, and original ways you can present your content in a fun, unusual, or memorable way.

Then, before investing too much time or money as you move forward in the pre-production phase, perhaps bounce your ideas off other people who are familiar with you, your company, its products/services, your target audience, and your online goals. Sharing ideas with other creative people whom you trust is always a good strategy, plus it'll help you consider things from different perspectives that could impact how your videos are perceived and/or accepted by your audience.

If your goal is to launch a YouTube channel and populate it with new videos on a regular basis, whether it's daily, weekly, or monthly, during this early phase of idea generation, develop a list that outlines concepts for your first 10 or so videos. Then, as you brainstorm ideas in the future, be sure to write them down so you can later refer to your ideas.

Make sure that what you intend to do with your YouTube channel is sustainable and consistent with your brand, online business reputation, and overall business model. For example, you may have great ideas for your first few videos, but what will you do to maintain and build your audience several months or even several years down the road? Keeping YouTube channel content fresh over the long term proves to be a huge challenge for many companies and individuals.

TAKING YOUR IDEA INTO PRE-PRODUCTION

After you develop what you think is a great idea for a YouTube video, before creating the storyboard and writing the script, choose what approach you want to take with the video. For example, will it be how-to related, informational, tell a story, showcase an interview, offer a product demonstration, or focus on entertainment? As you've already discovered, the possibilities are limited mainly by your imagination, skills, production budget, and the capabilities of the video equipment that's at your disposal.

At this point, it's a good strategy to create a storyboard for your video concept. On a sheet of paper, draw a series of boxes, like a cartoon strip, and within each of the boxes, sequentially sketch out what will happen in each scene of your video. Use stick figures, if necessary. The appearance and artistic quality of your storyboards is far less important than the raw ideas your storyboard conveys.

As you do this, below each box, write the scene number and a few words about what multimedia elements will be incorporated into the screen. So, the first box on your storyboard might contain the main title of the video or a sketch of the opening shot, along with a brief description of what will be said in a voice-over and what music will be heard.

Depending on the complexity of your overall video concept, the storyboard for a three- to six-minute video might be spread out between five and ten storyboard boxes. Creating a storyboard will help you expand on your video idea and develop it into a graphic and text-based outline for what will ultimately be shot.

Later, as you write the script for your video, if applicable, you can add the script elements under the appropriate frames in your storyboard. Especially if you'll be working with multiple people on your video production team, a detailed storyboard in conjunction with a script will help everyone develop a good understanding of the video's concept and content before you begin shooting.

Sometimes the core concept for a video may seem viable when it's written out in one or two sentences, but once you expand the concept into a rough storyboard, you may discover that everything you want to include within the video either won't take up three to six minutes or you'll need way too much time to convey your video's core message to the viewer.

Within your storyboard, plan each scene and shot, associate each scene or shot with dialogue, and determine when and where titles, animations, graphics, music, and sound effects, for example, will be used.

Many art supply stores sell oversize pads that have pre-printed storyboard grids on them. Levenger (www.levenger.com/Special-Request-Storyboard--Unpunched-Ltr-Core-8106.aspx), for example, offers 8.5-by-11-inch storyboard paper with three-ring binder holes, while Moleskine (https://us.moleskine.com/en/storyboard-notebook/p0438) offers 5-by-8.25-inch hardcover notebooks containing preprinted storyboard grids on each page.

Write a Compelling Script

By focusing in on your video's goal, then reviewing your storyboard, at this point you should be able to determine the approximate length your video will be, then be able to begin drafting a shooting script, which contains exactly what will be said, word for word, within the video. A script also describes who will say each line. Not all videos will require a script. If you deem a script to be unnecessary, it's even more important to create a detailed storyboard for your video idea before you begin shooting.

Assuming your video requires a script, be sure to write it in a style that caters to your audience, using language, phrasing, and an approach that viewers will easily relate to and understand. Within your script, make sure your message is presented clearly and you present your call to action multiple times.

Scriptwriting is a skill unto itself that takes years to master. Your best bet as you start out is to focus on what you're most familiar with and knowledgeable about. In addition to being a skill, scriptwriting is also a creative art form. Even a script for a three- to six-minute video could take hours, possibly days, to write, rewrite, and fine-tune. You want the wording and approach to be succinct and compelling. It also should sound natural for the people who will be saying the words on camera—whether it's you, an actor, voice-over announcer, or your company's spokesperson.

As you're writing your script, keep that age-old saying, "A picture is worth a thousand words" clear in your mind. When possible, use video images, photos, charts, graphs, or other graphic elements to convey concepts or ideas quickly and visually. Remember, you're creating a video that can include many visual and audible elements simultaneously to get your message across. Don't be afraid to use what's at your disposal during the shooting of a video as well as in post-production.

For a short video, your script can be written using any word processor. However, if you'll be crafting a more elaborate script and want to format it the way scriptwriters for commercials, TV shows, and movies do, consider acquiring special script-writing software to help you organize and format your script accordingly.

Final Draft 10 (https://store.finaldraft.com/final-draft-10.html), Movie Magic Screenwriter 6 (www.screenplay.com), and the screenwriting software available from Celtx (www.celtx.com) are three examples of specialized software packages for script writing. You'll find details about additional software at http://en.wikipedia.org/wiki/List_of_screenwriting_software. In addition to helping you properly format and print the scripts for your video productions, these software packages offer tools to help you flesh out ideas and assist with the creative process of script-writing.

Within your script, be sure to include as much direction and detail as possible related to shooting locations, camera angles, and types of shots. Describe the actions that the performers in the video take and how music and/or sound effects will be used.

Indicate when special props, charts, graphics, or other animated or multimedia content beyond live-action video footage will be used.

If your video will include dialogue between two or more people, ensure that the words you're writing in the script sound natural and can be easily understood when they're said aloud by the people featured in your video. How something reads on a page is very different from how it sounds when spoken, especially if it's a conversation between two or more people.

Develop a Budget

After the idea for a video has been fleshed out and storyboarded and/or scripted, sit down and develop a realistic production budget for it based on what will be involved in producing the video you're envisioning. Every element of the video's production should be considered in advance. Use the "Video Production Budget Worksheet" in Figure 4–1 to help you calculate your costs.

Expense Description	Cost per Day ($)	Total Cost
Actors/Presenters		
Crew—Writer, Director, Camera Person, Sound Engineer, Set Designer, Hairstylist, Makeup Artist, Production Assistants, etc.		
Location/Set-Related Costs		
Wardrobe, Costumes, Makeup, and Props		
Microphones and Sound Equipment		
Lighting Equipment		
Music/Sound Effects Licensing and/or Royalties		
Animation and Graphic Development		
Editing and Post Production		
Camcorder/Camera Equipment Purchase or Rental		
Catering/Food		
Shooting Permits		
Other Special Needs or Considerations		
	Total Budget	

FIGURE 4–1. Video production budget worksheet

Depending on the scale of your video production, you may need to use a professional and highly trained crew, including a director, writer, camera operator, sound engineer, production assistants, and video editor. These people are typically paid a daily rate, which will vary greatly based on their skill level, experience, your geographic region, and whether they're in a union.

Using professional vs. amateur actors and/or voice-over talent will also have a huge impact on your budget, as will the type of camera and related equipment you'll be using for your productions.

Keep in mind the costs outlined in the budget worksheet relate to pre-production, production, and post-production costs. You will still need to include video promotion costs into your overall budget. It's not uncommon for a promotional budget to be greater than the production budget for a video being published on YouTube by a company or organization. More information about planning the promotional budget for your videos can be found in Chapter 14, "Promoting Your YouTube Videos."

Use the worksheets provided in Figures 4–2 and 4–3 on page 55 to help you determine what will be needed during a video's production.

Set Your Production Schedule

Again, based on the complexity of your video, you may be able to shoot it in one take and wrap up production in less than one hour. Or, for more elaborate productions, the shooting alone might take several days. Once you have the concept for your video finalized, sit down and figure how much time will be required for pre-production, production, and post-production. If multiple people will be involved in various phases of the production, try to calculate how much time will be required of each person and when they'll be needed.

Actor / Performer	Cost ($)	Date(s) Needed
Wardrobe		
Hair		
Makeup		
Props		
Transportation		
Other:		

FIGURE 4–2. Actor/performer-related needs

Set	Item Details	Cost ($)	Date(s) Needed
Background			
Furniture			
Accessories/Accents/Décor			
Special Lighting			
Production Crew Members Needed on Set			

FIGURE 4–3. Set-related needs

Next, set dates and times for each phase of the video's production, and mark your calendar. Be sure that everyone involved is kept in the loop and that people know exactly when and where they'll be needed. If everyone shows up for filming except one of your actors or one or two key people on your production crew, this can result in costly production delays and frustration.

As you plan your production schedule, allow for last-minute problems, unforeseen issues to arise, and for other types of delays. For example, if you'll be shooting on location, expect that at least one or two people involved in your production will get stuck in traffic, get lost, or have car trouble. Also assume you'll run into some type of problem with your video equipment (which will hopefully be easily solvable) or that as you're shooting, you'll want to take a break to fine-tune your script or rework how a scene is being shot.

To help you save time and avoid frustration during your video shoots, plan on recording each scene a handful of times, and shoot scenes out of order if necessary. If several scenes will take place on the same set or at the same location, shoot those scenes back-to-back. You can always reorder your raw footage during the post-production (editing) phase. Also, make sure there's someone in charge at the shoot—whether it's the producer or director—then try to keep your cast and production crew streamlined so it's easily manageable.

YOUTUBE COMMUNITY GUIDELINES AND COPYRIGHT INFRINGEMENT

When producing your videos, make sure that all elements of your video are original or that you have the proper permission to use content or production elements that you don't own outright, such as music, sound effects, logos, and/or artwork. YouTube uses advanced technology to automatically scan videos as they're being uploaded to thwart the illegal use of copyrighted material.

YouTube prohibits certain types of material from being published on the service, including any type of pornography. All the rules pertaining to what is and isn't permissible within a YouTube video can be found within the YouTube community guidelines (www.youtube.com/t/community_guidelines).

As a YouTube channel operator and/or content producer, it is essential that you read and understand these guidelines before you begin filming your videos and uploading them to YouTube. Violating YouTube's community guidelines could result in your videos being taken offline or your channel being suspended.

For example, in addition to prohibiting pornographic material on YouTube, any type of child exploitation, animal abuse, or videos portraying drug use or underage drinking or smoking, as well as topics such as how to make a bomb, are also forbidden. You'll also discover that YouTube does not permit graphic or gratuitous violence.

While YouTube does support freedom of speech, it does not permit videos that attack or demean people based on race, ethnic origin, religion, disability, gender, sexual orientation, or age. You're also not allowed to issue threats, invade someone's privacy, stalk, or reveal someone else's private information using a YouTube video.

Another thing YouTube is strict about enforcing is that video producers and publishers use accurate titles, descriptions, tags, and thumbnails when uploading and listing their videos on the service. In other words, you can't use misleading or inaccurate information with the hope of attracting viewers for your videos who might otherwise have no interest in it if it were listed and titled accurately. This practice is called "click baiting," and while it's common for YouTubers to do this, it's inappropriate for small business operators to do it.

The most common violation of the YouTube community guidelines involves someone incorporating copyrighted music within their production without the proper permission. If you don't know whether you're about to violate a copyright by including something in one of your videos, visit YouTube's Copyright Help Center (www.youtube.com/t/howto_copyright) and/or consult with an attorney before publishing the questionable video content online. You can also visit the Library of Congress' Copyright website (www.copyright.gov) for more information about filing your own copyrights and to learn how to avoid violating copyrights owned by others. For a quick and animated primer about copyrights, watch *Take the Mystery Out of Copyright* by visiting: www.loc.gov/teachers/copyrightmystery.

In addition to YouTube's automated tools that seek out videos that violate the service's community guidelines, the YouTube community helps police and monitor the service. Anyone who discovers a video that violates YouTube's community guidelines can flag a video by clicking on the "Report" icon that's displayed below every video as it is being streamed/watched. Once a video is reported, within 24 hours, someone from YouTube will personally review the video and determine if it violates community guidelines.

Even if a video does not violate YouTube's community guidelines, it may be deemed inappropriate for viewers below a certain age and will then have restrictions and warning labels placed in conjunction with the video that pertains to who can and should watch it.

CREATE A YOUTUBE CHANNEL AND POPULATE IT WITH CONTENT

You can create, brand, and customize a YouTube channel for free. While you can create a channel right away, a better approach is to understand what's possible using a YouTube channel, then focus on producing a few individual videos first.

Then, when you create your YouTube channel and are ready to populate it with the first few videos, you'll be better equipped to customize and brand the channel itself, based on the initial content you've created and that's ready to share.

In terms of the steps you need to take, a YouTube channel must be established before you can upload, publish, and share videos on YouTube, which is why the step-by-step directions for creating your channel are covered first. However, until you have video content that's ready to publish, there's no point creating your YouTube channel and making it available to viewers, since there's nothing yet for them to watch.

Chapter 5

How to Start Your Own YouTube Channel

IN THIS CHAPTER

- What is a YouTube channel and how can it work for business?
- Benefits of starting a YouTube channel
- The importance of branding your YouTube channel
- Organizing content within your YouTube channel
- Strategies for making your YouTube channel successful

When you upload a video to YouTube, there are many ways for your potential viewers to find and enjoy it. Every video has a title, keywords (tags), and a description associated with it. It's also categorized by subject matter and given its own unique URL (website address). Plus, links for the channel (or the videos themselves) can be embedded into websites, blogs, a Facebook page, emails, and/or social media posts.

One of the most common ways your potential viewers will be able to find your content is by visiting your YouTube channel, which you should plan on branding with your company logo and contact information. Establishing a YouTube channel is free, and there are many reasons why it makes sense, especially if you're trying to establish a large audience for your videos.

Establishing a YouTube channel is separate from creating a free Google account, which is used to access the YouTube service. To establish a YouTube channel, however, you first need to set up a Google account, or you can use your existing Google account as the YouTube identity for your new channel. If multiple people within your company will be managing or contributing to your company's YouTube channel, set up a new and separate Google account, as opposed to using your personal Google account to create the company's YouTube channel.

A YouTube channel is a special area of YouTube that's dedicated to you (or your company)—the channel's host. When someone visits your YouTube channel, they will see descriptions and links to all the videos you've published as part of that channel, as well as information about you (or your company), and other channel-oriented details, which we'll focus on shortly.

One of the biggest benefits to hosting your own YouTube channel is that people can subscribe to it. Then, if they choose, subscribers can click on the "Alert" icon associated with your channel to automatically receive a notification whenever you publish a new video on your channel. Through a YouTube channel, you can develop and promote your brand, personalize your channel, and organize its contents for your audience. Your channel's main page can also offer links to your primary website(s), blog, Facebook page, your company's other social media accounts, and/or an online store, for example.

If you're selling a product, you want someone to find your video on YouTube and watch it, learn about your product, and either click on the link within the video window itself or on your YouTube channel page, which leads to your online store so that the viewer can immediately purchase the product online. However, research has shown that videos that use a hard-sell approach are not nearly as effective as an informational or product demonstration video, for example, that uses a soft-sell message.

While big companies often use videos that are in essence slickly produced commercials or infomercials to promote brand awareness or showcase a product, as a small-business operator who's trying to cater to a niche or targeted audience, spending $10,000 to $100,000 or more for a 30- to 90-second, professionally produced video that looks like a commercial is typically not the most cost-effective strategy.

Every YouTube channel page is customizable, allowing you to showcase you or your company's brand, corporate image, or your own personality to cater to your audience. As you develop your YouTube channel and ultimately populate it with videos, some of your goals for the overall channel should be to:

- Get people who watch one or more of your videos to subscribe to your channel.
- Encourage viewers to "like" your videos.
- Solicit comments about your videos from viewers.
- Persuade your viewers/subscribers to share links to your videos with their online friends (via Facebook, Twitter, Instagram, LinkedIn, email, etc.). This serves as

free and powerful word-of-mouth advertising for your videos and is one of the keys to helping a video go viral.

■ Entice your audience to follow the links on your YouTube channel page to your primary website, online store, blog, Facebook page, etc.

More information about how to achieve these goals is covered in Chapter 13, "Interacting with Viewers and Subscribers," as well as in Chapter 14, "Promoting Your YouTube Videos." Ultimately, you want traffic from your primary website(s) to visit your YouTube channel page and watch your videos, while you want people who access your videos via your YouTube channel page to visit your other websites, especially if you're trying to sell a product or service.

HOW TO CREATE YOUR OWN YOUTUBE CHANNEL

The process for establishing and customizing your own YouTube channel takes just a few minutes. You'll then want to customize the channel by adjusting a handful of options, uploading your photo or logo, and linking your channel with your other online social networking accounts, like Facebook, Twitter, Instagram, Pinterest, and/or LinkedIn.

First, Create Your Free Google Account

If you are starting a YouTube channel for your business, set up a separate Google/YouTube account from scratch, using a unique and nonpersonal email address. That way, someone else from within your organization can run the channel without you giving out your personal Google account username and password, which may also be associated with other Google services, such as G Suite or Gmail. Keep in mind, only one YouTube channel can be associated with each Google account.

There is no such thing as a specialized business account or YouTube channel for businesses. You'll need to customize a standard YouTube channel's settings so that it best caters to your audience and showcases your business, its image/brand, and your videos.

To create a unique Google account, follow these steps:

1. Launch any web browser on your computer that's connected to the internet and visit www.youtube.com.
2. From the YouTube homepage, click on the "Sign In" link that's displayed near the top-right corner of the screen (shown in Figure 5–1 on page 62).
3. When the Google "Sign In" screen appears, enter your email address, click on "More Options," then click on "Create Account" (shown in Figure 5–2 on page 62).

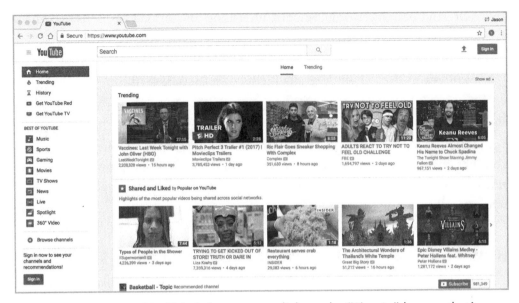

FIGURE 5–1. From YouTube's homepage, click on the "Sign In" button that's displayed near the top-right corner of the screen.

FIGURE 5–2. Click on "Create Account" to establish a new Google account that will be used to log in to YouTube and manage your YouTube channel.

4. At the "Create Your New Google Account" screen (shown in Figure 5–3 on page 63), fill in the fields. You'll be asked to enter your first and last name. Then, you'll be instructed to enter an email address. If you're creating a YouTube channel for

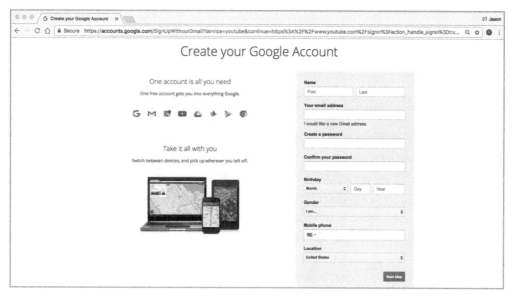

FIGURE 5–3. Fill in each field of the "Create Your New Google Account" screen with the appropriate information.

your business, for example, do not use a personal email address when prompted for your current email address.

5. Create and confirm a password for the new account, enter your birthday and gender, as well as a mobile phone number. Select your location from the pull-down menu, then click on the "Next Step" button.

6. When the "Terms of Service" window is displayed, scroll down. Click on the "I Agree" button to continue.

7. The web browser you're using will ask if you want the computer to remember the email address and password associated with the Google account. Whether you accept this option is a personal decision that should be made based on whether other people will be using your computer in the future. If your computer (and web browser) saves your email address and password for your Google account, every time you access YouTube in the future, you will automatically get signed it. However, if someone else is using your computer and web browser, they, too, will automatically be signed in with your account information. So, if other people will be using your computer and web browser in the future, reject the option to have your email address and Google password saved.

8. To verify your account, Google will either send a text message to your smartphone or call your voice line and provide a verification code. When prompted, choose the phone number you want Google to contact, and select between the "Text Message" (SMS) and "Voice Call" option.

9. Once you receive the six-digit verification code, enter it into the "Verify Your Account" field that's displayed within the web browser window. Unless you later turn on two-factor authentication for your account, this step needs to be done only once.

10. Next, a verification email will be sent to the inbox of the email address you provided. Click on the link that's embedded within your email. Upon doing this, your new Google account will be set up.

11. Return to the YouTube website (www.youtube.com), click on the "Sign In" button, and enter the email address and password you just used to create your Google account. This is how you'll log in to YouTube from now on.

12. Once you've signed into your newly created YouTube account, you'll need to populate your Google account profile. This includes uploading an optional profile photo. Start by clicking on the profile icon that's displayed near the top-right corner of the browser window. The email address associated with your account will be displayed (shown in Figure 5–4).

13. Click on the profile photo icon that's empty, then select and crop the profile photo you want to use in conjunction with your account (shown in Figure 5–5 on page 65). This photo will be displayed publicly. If you're creating an account for your business or organization, upload a company logo or product photo, as opposed to a personal photo or headshot. This will be a visual identifier for you (or your business) when you're doing anything related to your YouTube channel

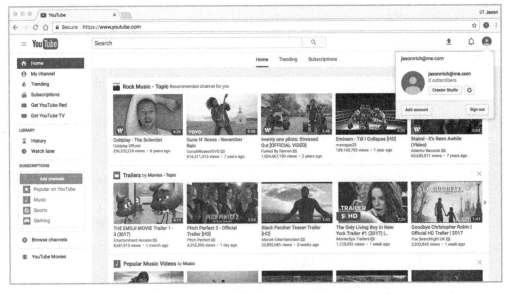

FIGURE 5–4. Click on the empty profile icon to add a photo or company logo as your account's profile image.

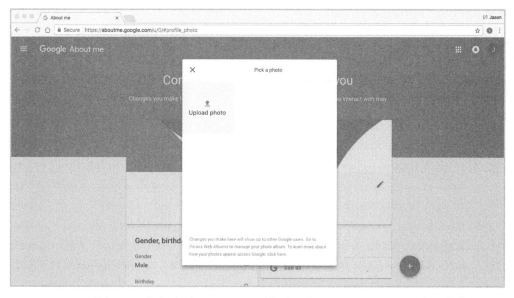

FIGURE 5–5. Select a digital photo or graphic (such as your company logo) that's stored locally on your computer to use as your account's Profile image.

or your Google account. If you're using a logo, for example, make sure you own the legal rights to use it online.

14. After saving your profile image, click on the circular "+" icon to provide additional public information for your profile (shown in Figure 5–6).

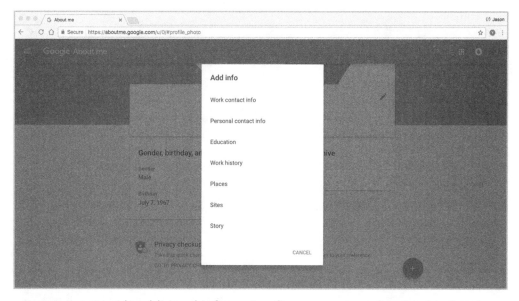

FIGURE 5–6. Provide additional information for your account, keeping in mind that the details you provide will be public and searchable.

Create Your YouTube Channel

Using your Google account (which also serves as your YouTube account for watching videos), you can now easily establish and customize your YouTube channel, then populate it with your own videos. Follow these steps to create a free YouTube channel once you have a valid Google account set up.

1. Access www.youtube.com, and sign in using your Google account username and password. The main YouTube home screen will be displayed.

2. Near the upper-right corner of the screen, you'll see your account profile picture. Click on it to reveal the Google account menu, which will also be displayed near the top-right corner of the screen (refer to Figure 5–4 on page 64).

3. Click on the "Creator Studio" button that's displayed below your email address and profile photo. When the "You must create a channel to upload videos. Create a channel" message is displayed, click on "Create a Channel" (shown in Figure 5–7).

4. When the "Use YouTube as . . ." window pops up, enter your first and last name into the appropriate fields (shown in Figure 5–8 on page 67). Click on the "Create Channel" button to continue.

5. Your empty YouTube channel has now been established. The next few steps involve customizing and branding the channel's appearance. At any point moving forward, you can click on the "Upload" icon (the upward-pointing arrow

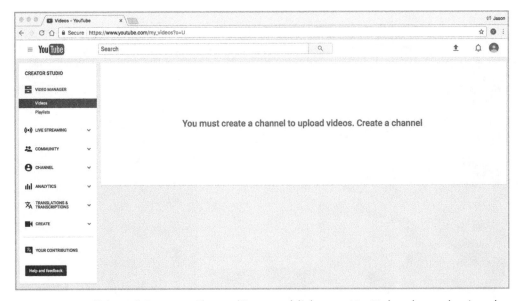

FIGURE 5–7. Click on "Create a Channel" to establish your YouTube channel using the Google account information you used to sign into YouTube.

FIGURE 5–8. Enter your name in the "Use YouTube as . . ." fields, then click on the "Create Channel" button.

icon that's located near the top-right corner of the browser window) to begin populating the channel with videos that are ready to publish online (shown in Figure 5–9).

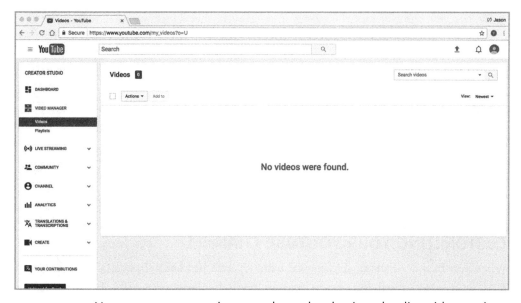

FIGURE 5–9. You can now customize your channel or begin uploading videos to it.

GIVE YOUR SUBSCRIBERS A CHANCE TO INTERACT WITH YOUR CHANNEL

Any time someone watches a video on YouTube, if the "like" option is enabled, they can click on the thumbs-up icon to "like" the video. If a video earns a lot of "likes," it means you're doing something right.

Beyond just liking a video, a viewer can also be given the opportunity to "dislike" a video, as well as comment on a video (if this option is enabled) by composing a text message that is related to the video. As the YouTube channel operator, you can decide if the comments posted by others will be published online for everyone to see by adjusting the Sharing Settings associated with your YouTube channel. To customize these settings, from the Creator Studio main screen, click on the Community option (displayed along the left margin of the browser window) to expand this menu, then click on the gear-shaped Community Settings icon that's displayed near the top-right corner of the browser window. Scroll down to the Default Settings heading, then adjust the options related to "Comments on Your Videos," "Comments on Your Channel," and "Creator Credits on Your Channel."

Anyone who creates a Google account (with its associated YouTube account) can create their own personalized collection of favorite videos, which they can watch whenever they wish. By activating the "Favorite a Video" option for your channel, people who watch your videos will be able to add them to their own "Favorites" list. By default, when someone then views your video(s), they'll be able to see how many people have added it to their "Favorites" lists.

You, as the YouTube channel operator, can decide whether to allow other people to subscribe to your channel. If you're creating a YouTube channel to build a large and dedicated following for you, a product, event, service, or your business, you'll want to encourage people to "like" your videos, add their own comments, "Favorite" your videos, and subscribe to your YouTube channel. You'll also benefit greatly if you convince your viewers to share your video with their online friends via email and their social media accounts, for example.

CUSTOMIZING YOUR YOUTUBE CHANNEL

When you first access your newly established YouTube channel page (shown in Figure 5–10 on page 69), it will look pretty barren. It will display your profile photo, name, and a few details like your latest activity, date joined, age, and country.

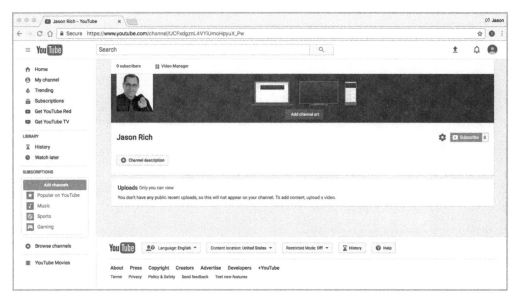

FIGURE 5–10. Initially, your YouTube channel page will look barren. You need to add a profile photo (if you haven't already done so), as well as custom Channel Art.

To begin customizing your channel page, click on the "Add Channel Art" option and upload artwork that will be displayed as banner artwork along the top of the page. This is in addition to your profile photo. The custom channel art (wallpaper) can be a digital photo or a graphic image you create or edit using Adobe Photoshop or another graphics program. You can also pay a small fee to a graphic artist and have them create a professional-looking graphic for you.

When selecting a photo to use as channel art, be sure it's not too busy, or it will distract or confuse your visitors. It's also essential that you own the rights to the image/photo you'll be using. Otherwise, you could get into trouble for copyright violations.

Next, click on the "Channel Description" button and compose a text-based description of your channel. Keep in mind, this is a description of your YouTube channel as a whole—not specific video content. Use this Description option (shown in Figure 5–11 on page 70) to tell visitors about your company, yourself, and/or your goal for the channel. Describe the type of content people can expect to see, who it will appeal to, and why people will find your content relevant and compelling.

After typing your channel description, be sure to proofread the text carefully before publishing it. Spelling mistakes, grammatical errors, or poor use of the English language, for example, are not acceptable and will make you look unprofessional. Incorporate into your description a series of keywords or phrases that best describe your YouTube channel, as well as your product, service, company, or event. When someone performs a search on YouTube or Google, their search terms are automatically compared to the

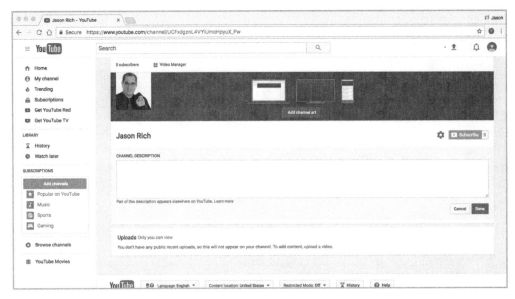

FIGURE 5–11. Compose an attention-getting Channel Description. Keep it short, but make people want to spend time watching your videos and subscribe to your channel.

description you've created for your YouTube Channel. If Google discovers a match or matches, your channel will be listed in the user's search results. This is a powerful tool for attracting traffic to your channel and increasing your views.

Click on the "Done" button to save your description and continue. Keep in mind, YouTube, Google, and other search engines will use this information when it comes to your channel's search engine optimization rankings and listings. Be sure everything you include in your channel's description appeals to your audience.

Next, click on the gear-shaped "Channel settings" icon that's located to the immediate left of the "Subscribe" button. As you're viewing the Channel settings window (shown in Figure 5-12 on page 71), click on the virtual switch associated with the "Customize the layout of your channel" option, and then click on the "Advanced settings" option.

From the "Advanced Settings" page that's displayed within your browser window, one of the first empty fields you'll see is labeled "Channel Keywords" (shown in Figure 5-13 on page 71). Here, you should include a comprehensive list of keywords and phrases that accurately describe your channel and are relevant to your target audience. In addition to the text included within your Channel Description, these keywords will be used by YouTube and Google to help match your channel with potential viewers/ subscribers who are using the Search field to find content that's relevant to their interests. As you enter keywords, separate them with commas.

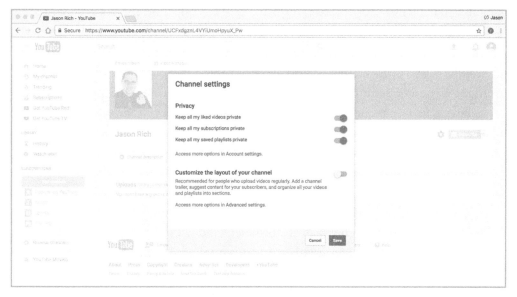

FIGURE 5–12. YouTube offers a variety of additional settings that you should adjust and customize.

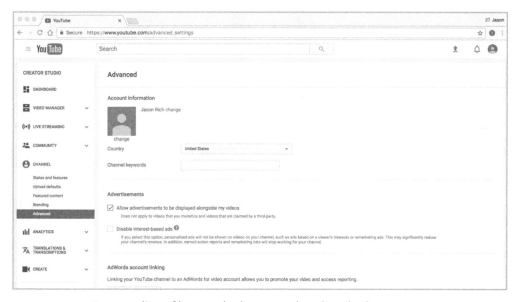

FIGURE 5–13. Create a list of keywords that are related and relevant to your company, YouTube channel, and its content.

Also from the Advanced settings page, you're able to determine whether you want your YouTube channel to be able to generate revenue by displaying ads to your viewers. Whether you turn on this feature or not will depend on your goals for the channel. Be sure to reach Chapter 12, "Monetizing YouTube: Getting Paid for Your Video Views," before turning on this feature.

When you first launch your channel, you'll have zero subscribers. It could take weeks or months before your channel attracts an impressive number of subscribers. Until then, from the Advanced Settings page, turn off the feature that's labeled Subscriber Counts, so visitors to your channel can't see how many subscribers you have. Later, when you have an impressive subscriber base, turn this feature on since it will help show new visitors that your content is well liked and has developed a strong following.

Be sure to click on the "Save" button at the bottom of the Advanced settings page to save your changes and put them into effect. Now, you're ready to create videos and populate the channel. Click on the Upload icon (the upward-pointing arrow icon that's located near the top-right corner of the browser window) to begin the video uploading process. How to do this is covered within Chapter 11, "Uploading Your Videos to YouTube."

One other element of your YouTube channel that you'll want to customize is the channel's unique URL (website address). By default, your channel is assigned a long, but unique, URL. To customize it, from the Creator Studio Dashboard, click on the "Channel" option that's displayed in the left margin of the browser window, and from the Status and Features screen, scroll down and click on the "Custom URL" option. If an "Ineligible" message is displayed, click on the "See Eligibility Requirements" link, and follow the on-screen directions for creating your channel's custom URL. Ultimately, the custom URL you choose will take on this format: http://www.youtube.com/[your custom channel name].

A second option is to visit any domain name registrar, such as GoDaddy (www.godaddy.com) and register the easy-to-remember domain name you want to use for your YouTube channel. Then, once you've acquired the desired domain name (an annual fee will apply), forward that domain name to your assigned YouTube channel's URL.

When creating a custom YouTube channel URL or purchasing a domain name, be sure to choose something that's easy to remember, spell, and identify. It can be your full name, the name of your company, or something short and clever.

As you customize your YouTube channel from the Creator Studio main screen, click on each of the options displayed along the left margin of the screen to access a different selection of options that can be personalized. For example, the channel title should include your company's name. While you cannot change your Google account username once it's set up, or the YouTube channel's custom URL (once you set it initially), you can modify the channel title at any time.

Once you begin publishing videos on your YouTube channel, you can embed those videos directly within your website, blog, or Facebook page, for example. If you want the

THIRD-PARTY COMPANIES CAN HELP BRAND YOUR YOUTUBE CHANNEL

One of the easiest ways to brand your YouTube channel and make it look professional is to take advantage of the services offered by a third-party company, like Creative Market (https://creativemarket.com/search?q=YouTube). This company, for example, offers a selection of fee-based templates that make it easy to use your artwork with pre-designed channel layouts and provide your channel with a professional appearance, with no graphic arts or artistic skill required.

To find additional third-party resources that can help you brand your YouTube channel, within any search engine, enter the phrase, "YouTube Channel Templates," or access YouTube's own Creator Services Directory by visiting: https://servicesdirectory.withyoutube.com.

ability to do this, be sure to turn on the "Embed" option when you upload and publish a video to your YouTube channel. You'll learn more about uploading and embedding YouTube videos in Chapter 11, "Uploading Your Videos to YouTube."

Then, once your videos are online, you can access real-time details about viewers for free, using the online (and free) YouTube Analytics tools. To access these tools, from the main Creator Studio page, click on the "Analytics" option that's displayed along the left margin of the browser window. Chapter 14, "Promoting Your YouTube Videos," explains how to use YouTube's own Analytics tools, plus recommends a handful of third-party tools, like SocialBlade (www.socialblade.com), which provide even more information that can help you track the success of your channel and the appeal of your individual videos.

CUSTOMIZING YOUR GOOGLE ACCOUNT PROFILE

As you now know, your Google account is used to manage your YouTube Channel account. By default, it also establishes your online identity on YouTube and on all of Google's other online services. Every Google account has a profile that contains your full name and/or a nickname (which can be your company name).

Your Google account can also display your profile picture (a photo of you or your organization's logo), as well as additional details about you or your company. To edit your Google account profile, log in to your Google account (https://myaccount.google.com)

FIGURE 5–14. Be sure to customize the content within your Google profile. It's viewable by people who visit your YouTube channel and searchable by anyone.

and click on your profile picture that's displayed in the upper-right corner. Next, click on the "Profile" icon.

When your "Profile" page is displayed (shown in Figure 5–14), click on the "Edit" option (the pencil-shaped icon) that's displayed near the center of the screen to the right of your name and profile photo. You'll now discover additional fields into which you can add information about you (or your company) that will become publicly viewable and searchable.

Only enter information into fields that allow you to convey information that you want to share with the public and your audience, and stick to the information that's requested by each field. Your YouTube channel page, your account profile, and each of your videos should contain your contact information. Always make it as easy as possible for your potential and existing customers/clients to find and contact you. Click on the "Done Editing" button to save your changes and publish them online.

START BRANDING YOUR YOUTUBE CHANNEL

Before promoting your YouTube channel to the public and uploading videos to it, make sure you've customized all available aspects of the channel's page so it appeals to your audience and displays appropriate and relevant information, as well as links to your website, blog, and other social media accounts (Facebook, Twitter, Instagram, LinkedIn, etc.).

As soon as you establish a YouTube channel, it automatically becomes searchable via YouTube and Google, for example. Thus, depending on how good your channel name, description, and keywords are, your target audience will be able to find you. Again, it's essential that everything on your YouTube channel page, as well as within your videos, use consistent branding and messaging with whatever is used in your company's other online and real-world endeavors.

The logo, color scheme, slogans, product descriptions, company information, and other content that you showcase on YouTube should all work toward building and promoting your overall brand, while simultaneously enhancing your company's online reputation and credibility. To accomplish this successfully, consistency and synergy is essential. Remember, having an attractive or eye-catching YouTube channel page is important. It sets the tone for your videos and the online brand or image you're trying to convey. However, what's even more important is your ability to populate the channel with videos that will appeal to your target audience.

When designing your YouTube channel page, always focus on your target audience and what will be of interest and visually appealing to them. This includes thinking about your target audience when designing your page's channel art, as well as when writing your channel's description, compiling a list of keywords, deciding what links will be displayed on the YouTube channel page, and choosing what interactive elements you'll allow your viewers to have when they're viewing your page and/or videos.

See How Established Companies Have Branded Their YouTube Channels

The following is a list of popular companies and channels on YouTube (listed alphabetically) that have customized and branded their respective YouTube channels. As you visit these channels, look at how they've been branded (using a logo and channel artwork), how the channel page promotes links to other social media accounts (or a website), and how the channel operator has organized individual videos into categories and/or playlists. Also take a moment to read the "About" section for each channel.

- *American Heart Association:* www.youtube.com/user/americanheartassoc
- *Apple:* www.youtube.com/user/Apple
- *ASPCA:* www.youtube.com/user/aspca
- *Bright Sun Films:* www.youtube.com/user/BrightSunGaming
- *CNN:* www.youtube.com/user/CNN
- *Coca-Cola:* www.youtube.com/user/cocacola
- *Entrepreneur:* www.youtube.com/user/EntrepreneurOnline
- *Honda:* www.youtube.com/user/Honda
- *Katy Perry VEVO:* www.youtube.com/user/KatyPerryVEVO

- *Nintendo:* www.youtube.com/user/Nintendo
- *Royal Caribbean International:* www.youtube.com/user/RoyalCaribbeanIntl
- *Saddleback Leather:* www.youtube.com/user/saddlebackLeather
- *Star Trek:* www.youtube.com/user/startrek
- *Superwoman:* www.youtube.com/user/IISuperwomanII
- *The Tonight Show Starring Jimmy Fallon:* www.youtube.com/user/latenight
- *Tyler Oakley:* www.youtube.com/user/tyleroakley
- *Warby Parker:* www.youtube.com/user/warbyparker

By visiting this small sampling of channels, you'll see what's possible and perhaps generate your own ideas for how to brand your YouTube channel.

KEEP YOUR CHANNEL CURRENT AS YOUTUBE EVOLVES

YouTube is continuously evolving, and each time the service launches new functionality, businesses like yours discover how to best use the latest tools to achieve their online goals.

Using online-based tools, your business can customize its YouTube channel page using its own logos, photos, and artwork, plus ensure that the branded page looks consistent on any computer, smart TV, or mobile device.

One feature that's available to you can become active when someone new visits your channel page. If you choose, they'll automatically see a special trailer video that you produce. This video is shown only to first-time visitors. Return visitors directly access your main YouTube channel page. Use this trailer video to quickly introduce people to your business and your channel in a way that goes above and beyond what's offered by the text-based channel description.

Another feature allows you to manually arrange the order videos are showcased within your YouTube channel page. They no longer need to be displayed in reverse-chronological order. This makes it easier to group together related videos and to put together custom playlists for your visitors. This tool can also be used to introduce or reintroduce your subscribers to older videos they might have missed or to group together videos that cover a related topic.

Now that you've established and customized your YouTube channel, you need to focus on creating the very best content possible. The next section of this book (Chapters 6 through 11) focuses on gathering the equipment you'll need to produce professional-quality videos, and then explains how to start creating your original content.

MEET JILL SCHIEFELBEIN, CHANNEL HOST OF DYNAMIC COMMUNICATION

YouTube Channel URL: www.youtube.com/user/impromptuguru

As an experienced public speaker and expert communicator, Jill Schiefelbein is both the author of *Dynamic Communication* (Entrepreneur Press) and the host of the Dynamic Communication YouTube channel, on which she offers advice on how anyone can easily improve their public speaking skills, plus communicate with more confidence.

The Dynamic Communication YouTube channel is populated with more than 52 instructional and tip-oriented videos that are just over one minute each. "In 2012, my first business was called 'Impromptu Guru,' and that's the name used in my YouTube channel's URL. That was my first mistake. Unless you plan to use the same business name your entire professional life, I recommend using your own name if you're planning to build a brand around yourself and promote yourself using YouTube," said Schiefelbein.

Based on her experience as a professional communicator, Schiefelbein discovered first-hand that one minute is an ideal length to communicate information within a YouTube video. "You can deliver one actionable item and one single takeaway. Right from the start, more than 88 percent of my viewers watched the entire videos, as opposed to clicking away early. In some cases, I later combined two or three related one-minute videos into a single video that was under three minutes, and that, too, helped viewer retention," says Schiefelbein, who credits using YouTube Analytics for helping her discover insight into the attention span and interests of her audience.

She notes that watch time (in other words, how much of your video someone watches before clicking away) is as important on YouTube as video views. These days, YouTube offers more tools than ever that content providers can use to engage with their viewers. There are many ways to use these tools, and a channel operator should not overlook using them. "I have recently gone back and retrofitted my older videos with these tools and have experimented to see which ones resonate the most with my audience," she adds.

"Using YouTube, one of my goals was to expand my own popularity and personal brand by demonstrating communication and presentation skills to my perspective clients. I created a 52-video series, called '60 Second Guru.' By watching just one one-minute video per week, anyone could improve their presentation skills. I filmed all the videos in one day at a studio. I hired a professional camera crew, makeup artist, hair-stylist, and video editor to help with the project. Initially, I started to publish the videos once per week. If someone wanted to see all 52 videos back-to-back, they could purchase a complete DVD. I think I wound up selling a total of three DVDs," recalled Schiefelbein.

Starting in 2012, the videos were promoted using social media and direct email. While she obtained about 60,000 views for the video series, based on the time and money she invested, Schiefelbein expected better results. "What I wound up doing was repurposing the videos and using them as follow-up upsells to my clients. After I did in-person training, I'd offer three months' worth of these videos as 'drip training' afterward to reinforce what I taught in person. This approach allowed me to almost immediately recoup my video production costs.

"At the same time, I invested time learning all I could about YouTube Analytics and discovered tips for improving the audience for my videos on YouTube. I changed all the titles to make them more attention getting, and I selected thumbnail images that were more consistent with everything else featured within the channel. I also rewrote each video description, focusing more on keywords. These activities allowed me to go from about 60,000 views to more than 800,000 views in a relatively short time," says Schiefelbein.

"YouTube Analytics and the information this free tool set provides is a way for your audience to communicate with you, without directly communicating," she adds. "Pay attention to the information YouTube Analytics provides. You will learn all sorts of useful information about your audience and their viewing habits. You can also see what video titles, keywords, and video descriptions generate the most interest and best results. Most important, you can determine how well you're reaching your target demographic."

As of mid-2017, the Dynamic Communication YouTube channel only had about 7,000 subscribers, but the individual video views continue to increase. "Once my videos reached about 300,000 views, media syndicators began to take notice of my content. For example, I was one of the first YouTube channel hosts to become part of The Entrepreneur Network (www.entrepreneur.com/watch). This lead to me hosting several live streams, then I wrote the *Dynamic Communication* book for Entrepreneur Press. Today, my focus is on creating YouTube content that will get syndicated, so I am more concerned about video views for my content across the internet, not necessarily the traffic on my own YouTube channel," explains Schiefelbein.

The most recent content added to Schiefelbein's channel is a collection of video snippets from interviews she conducted for her *Dynamic Communication* book. "Right now, I am negotiating with a sponsor to create a new video-based series for YouTube that will also focus on business communication," says Schiefelbein. "In terms of new content, when developing ideas for videos, I am asking what questions people have about public speaking, then framing my content around how I can answer those questions in an informative, fun, easy-to-understand, concise, and engaging way."

Chapter 6

The Equipment You'll Need

IN THIS CHAPTER

- The equipment you'll need to produce, edit, and publish videos
- Other video production-related accessories, tools, and essentials you may need
- Strategies for saving money on your equipment

Just a few years ago, it would have cost you thousands of dollars and required a significant level of video production expertise to shoot, produce, and edit professional-quality videos with good-quality lighting and sound. All that has changed.

Today, many smartphones, as well as low-cost point-and-shoot digital cameras, are equipped with a video recording function that's capable of shooting stunning HD-quality video. There are also many low-cost, consumer-oriented video cameras available that offer close to broadcast quality. However, if your goal is to produce truly broadcast-quality videos, there are also a plethora of options available when it comes to acquiring the right equipment.

This chapter focuses on the video production equipment you'll probably need to shoot, edit, and publish videos for YouTube. The first step, however, is to carefully define your needs and determine what you're trying to accomplish. A few basic questions to consider are:

- What types of videos will you be shooting?
- Where and when will you be shooting?
- Do you need a specialized camera to record specific types of video, such as a portable action camera, like the GoPro HERO6, to capture first-person action; a 360-degree camera; or a drone with a built-in camera for aerial shots?
- Will you be shooting indoors or outdoors?
- Will you shoot your videos in 1080p or 4K resolution, or in a lower- or higher-quality resolution? If your audience is people who will be viewing your videos

SAVE MONEY BY BUYING USED EQUIPMENT

You can always start with low-end, inexpensive equipment. Then as you become successful and gain experience producing videos for YouTube, you can always upgrade your equipment over time. It's also possible to save a fortune by purchasing used equipment, such as a used or refurbished video camera, lights, a tripod, and microphone(s). You'll find used, consumer-quality video production equipment for sale on eBay, for example.

To find and purchase higher-end used or refurbished equipment, visit websites like:

- Adorama: www.adorama.com/catalog.tpl?op=category&cat1=Used
- OneQuality.com: www.onequality.com
- Full Compass: www.fullcompass.com
- NewPro Video: http://newprovideo.com
- B&H Photo-Video: www.bhphotovideo.com
- UsingLighting.com: www.usedlighting.com

These are just a few of the countless companies on the internet that sell used equipment. Before purchasing used equipment from a company you're not familiar with, pay careful attention to the seller's online ratings, as well as the comments posted by previous customers to make sure they're reputable.

Do your research so you know exactly what equipment you want and need. Make sure you know exact make and model numbers, for example, so you wind up acquiring the right equipment, and not an older version of a camera or a less feature-packed "gray market" version of a camera, for example.

exclusively on smartphones with small screens, or if you're striving to capture a "grass-roots" or "homemade" look to your videos, using a lower-quality resolution may be acceptable. In general, however, people using YouTube now expect content to be offered in 1080p (or higher) HD resolution.

- What are your set, lighting, and audio requirements?
- Will you be shooting mainly people in your videos, or will you be demonstrating products that require detailed close-ups?
- Will your videos require special effects, animated titles, or other graphics?

Next, consider your budget. Do you need to produce the highest-quality videos possible with a low-end camera and no special lighting or sound equipment, or can you afford to invest in basic video production equipment that, if used correctly, will greatly improve the overall quality of your productions?

WHAT YOU SHOULD KNOW ABOUT VIDEO RESOLUTION

When it comes to shooting HD video and choosing the right equipment, you'll hear a lot about resolution. This relates to how many individual pixels are used to make up each frame of the video. A standard definition TV set (SDTV) offers a resolution of 640 by 480 pixels. When video is shot in standard definition (SD), it can be shown on any standard definition TV set, regardless of its screen size. Thus, an SD video will look the same on a 15-inch screen as on a 32-inch screen, for example.

The world has progressed well beyond standard definition, however. In most homes these days, you'll find high-definition, flat screen TV sets (HDTVs). When it comes to shooting HD video, there are several industry-standard resolutions—720p, 1080p, and 4K resolution. Ultra HD, 4K resolution, and 4K Ultra HD are very similar but not identical from a technical standpoint. However, these terms are often used interchangeably.

Video shot in 720p HD uses a 720 by 1280 pixel resolution, while 1080p uses a resolution that comprises 1080 by 1920 pixels. Ultra HD uses 2,160 by 3,840 pixels, and 4K resolution has a horizontal resolution of 4,096 pixels, but the vertical resolution is unspecified. As of mid-2017, Apple's higher-end iMac Pro computers were equipped with monitors capable of displaying 5K resolution content. High-end, 8K resolution television sets and video monitors will likely start to become available in 2018, but probably won't become popular with consumers for at least two to three years due to their high price point.

Keep in mind, in addition to SD and HD video using a different number of pixels, the aspect ratio of the video is also different. An SD video, for example, has an aspect ratio of 4 to 3, meaning that the width of the picture is 4/3 the height. However, an HD video has an aspect ratio of 16:9, meaning that the width of the picture is 16/9 the height.

Shooting videos in HD resolution results in much more detailed, colorful, sharper, and vibrant pictures than what you'd see in standard resolution video. As a YouTube content creator, plan on shooting in at least 1080p, or maybe 4K, depending on your audience and objectives. It's always advisable to shoot in the highest resolution possible. As you're editing your newly shot video and preparing to publish it online, you can always downgrade the resolution with a few mouse clicks. However, you cannot easily upgrade resolution.

Some TV sets connect directly to the internet or have a set-top box or video-streaming accessory (such as an optional Apple TV, Amazon Fire TV, or Google Chromecast device) that does. This grants a viewer the ability to stream and watch YouTube videos on their HDTVs. However, plenty of people still watch YouTube videos on their computer, tablet, or smartphone screen.

YouTube currently supports 16:9 aspect ratio players and automatically adds black bars to the right and left side of video windows (referred to as pillarboxing) to compensate, when necessary, for videos that use a 4:3 aspect ratio. YouTube does not crop or stretch a video's aspect ratio to make it fit the standard 16:9 aspect ratio. You'll discover that YouTube is compatible with many different video resolutions, and support for higher resolutions and new video formats, such as 360-degree video, are constantly being added.

The decision about what resolution to shoot your videos in will depend on a variety of factors, including your budget, your target audience, and what type of equipment you anticipate your audience will typically use to stream your videos—an HDTV set, computer, tablet, or smartphone.

Again, to adhere to current technology standards, seriously consider shooting and uploading your videos in at least 1080p HD resolution. This will allow people to experience an excellent picture quality, regardless of what internet-enabled device they're using.

Virtually all consumer-oriented digital video cameras, as well as the video capabilities of point-and-shoot cameras, higher-end digital SLR cameras, and the cameras built into most smartphones and/or tablets, are all now capable of recording in 1080p (or higher) HD resolution. The Apple iPhone 8 or iPhone X, for example, can capture video at 720p, 1080p, or 4K resolution using the camera app that comes preinstalled on the phone.

When using any digital video camera to record, your video content is captured by the camera and stored as a digital video file. The higher the resolution, and the higher the frame rate the video is shot in, the larger the raw (unedited) video file size will be. Frame rate refers to the number of frames per second (fps) that the video is shot using. You'll typically shoot using 25fps or 30fps, unless you'll be capturing video to be shown in slow motion or if you're shooting high-action sequences. In this case, a higher fps rate should be used.

Editing HD video that's more than a few minutes in length will require a significant amount of local storage space on your computer's hard drive, as well as a fast microprocessor and a lot of RAM within your computer. But because most YouTube videos are less than ten minutes long, a typical home computer, or even a tablet or smartphone, can be used to edit shorter HD videos.

Video File Formats

Beyond just choosing a resolution, fps rate, and aspect ratio when shooting your videos, you'll also need to choose a file format that uses compression. Raw digital video footage uses a tremendous amount of data that results in massive digital video file sizes. However, when you transfer your video footage to your computer for editing, you can save it in a specific, industry-standard video format and later upload your videos to YouTube in a compatible video format that uses file compression to make the file sizes smaller and more manageable.

Each video file format uses a different method of data compression, and the latest video-compression technologies allow for video resolution to stay extremely high but for file sizes to be shrunk dramatically. When a file is compressed, the compression rate is measured in kilobytes per second (Kbps). The more Kbps used for the compression, the better the quality of the compressed video. As you begin using specialized video-editing software, then uploading your videos to YouTube, you'll discover that many different file formats and compression rates exist. As of mid-2017, YouTube supports the following file formats: .MOV, .MPEG-4, .MP4, .AVI, .WMV, .MPEGPS, .FLV, .3GPP, and .WebM.

Using video-editing software or the online tools available from YouTube, it's easy to take digital video files that have been saved in almost any format and convert them into a file format that offers better compression and/or that works better with YouTube. You can also use specialized video conversion software for a PC or Mac.

For example, Movavi (www.movavi.com/videoconverter) offers powerful video-conversion software for the PC and Mac. You'll find a handful of other commercially available software packages that can be purchased and downloaded at CNET's Download.com website (http://download.cnet.com/windows/video-converters).

If you don't want to buy video-conversion software, there are plenty of "freeware" applications available for the PC and Mac, such as the Freemake Video Converter from Freemake.com (www.freemake.com/free_video_converter). It supports more than 500 video formats.

GETTING THE RIGHT EQUIPMENT

How to choose the best video camera is covered within Chapter 7, "Selecting the Right Video Camera." However, beyond choosing a camera, you'll need additional equipment to achieve semi-professional or professional production quality. Based on where you'll be shooting, the background you choose, as well as the ability to capture good lighting and high-quality sound, are extremely important considerations. You'll also need a computer for editing, viewing, uploading, and managing your video files. Your computer needs a large internal hard drive or a high-capacity external hard drive, a decent microprocessor, plenty of RAM (for processing video), and specialized video-editing software installed. Choosing video-editing software is the focus of Chapter 9, "Editing Your YouTube Videos."

Because the file size of your edited HD videos will be massive, the computer used to edit your videos will need access to a high-speed internet connection so you can upload the videos to YouTube within a reasonable time frame.

The following is a summary of the core video production equipment you'll need to produce semi-professional or professional-quality videos for YouTube. If you're just starting, you can easily get away with using low-end equipment. However, if your videos will be representing your company, product, or service, and the quality of the videos is important to maintain your business's image and reputation, and to meet the expectations of your audience, investing in higher-end equipment will be necessary.

Everyone's video content and production needs will be different. From an equipment standpoint, here's a rundown of what you'll probably need:

- A digital video camera that's capable of shooting 1080p (or higher) HD video
- A tripod or Steadicam to hold the camera steady while shooting
- Proper lighting that does not cause unwanted shadows
- A simple background; typically, a seamless, solid-color wall, or a cloth, paper, or vinyl backdrop works best
- External microphone. The microphones that are built into low-end cameras tend to offer low audio-recording quality. An external microphone can be placed on or near the audio source, or the person you're filming, and can dramatically improve the quality of the audio being captured, while cutting out ancillary and unwanted background noise.
- An internet-connected computer for editing and managing your video files, then uploading them to YouTube
- Specialized video-editing software
- A teleprompter to display your shooting script. It's hard for some people to memorize scripts. Instead, using a teleprompter allows you or your subject(s) to read

a script as you're shooting. A professional teleprompter can be expensive, so consider using a low-cost app on a tablet to function as a full-featured teleprompter.

Choosing the Right Tripod

One of the easiest ways to make your videos look more professional is to ensure the camera is held steady, even when capturing shots requiring the camera to be in motion. To achieve this, a tripod or Steadicam is required. Do not simply hold the camera in your hands as you're shooting.

You'll quickly discover that all tripods are not alike. The price can vary from below $40 to well over $1,500, depending on what it's made from and what it's designed to do. The main function of a tripod is to hold your camera steady, in a single location while shooting as well as to allow for smooth pans and zooms.

It's almost impossible to hold a video camera absolutely still in your hands as you're shooting. Any movement, and your videos will shake. Without a tripod, it's also very difficult to execute smooth pans and zooms as you're shooting. Choose a tripod designed for your camera's size and weight, plus any equipment that's attached to the camera, such as a large telephoto lens, light, or an external microphone.

Most inexpensive tripods are sold as a single unit. However, mid- to high-end tripods have three components—legs, feet, and a detachable (and selectable) head. The tripod head is located at the top of the tripod and attaches to your camera. There are two main types of tripod heads—a ball head and a pan-tilt head. The type of tripod head you use determines how you can rotate and position the camera at various angles, as well as pan or tilt the camera up and down, or from side to side.

In some cases, the tripod and head are one piece. It is also common for them to be offered as two detachable pieces that are sold together. Some manufacturers, however, sell tripod legs and heads separately, allowing you to customize the equipment as needed.

The legs hold the tripod steady. On most tripods, the legs can be expanded to be different lengths so you can adjust the height at which the camera is positioned. Others allow for the legs to be positioned at various angles. The feet of some tripods are also changeable or adjustable, and should be selected based on the type of surface it will be placed on when in use. For example, rubber feet will keep the tripod from sliding on a flat, smooth floor, while spiked feet will prevent movement if the tripod is placed on grass or dirt.

Other options include an easy-on/easy-off mount, so you don't have to screw the camera on and off the tripod head each time you need to attach or remove it. An easy-on/easy-off mount simply clicks into place, allowing you to attach or remove the camera from the tripod quickly, without compromising stability.

Another useful tripod feature is a level gauge. Accidentally positioning the camera at even the slightest angle could result in your video looking strange or crooked. The size and weight of the tripod should also be a consideration if you need to carry equipment to many locations. Some tripods are made from very lightweight aluminum or titanium, yet are strong enough to hold heavy and large cameras. The component materials, as well as the features the tripod offers, will determine its cost.

Tripods are available from consumer electronics stores, photo and video specialty stores, as well as online. Some mid- to high-end tripod manufacturers include:

- *Gitzo:* www.manwww.manfrotton.us/gitzofrotton.us/gitzo
- *Joby:* https://joby.com
- *Libec:* www.libecsales.com
- *Manfrotto:* www.manfrotto.us
- *Slik:* https://slikusa.com
- *Vanguard:* www.vanguardworld.com

Another option is a handheld image stabilization system, such as the Merlin 2 Steadicam from Tiffen Company (www.tiffen.com). A Steadicam device allows the camera operator to move the camera slowly and steadily as he's holding the camera and shooting. Similar products are available from:

- *Glidecam Industries:* www.glidecam.com
- *JAG35:* www.jag35.com
- *Redrock Micro:* http://shop.redrockmicro.com

Of course, you may have simple needs in this department, and a stabilization system may not be necessary just yet. That said, the more professional your videos look, the better your ability to market in the future.

Choosing the Lighting

Just as with still photography, proper lighting is an extremely important component when it comes to shooting video. Your worst enemy will be shadows. Ideally, you want your primary light source—whether it's the sun or artificial lighting—to be positioned in front of your subject and behind the person holding the camera.

The primary light source should not be shining directly or indirectly into the camera's lens while you're shooting. This will cause glare, silhouettes, or overexposed footage. When shooting indoors, the "natural lighting" will seldom be suitable for shooting decent-quality video, so you'll need to use additional (artificial) lighting.

Many video cameras have either a built-in or attachable light, but they can present problems. These often cause harsh shadows, depending on how the camera and light are positioned. If the light's too bright, it can wash out your subject; if you're too far away, the subject will be underexposed or engulfed in shadows. It can also limit the cameraperson's mobility.

Consider investing in a studio lighting kit that includes two, three, or four lights that can be positioned independently and evenly light your subject when shooting indoors. A lighting kit will typically allow you to adjust each light's brightness, which can help to eliminate shadows, while surrounding your subject in even lighting.

Make sure that the lighting kit will provide continuous lighting at an intensity that's suitable for the situation in which you'll be shooting. The type of light bulbs will also affect how colors appear within your videos. Incandescent bulbs, fluorescent bulbs, or LED bulbs, for example, each offer pros and cons.

You may need to adjust the white balance feature within your video camera to compensate for lighting warmth or coolness. Unless you plan to shoot broadcast-quality videos, you can probably get away with initially investing in a basic three-light system that will cost between $300 and $400.

B&H Photo-Video (www.bhphotovideo.com) and Adorama (www.adorama.com) both offer many types of lighting kits, as well as individual lights and stands that can be mixed and matched to meet your needs in any indoor situation. Other companies worth checking out for more versatile lighting kits include:

- *Cowboy Studio:* www.cowboystudio.com/category_s/226.htm
- *K 5600 Lighting:* www.k5600.com
- *Kino Flo Lighting Systems:* www.kinoflo.com
- *Tiffen:* www.tiffen.com (click on the "Lighting" menu option.)
- *Studio 1 Productions:* www.studio1productions.com

PhotoBasics (http://fjwestcott.com), a division of Westcott, which makes professional video lighting equipment and related products, offers a handful of lower-end lighting

FOR TALKING HEAD SHOTS, USE A RING LIGHT

One of the easiest ways to properly light a person's face for midshots and close-ups is to use a ring light. This is a favorite and low-cost lighting technique used by YouTubers. For example, the Smith-Victor 19-inch LED Ring Light is $169.99 (www.smithvictor.com/products), but you'll find ring lights offered in different diameters that use different types of bulbs, at varying prices.

systems for amateur and semi-professional videographers. Photo Basics offers several two- and three-light kits that use fluorescent or tungsten light bulb options, starting at just under $300.

For shooting outdoors on a sunny day, consider using a silver or gold reflector and a stand to evenly bounce sunlight onto your subject. Some reflectors are large enough so you can redirect sunlight evenly onto multiple subjects at once. They're available from photo and video specialty stores and online. Prices range from under $30 to several hundred dollars. Photo Basics, for example, offers many reflector and backdrop options that are versatile and affordable, and can yield professional-quality results while using semi-professional level equipment.

Choosing Your Background

Any location, indoors or outdoors, can be used for shooting your videos. However, using random locations poses a handful of challenges when it comes to lighting and audio. And you never want to use a background that's too busy, or that will distract your audience.

Using lights and specialized microphones, any location can be made optimal for shooting video. However, it's much easier to choose or create a location that allows you to control the shooting conditions. One way to do this is to set up a solid backdrop.

A backdrop can be made from seamless paper, vinyl, or cloth. They're available in a wide range of sizes and in virtually any color from photo and video specialty stores, including B&H Photo-Video and Adorama. There are also companies, like Backdrop Source (www.backdropsource.com) and Backdrop Outlet (www.backdropoutlet.com) that offer hundreds of different backdrop options.

These backgrounds are created using materials and dyes designed to work perfectly with lighting kits. In some cases, these backdrops can help to absorb the lighting and dramatically reduce shadows. They also make it easy to evenly light your subjects, while offering a visually simple, nondistracting background.

For a good-quality backdrop made from paper, vinyl, or cloth (these are referred to as "muslins"), plan on spending between $50 and $300, depending on the size. Common sizes are 5 by 7 feet, 5 by 9 feet, 10 by 10 feet, 10 by 20 feet, or 20 by 20 feet. If you're using paper or a cloth backdrop, keep them crease- and wrinkle-free.

Using an External Microphone

When was the last time you tried to hold a conversation on a cell phone while you or the other person were in a noisy area? Could you hear everything that was being said?

Probably not. The microphone built into the cell phone picked up all ambient noises and probably drowned out the person speaking.

If you don't use proper microphones when shooting your video, you'll wind up recording audio that's as bad as the worst cell phone connection. When you rely on your camera's built-in microphone, the result will almost always be poor audio quality. That tiny microphone is designed to pick up all the sound in the immediate area, plus the quality of the microphone typically isn't too good to begin with. If the microphone is part of or connected to the camera, but the subject is located on the opposite side of the room, the microphone often won't adequately pick up the person's voice, and the sound will be hollow.

Most video cameras allow you to connect one or more external corded or wireless, microphones. When you use an external microphone, you can:

- Pick the type of microphone you use.
- Choose the quality of the microphone.
- Select the position of the microphone.
- Independently control audio levels while shooting or editing.

External microphones can cost hundreds or even thousands of dollars. Before investing any money, determine the situations in which you'll be shooting video, and what your audio recording needs will be. Then, consult with an expert at an audio/video store who can help you select a microphone that's best suited to your needs.

In most cases, a handheld microphone, or a lavaliere microphone that attaches to someone's lapel, will work well when you're shooting video that includes people talking. The appropriate microphone can also eliminate unwanted background noise and ambient noise. Keep in mind, some types of microphones are designed to pick up and record only what's directly in front of them, while other microphones will pick up all audio that surround them.

Plan on spending between $100 and $300 for a good quality external microphone that connects to your video camera. When choosing a microphone, try to select one that can also connect to your computer via an adapter so that when you're editing your video, you can use it to record any necessary voice-overs.

For less than $200, you can also purchase a separate studio-quality microphone that connects directly to a computer via its USB port, or a microphone that connects to the Lightning or micro- or mini-USB port that's built into your smartphone or tablet. One example of a microphone that connects to a computer using a USB cable is the Snowball microphone from Blue Microphones (www.bluemic.com/snowball). This company also offers external microphones for use with mobile devices, such as an iPhone or iPad.

Choosing a Teleprompter

A standalone teleprompter, or one that connects to a video camera, can cost anywhere from several hundred to several thousand dollars. There are a handful of online retailers, including B&H Photo-Video (www.bhphotovideo.com), Adorama (www.adorama.com), and Prompter People (www.prompterpeople.com) that specialize in this type of equipment and offer teleprompters from various manufacturers.

A far simpler and lower-cost solution is to create oversized cue cards using poster board and markers, or download and use a teleprompter app on your tablet. Search for the phrase "teleprompter" in the App Store, and you'll discover dozens of teleprompter apps, ranging from free to about $15. You can then use a specialized stand to position the tablet at eye level near the video camera as you're shooting.

Other Video Production Essentials

Keep the following additional needs in mind so you can create the most professional looking videos possible. Remember, the more professional your videos are, the more your credibility (and monetization potential) will soar.

- *Set and props.* Based on what type of video you'll be shooting and where, you may decide you need a set and props. A set can be a table or desk positioned in front of your backdrop, or it can be something elaborate that you design and construct from scratch.
- *Wardrobe, hair, and makeup considerations.* If you'll be featuring people in your videos and shooting in HD, the appearance of the people in your video is important. You'll need to choose what they'll wear and how they'll style their hair, and make sure they wear appropriate makeup that looks natural in the lighting conditions in which you're shooting. When using artificial lighting, even guys should wear basic makeup to keep from looking pale, washed out, or sweaty.
- *Background music and sound effects.* You can record your own music and/or sound effects; however, you'll probably find it much easier to license or acquire royalty-free production music and/or sound effects that you can incorporate into your productions. Appropriate music and sound effects can add a tremendous amount of production value to your videos. These production elements are typically added during the video editing (post-production) phase.

The adage, "You get what your pay for," certainly applies here. These extras are, in my opinion, worth it to help you boost the quality of your videos, whether you are using them to promote a service, product, or yourself as a subject matter expert.

Adding Music and Sound Effects

When you're editing raw video and adding post-production elements, you'll probably want to add sound effects and music. These audio elements, if used properly, will add tremendous production value to your videos. However, there are a few things to consider.

First, the music and sound effects used should be appropriate to the production. Music and sound effects can set a mood, and add excitement or anticipation to a video production, or simply make it more pleasant to watch. If used incorrectly, however, music and sound effects can be distracting or annoying.

Second, the music and sound effects incorporated into your video should be properly mixed so the audio levels are just right. Your video-editing software will offer controls for adding and controlling the music and sound effect levels.

Third, you need permission from the copyright holder to use the song or music, and the recording itself. YouTube has very strict rules for using music and sound effects in videos, based on who owns the copyright. If you violate these rules, your videos could be blocked, or YouTube could automatically remove all the audio from your videos.

If you discover that YouTube has removed the audio track from your video, it's probably because you've violated a copyright. Refer to this page on YouTube's website for more information on how to avoid this situation and to learn about your options if this happens: https://support.google.com/youtube/answer/2797449.

Potentially infringing content includes audio from albums, TV shows, music videos, movies, and movie trailers, or music from live concerts—even if you captured the video yourself.

To learn more about what production music and sound effects you can legally use, participate in the free, online YouTube Copyright Workshop (https://support.google.com/youtube/answer/6364458). This is particularly important if you're a business operator who is planning to use your videos for promotional or marketing purposes.

If you're having trouble finding music and sound effects that you're allowed to use, refer to YouTube's own library of pre-approved audio tracks by visiting: www.youtube.com/audiolibrary/music.

From third-parties, it's also possible to purchase, license, or acquire royalty-free production music (in some cases for a flat, one-time fee). For example, there's Stockmusic.net (www.stockmusic.net) that has a library containing thousands of available music tracks that can be acquired on a royalty-free basis for between $14.95 and $39.95 per track. Other sources include:

- *AudioBlocks:* www.audioblocks.com
- *Getty Images Music:* www.gettyimages.com/music

- *Killer Tracks:* www.killertracks.com
- *Music for Productions:* www.musicforproductions.com
- *Premium Beat:* www.premiumbeat.com/production-music
- *Shutterstock Music:* www.shutterstock.com/music

You can use any internet search engine and enter the search phrase "royalty-free production music" to find links to vast libraries of music like these.

Adding Professional Voice-Overs

Off-screen voice-overs can be used in videos, in conjunction with graphic titles, to narrate content, or to emphasize key points (when content other than people is being shown). Basically, a voice-over is used when you want your audience to hear someone speaking but not show the speaker in the video.

Many (but not all) video-editing software packages will allow you to add voice-over content to your footage by connecting a microphone to your computer. Another option is to hire a professional announcer to record your script digitally, which you can then import into your video.

Many radio announcers and actors record voice-overs on a freelance basis to supplement their income. There are also production houses that specialize in recording voice-overs based on customers' scripts. The cost will vary greatly, based on the length of the script and how much production work is involved.

Radio Voice Imaging (www.radiovoiceimaging.com) is one of many voice-over production companies you can hire by uploading your script to their service, then providing some basic direction. The company will then use their professional announcers to record your script. The recorded audio file will be emailed to you within a few business days. It can then be imported directly into your video production using your video-editing software.

To find voice-over announcers and production studios, enter "voice-over production" into any internet search engine. You'll find hundreds of options, including:

- *Agent 99 Voice Talent:* www.agent99voicetalent.com
- *InternetJock.com:* www.internetjock.com
- *Mood Media:* http://us.moodmedia.com/messaging-samples/voiceover-web-audio
- *Voice Talent:* www.voicetalent.com
- *Voice Talent Now:* http://store.voicetalentnow.com

Before hiring any voice-over actor, always listen to their demo to determine if their voice is suitable for your production.

PUTTING THE PIECES TOGETHER

Having the right equipment to create your videos is only one of the key steps in a video's production. However, it's essential you choose equipment that's suitable based on your budget, experience level, what you're trying to accomplish, and what your videos' content will include.

When you're first learning about video production and producing your initial YouTube videos, keep things as simple as possible. Don't spend money on equipment you don't need and don't know how to use properly, unless you also plan to spend time learning how to use it.

As you gain more experience and enhance your skills, you can always incorporate more advanced video production techniques, upgrade your equipment, add special effects, and work toward enhancing the quality of your videos. YouTube offers free tutorials for improving your skills as a videographer. To watch these tutorial videos, visit: www.youtube.com/yt/creators. There's also YouTube Creator Academy that can be found online by visiting: https://creatoracademy.youtube.com/page/education.

Chapter 7

Selecting the Right Video Camera

IN THIS CHAPTER

- Using your computer's webcam or a smartphone or tablet's camera to shoot video
- Using the video mode of your point-and-shoot or digital SLR camera
- Choosing an HD video camera to meet your needs and budget

In Chapter 8, "Filming YouTube Videos," we'll explore the production steps that go into the creation of a video. However, before you can start filming, you'll need one key piece of equipment—at least one HD video camera.

If you want your video to be viewable on any computer screen, HDTV set, tablet, or smartphone, you'll need a camera capable of shooting in 1080p (or higher) HD resolution. There are many options, starting with the camera that's built into your computer (or an external webcam), smartphone, or tablet. The latest models of the Apple iPhones and iPads, for example, can capture HD video in 720p, 1080p, and 4K resolution, as can most popular Android-based smartphones and tablets. Likewise, the latest iMac and MacBook models have built-in cameras capable of capturing HD video, as do most of the more recently released Windows PCs.

If you've already invested in a good-quality point-and-shoot digital camera, or a higher-end digital SLR camera, chances are it also has a video recording mode, as well as some basic video-recording features, such as zoom capabilities. Plus, virtually all digital SLR cameras released within the past few years, from companies like Nikon and Canon, can not only shoot HD-quality video, but they also have interchangeable lenses, plus the ability to attach external microphones and portable lighting equipment.

As you learned in the previous chapter, optional external microphones with a USB, micro/mini USB, or Lightning port are available, so they can be connected directly to a computer, smartphone, or tablet, allowing you to dramatically improve the audio you capture in conjunction with your video content when filming.

Assuming your sole purpose for the camera is to shoot HD-quality video, a stand-alone digital video camera offers the most flexibility and recording features. These are available from many different manufacturers and can be purchased from consumer electronics stores, photo/video specialty stores, or online. However, many YouTubers achieve professional quality results using a digital SLR camera (with interchangeable lenses) from Canon or Nikon, for example, to shoot their videos.

RENTING EQUIPMENT

If you plan to film only a handful of videos within a short time period, you may want to consider renting high-end equipment from a photo/video specialty store. Typically, you can rent a camera on a daily or weekly basis.

Using any internet search engine, such as Google or Yahoo!, enter the search phrase "video camera rental" to find companies that rent mid- to high-end video cameras and related video production equipment. Some of the companies you'll find include:

- *Adorama:* www.adoramarentals.com
- *BorrowLenses.com:* www.borrowlenses.com/category/Video
- *HD Rental:* www.hdrental.com
- *LensRentals:* www.lensrentals.com
- *Radiant Images:* www.radiantimages.com
- *Rule Boston Camera:* www.rule.com

Any of these would be a great choice if you are working on a limited-time project or if you're simply not yet ready to invest in production equipment.

Low-end but decent-quality digital video cameras capable of shooting HD-quality video start at around $200. However, if you're looking for professional-quality equipment and features, you can easily spend thousands of dollars for a high-end camera. Regardless of your budget, it's essential that you use a video camera that allows you to attach external corded and wireless microphones so that you can record good quality audio in conjunction with your video. This chapter explores your many options when it comes to finding and purchasing a digital video camera that will meet your needs.

Keep in mind, your camera is a key component needed for your video production, but you'll need other equipment as well, including microphones, lighting, and video-editing software, so don't spend your entire production budget on just a good-quality camera.

THE PROS AND CONS OF SHOOTING WITH A WEBCAM

The benefit of using a webcam that's built into your computer (or that connects directly to your computer) to record your videos is that the raw video footage is stored locally, directly on your computer, where you can edit, view, and publish it. This type of camera works best if you're sitting at a desk, for example, and want to record yourself talking directly to the camera. For this, the microphone that's built into your computer

BLUE OFFERS MICROPHONES FOR COMPUTERS AND MOBILE DEVICES

Blue (www.bluemic.com) offers a collection of semi-professional and professional-quality microphones that use a USB and/or Lightning port so they can connect directly to a PC or Mac computer, or directly to almost any smartphone or tablet. As you'll discover, certain types of microphones work better when recording people speaking, while others are better at recording singing, music, or more robust types of sound.

Choose a microphone that's compatible with the equipment you'll be using and that's suitable for the type of audio you'll be recording in conjunction with your video. Other sources for microphones with various types of USB ports include: Adorama (www.adorama.com), B&H Photo-Video (www.bhphotovideo.com), and Sweetwater: www.sweetwater.com/c981--USB_Microphones.

may provide adequate sound quality, although most computers also have a USB port through which you can attach a higher-quality external microphone for better audio quality, which is a recommended option.

The drawback to recording video with a webcam that's connected to your computer is you'll have limited movement options and no optical zoom capabilities. Keep in mind, if you plan to record yourself facing your computer and talking to your audience by looking directly into the camera, your audience may get very bored looking at "talking-head" footage for more than a few minutes at a time. Keep your talking-head videos very short, or intersperse other types of footage or content within your edited videos.

If your computer doesn't have an HD-quality video camera or webcam built in, you can purchase an external webcam that will connect to your computer via its USB port. Several companies, including Logitech (www.logitech.com), offer webcam accessories that are sold online or through consumer electronics stores, such as Best Buy (www.bestbuy.com).

The software you use to record videos using your computer's webcam will offer a variety of effects that can be added as you're recording, in addition to the effects that can be added using video-editing software during the post-production phase.

SHOOTING VIDEO USING THE CAMERA BUILT INTO YOUR SMARTPHONE OR TABLET

Many of the latest smartphones and tablets have one or more cameras that are capable of recording HD-quality video. These mobile devices also offer the ability to attach an external microphone and have apps available that offer a variety of shooting options—such as a digital zoom or the ability to add special effects—while you're shooting.

Videos shot using a smartphone or tablet can then be edited, viewed, and shared using specialized apps on the mobile devices themselves, or the raw footage can easily be transferred to a computer, where you can then use full-featured video-editing software to polish your raw video content.

Unlike your computer's webcam, a mobile device's built-in camera offers greater mobility, which makes it easier to pan and tilt the camera as you're shooting, adjust the shooting angle, and take advantage of the digital zoom. Assuming the camera that's built into your mobile device offers the HD resolution you need, this is certainly a viable option for shooting videos on a budget.

However, at best, you can expect to achieve amateur to semi-professional quality, even if you have optimal lighting and use an external microphone to capture the best possible audio.

USING THE VIDEO MODE OF YOUR DIGITAL CAMERA TO SHOOT HD VIDEO

Many point-and-shoot digital cameras and higher-end digital SLR cameras also have an HD video-shooting mode that can be used for shooting YouTube videos. Keep in mind, shooting video with these cameras typically drains the battery life quickly, so always have two or three extra, fully charged batteries for the camera on hand when filming. You'll also need higher-capacity memory cards for storing your raw video content as its being shot.

While you can use a camera's low-quality built-in microphone to record audio, you'll want to use a camera model that allows you to connect at least one or more external microphones (based on your needs).

The higher-end digital SLR cameras, from Canon and Nikon, on the other hand, have HD video-recording modes that allow you to capture professional-quality HD content using a wider range of video-recording features, including the ability to attach an external microphone and use interchangeable lenses. A mid- to high-end digital SLR camera will cost anywhere from $1,500 to $5,000, plus the price of optional lenses, microphones, and other accessories.

The video-recording quality of some mid- to high-end digital SLR cameras is often good enough to create broadcast-quality HD video, though the resulting digital video files will be massive; and any video longer in length than 10 to 15 minutes may generate a file size that's too big for most personal computers to handle. For long videos, you'll need a high-end computer (or a digital video-editing workstation) to properly edit your videos, even using the latest data compression.

SHOOTING VIDEO USING A STAND-ALONE CONSUMER-QUALITY HD VIDEO CAMERA

Unlike digital point-and-shoot cameras and digital SLR cameras that are designed to take still photos as well as shoot video, stand-alone HD video cameras are designed for one purpose—to capture video. Most consumer and semi-professional models are compact, all are battery-powered, and most also offer a built-in screen that serves as viewfinders and/or allows you to play back your video directly from the camera.

If possible, select a video camera that offers both a traditional viewfinder that you can look through as you're shooting and a large display screen. Using a traditional viewfinder will require much less battery power than a display screen, but having the option to use a large display screen as your viewfinder, as well as to play back your footage, is always nice. The viewfinder screens are also sometimes very difficult to see when shooting outside on a bright and sunny day.

When choosing a video camera, pay attention to its zoom capabilities. Ideally, choose a video camera that offers at least a 10x optical zoom lens, as well as stronger digital zoom capabilities. Optical zoom is the physical lens' zoom capability. Digital zoom uses technology to digitally create a simulated zoom. While it often allows for stronger magnification, it's not always as crystal clear as an optical zoom.

All HD video cameras have a built-in microphone, but their quality is typically very poor, and they pick up ambient noise, as well as many camera movement-related noises. You'll want the option of attaching a corded or wireless microphone to the camera to capture the best audio quality possible. Be sure to select an optional microphone that's designed for the specific type of audio you're recording or that's designed to handle specific recording conditions.

The battery life a video camera offers is an important consideration. Buy at least two or three extra rechargeable batteries, and keep them fully charged and on-hand when you're filming. Brand-name replacement batteries can cost between $50 and $100 each. For generic batteries at a fraction of the cost, visit a price comparison website, such as Nextag (www.nextag.com) and search for replacement batteries for the exact make and model of your camera. (This money-saving strategy also works when shopping for replacement batteries for other types of cameras, as well as most types of consumer electronics that use rechargeable batteries.)

The Video Footage Storage Options Offered by Video Cameras

HD video cameras come in a wide range of shapes and sizes, and each model offers different options. Choose a model that shoots in at least 1080p resolution, but to stay current with technology, a 4K resolution camera is a better option.

Another consideration when choosing a camcorder is what type of media will be used to store your footage as it's being shot. Your options include digital video (DV) tapes, flash memory cards, or an internal hard drive or flash drive. The latest mid- to high-end camcorders feature internal flash drives for storing video footage as it's shot, and many have both an internal flash drive and a memory card slot.

Video Cameras with Flash Memory Cards, Internal Flash Drives, or Hard Drives

The majority of video cameras available today rely on an internal flash drive or hard drive for storing video. If you have a choice between a video camera with an internal flash drive or internal hard drive, choose the flash drive. It's more reliable and durable, especially if you'll be shooting in extreme weather conditions or at high altitudes, or will be shooting high-action sequences (requiring the camera to be in motion).

The amount of internal hard drive storage space that a camcorder has is measured in gigabytes (GB). Look for a camcorder with a 256GB or larger capacity hard drive or flash drive, even if you'll typically be shooting shorter videos that will then be transferred to a computer.

You'll discover that most consumer-oriented video cameras use interchangeable flash memory cards. When a memory card gets filled up, you transfer your files to your computer and then erase and reuse the memory card. What's great about this technology is that your footage is stored as a data file that can be easily transferred from your camera or its memory card to your computer.

One benefit of using a camera with a flash memory card is that you can choose the capacity and read/write speed of the memory cards you use. The storage capacity will dictate how much video you can store per card.

A 32GB memory card can hold approximately 480 minutes (8 hours) of 1080p HD video. You can find memory cards with very large capacities (512GB or more), but the higher its capacity, and the faster its read/write speed, the more you'll pay. Choose the highest capacity memory card with the fastest read/write speed you can afford. If you'll be shooting video at 4K resolution, a 256GB memory card (or one with an even larger capacity) is recommended, assuming it's compatible with your camera.

Another nice benefit of using memory card storage with a video camera is that you can swap out cards for each video project you're working on.

Action Video Cameras

For some YouTube video productions, an extremely portable action camera (such as the GoPro HERO6) may offer a viable option. These cameras typically cost less than $400, and they're designed for shooting action-oriented HD video while on the go. The content that's shot can easily be edited on a mobile device or computer, then uploaded to YouTube. These cameras are small, lightweight, often waterproof, and extremely versatile. In fact, they can be attached to someone's body to capture action video from a first- and third-person perspective while the videographer is engaged in a sport or activity, for example. Most use interchangeable memory cards for storage.

These action cameras have a built-in microphone and USB port to which you can connect a USB cable to transfer your raw footage to your computer or mobile device, although some of these cameras also allow content to be transferred from a memory card that's installed within a camera directly to a computer or mobile device using a wireless wifi and/or Bluetooth connection.

While GoPro (www.gopro.com) is a pioneer in the action camera category, dozens of other companies (such as Sony, Mevo, Polaroid, and Nikon) have also released highly portable cameras that are equally durable, but often less expensive. When choosing an action camera, considerations include the video resolutions it can shoot at, the battery life of its rechargeable battery, the highest capacity memory card it's compatible with, and the different video shooting modes it offers. Also pay attention to the optional mounts and housings that are available for it that allow the camera to be used in specialized shooting situations. Make sure the camera is designed to be used in the climate you plan to shoot in. Some are designed specifically for use underwater, at high altitudes, or in extremely cold temperatures, for example.

SEMI-PRO OR PROFESSIONAL-QUALITY VIDEO CAMERAS

Beyond the mid- to high-end consumer HD video cameras you'll find at consumer electronics superstores, such as Best Buy, there's another category of professional-quality cameras that start at around $3,000, and go up considerably from there. These cameras are used to film TV shows, commercials, and some movies.

These professional-level cameras offer many features not found in even the highest-end consumer camera models, including interchangeable lenses and powerful optical zoom capabilities. Professional cameras are typically heavier and more cumbersome, but offer unparalleled HD-quality filming capabilities.

In addition to buying or renting a professional camera, you'll probably need to hire an experienced camera operator and need a high-end tripod, lighting equipment, and external microphones. Beyond needing a substantial budget, you'll also need to learn how to use this type of equipment.

SPECIAL-PURPOSE HD CAMERAS

While a good quality and portable action camera, such as the GoPro HERO6, will allow you to capture visually stunning 1080p or even 4K resolution video from a first- or third-person perspective in a wide range of conditions (including underwater), specialized cameras can be also used to shoot 360-degree HD video, for example. Instead of capturing what's directly in front of the camera's lens, a 360-degree camera is designed to capture absolutely everything within a scene (in all directions), then allow the viewer to scroll up, down, left, or right to see a scene from any angle.

YouTube now supports 360-degree video content, since shooting this type of content has become much more affordable. For less than $500, many companies, including Samsung, Nikon, Kodak, Panono 360, Ricoh, and Giroptic, offer cutting-edge, 360-degree cameras that are extremely portable and durable.

In addition to 360-degree cameras, many YouTube content creators are looking at creating virtual reality (VR) and/or augmented reality content. YouTube will support the latest video formats as they become more accessible and as the price for the equipment that's required to create this type of content continues to quickly drop.

YouTube offers tutorials for publishing specific types of content. Visit the following YouTube webpages for the latest information:

- *Upload virtual reality videos:* https://support.google.com/youtube/answer/6316263.
- *Upload 360-degree videos*: https://support.google.com/youtube/answer/6178631.
- *Upload 3D videos*: https://support.google.com/youtube/answer/7278886

Consider Using Multiple Cameras When Shooting

If you want to capture actions that will be shown in your videos from multiple perspectives simultaneously, and have a wider range of editing options later, consider shooting with two or more HD video cameras simultaneously. This requires additional camera operators and a higher production budget, but when editing, being able to choose from multiple camera angles will give you far more creative options.

The extremely portable Mevo camera (https://getmevo.com) is a single handheld camera, but it captures multiple shots simultaneously, which you can quickly switch between during live video broadcasts or select from when editing your videos. The price of this unique camera is between $399 and $599, depending on the configuration.

TRANSFERRING VIDEO FOOTAGE TO YOUR COMPUTER

You'll need to transfer raw (unedited) digital video files from whatever camera you're using to your primary computer (or perhaps your mobile device) for viewing, editing, archiving, and publishing online. Depending on the camera you purchase, this can be done in one or more of the following ways:

- Connect a USB cable directly between the USB port of the camera and the USB port of your computer. Some cameras have a micro-USB or mini-USB port built in, so be sure to use the transfer cable that came with the camera or one that's compatible with the USB port built into your camera.
- Remove the memory card from the camera and insert it into an external memory card reader that's connected to your primary computer via its USB port. For less than $30, you can purchase a memory card reader that's compatible with the type of memory card(s) you'll be using.
- Wirelessly transfer the raw digital video files to your computer (or mobile device) if the camera and computer are connected to the same wifi network and/or Bluetooth connection.

When you purchase your camera, determine if the appropriate cables and equipment for transferring the video footage you shoot are included with the camera (they often are). If necessary, purchase the additional cables, a memory card reader, or other equipment you'll need to handle this important task.

Many video cameras have a built-in A/V port or HDMI port that allows you to directly connect a specialty cable between the camera and your HDTV set to view the raw video you shoot directly from the camera without first transferring it. This allows you to see exactly how your footage will look on an HDTV. When you do this, however, the footage remains stored on your camera. It will still need to be transferred to a computer or mobile device for viewing, editing, archiving, and publishing.

One of the very first things you should plan to do after you shoot important video footage is to transfer it to your computer (or to an online-based file storage service). Before you start the editing process, immediately make a backup of the raw digital video file(s), which you store on an external hard drive or in an online file storage service (such as Dropbox, Box, Apple iCloud, or Microsoft OneDrive). This way, if something goes wrong during the editing process or your computer crashes, you know you have a full backup of the original video files. Moving forward, as you edit your videos, make frequent backups manually, even if the video-editing software also automatically backs up your work.

Never delete the raw video footage from your camera or its memory card until you are certain that the file transfer was successful and you've backed up the footage somewhere other than your primary computer.

MONEY-SAVING TIPS WHEN CAMERA SHOPPING

Consumer-grade cameras are available from consumer electronics stores and photo/video specialty stores. While you will pay more at retail photo/video specialty stores, the expertise of the salespeople tends to be top-notch, so you will receive excellent advice and get hands-on product demonstrations prior to making a purchase.

However, if you're looking for the best deals on these cameras, you'll probably want to shop online. Camera/photo specialty stores, such as B&H Photo–Video (www. bhphotovideo.com) and Adorama (www.adorama.com), not only offer competitive pricing, but also tend to maintain a great inventory selection.

These companies also offer telephone sales and support departments, which you can call for advice about what to purchase. Online photo/video retailers also sell a wide selection of video-related accessories and other equipment, such as tripods, lighting, and sound equipment, so you can often acquire everything you need from one vendor.

If you already know the make and model of the camera you're looking for, or what additional equipment and accessories you need, consider using an online price comparison website, like Nextag.com (www.nextag.com). Enter the make and model of what you're looking for into the site's search field for a list of retailers and prices, plus view customer ratings for the retailer and product reviews. Also, be sure to check Amazon.com for competitive pricing on all your audio/video equipment needs.

Another savings option is to seek used equipment from a reputable photo/video specialty store. This equipment typically comes with some type of warranty, and you're guaranteed it will be fully operational when you take possession of it. Some camera manufacturers' websites, as well as photo/video specialty stores, sell refurbished equipment as well. This is equipment that has been returned by the original purchaser, but has been refurbished by the manufacturer to meet its original specifications.

Also, consider seeking the advice of experts. For example, you can hire a freelance camera operator or video producer, using a service like Upwork.com, then pick their brain. Or you can rely on the advice offered by the salesperson at a photo/video specialty store. You can also contact other YouTube video producers and discuss what equipment they use.

Learn More from Video Production Magazines and Websites

Reading special interest video production magazines, such as *HDVideoPro*, will also help you learn about the latest video equipment and provide you with reliable product reviews. *HDVideoPro* is a monthly magazine that's available from newsstands; however, the publication's website (www.hdvideopro.com) offers a vast amount of free information, including past articles and reviews.

Videomaker magazine is another must-read monthly publication if you're interested in learning more about video production and want access to reviews of the latest cameras and equipment that's available. This, too, is a print publication available on newsstands, but the publication's website (www.videomaker.com) offers a vast amount of useful and free information.

Creative Planet Network (www.creativeplanetnetwork.com/videoedge) is targeted to professional-level video production but is also highly informative.

Once you know which camera make and model you'll be using, you'll find plenty of free how-to information available from YouTube. Within YouTube's search field, simply enter the make and model of your camera, followed by the word "tutorial." You could also type something like "action videography, using the [insert camera make and model]."

Also, be sure to visit the camera manufacturer's website. You'll often find free video-based tutorials about how to use your specific camera, plus other useful information that can help you dramatically improve your video productions' quality.

Chapter 8

Filming YouTube Videos

IN THIS CHAPTER

- Putting the production elements together
- Getting ready to start filming
- Shooting your videos

Hopefully by now, you've put a lot of thought into the concepts for your first few videos and have invested additional time storyboarding the ideas and/or writing scripts. Now that the pre-production phase is completed, it's time to gather your production equipment, cast, and crew, and get ready to shoot your videos. This chapter focuses on the production phase (the filming aspect) of your videos.

PREPARING FOR YOUR SHOOT

First and foremost, you'll need to consider what approach you want to take with each of your videos, then consider how you'll want them to look and sound once you've finished editing them. Keep in mind, consistency between videos, your YouTube channel page, and your overall online presence on other services (including your website) is important. These initial decisions will also help you determine where you should do your shooting and what production equipment you'll need to achieve the best possible results.

GET ACQUAINTED WITH YOUR VIDEO-EDITING SOFTWARE

Before you start filming your first YouTube video, spend some time becoming acquainted with the video-editing software you'll be using to edit your raw video content to transform it into the YouTube videos you'll be proud to share with the public. Discover what key features and functions your video-editing software offers that will be beneficial to you. For example, preview the various scene transition, title creation, color correction, and audio manipulation tools, so you learn what's possible during the editing process.

From an editing standpoint, once you know what you'll be able to do with your raw video footage after it's been shot, you'll have an easier time envisioning what your final videos will look like. You'll also discover that the production phase will go smoother, because you'll quickly be able to determine if you've shot each scene in a way that can easily and seamlessly be edited into your final video production. The focus of Chapter 9, "Editing Your YouTube Videos," is on choosing and using the best video-editing software (or mobile app) to meet your needs.

Envision how you want the final videos to look and sound once you add titles, credits, background music, sound effects, and other production elements, such as animated graphics, digital photos, and/or graphic charts, which get added during post-production.

If you'll be shooting indoors, you'll need to set up and use proper lighting and sound equipment, plus a simple background—whether it's your office, factory, or a solid-color backdrop.

Especially if you're starting to learn about video production, the best strategy for success is to keep your videos simple from a production standpoint and really focus on the content—your key message, call to action, and whatever other important information you plan to communicate within your videos.

Videos for major corporations are much more likely to be professionally produced and suitable for broadcast on TV. Even their product-demonstration and promotional videos have a slick look that's almost like watching a high-budget TV show or music video. The Honda channel (www.youtube.com/user/Honda) and the Coca-Cola channel (www.youtube.com/user/cocacola) on YouTube both use this approach. Most of the videos on these channels are highly produced, extended-length commercials, created by well-known advertising agencies.

For small- to mid-sized companies, creating slick, commercial-like videos probably is not feasible from a budget standpoint, nor will this approach appeal to your target audience, which is probably not turning to YouTube to watch commercials or infomercials, like what they already see in abundance on television.

Figure out what approach will work best for your company and will allow you to effectively and efficiently communicate to your audience your core message and call to action as quickly as possible. Try to personalize your company and the people featured within your videos to quickly establish and build a connection with your audience.

During the production phase, your focus should be on shooting the live-action scenes or elements that will be used within your videos. "Live action" refers to the scenes or sections of your videos that will feature people or content shot in the real world. Titles, logos, graphics, music, sound effects, computer animation, and other multimedia content will be added during post-production.

Let's take a closer look at some of the things you'll need to consider as you begin shooting the live-action video elements of your productions. While you want to achieve the highest production quality you can, your content is what really matters.

Where You'll Be Shooting

Whether it's indoors or outdoors, select a shooting location that can help you tell your story, communicate your message, and set the scene without distracting your audience. As you choose your setting, consider what lighting and sound challenges you'll encounter, and make sure you have the right production equipment to overcome these challenges.

Ideally, you want to be able to control the environment within and around your shooting location, so you can easily light the set and capture only the sound you want to include in your videos, without cars, airplanes, machinery, or other distracting ambient noises.

As you're shooting, ensure what you're filming is in focus and well lit. While you can slightly improve some aspects of a video's quality in post-production, ideally, you want to capture the highest quality raw video footage possible.

Based on what will be happening in your video, make sure your location will allow you to achieve the shots you need, whether it's showing your subject in motion, sitting at a desk or on a stool, or positioned with your company's products in the foreground or background.

If you're shooting a product demonstration, a solid backdrop will be less distracting, because you want the audience to focus on the product or spokesperson. However, if you're shooting a news-style report or a tour of your factory, your background may be a key part of the message you're trying to convey.

There will be challenges wherever you shoot. Indoors, when using artificial lighting, you'll need to deal with unwanted shadows. When shooting outdoors, the challenges might include reflections from the sun, ambient noise, and wind. Again, using the right equipment is essential.

Consider the Stars of Your Video

Next, consider who will be appearing in your videos and how you want to present them. Pay attention to every aspect of each person's appearance, as well as how they'll be positioned, what they'll be doing, what persona or personality they'll convey, and what they'll be wearing. Wardrobe, makeup, and hairstyle will all play a critical role in establishing that all-important first impression and ongoing rapport with your audience.

People often come across best wearing solid colors and simple outfits that don't blend in with the background. Avoid flashy or shiny jewelry, including watches that reflect light. If your subject wears glasses, get anti-reflective lenses, especially if you'll be using artificial light, to avoid distracting eyeglass glare.

The people in your video should also have their hair nicely styled, so you may want to hire a professional stylist. Messy hair can detract from their professional appearance and be distracting to your audience. As for makeup, more is less, especially if you're shooting in HD or plan to use close-ups shots. You want the people in your videos to look natural. A professional makeup artist understands how to do makeup for video shoots. And even men should wear makeup to cover blemishes and remove shine, especially when shooting in artificial light.

Next, think about what your presenters will be doing, and how they'll be positioned. Figure out what props will be needed to help them appear natural in front of the camera. Will they be holding or interacting with specific products? If so, do their appearance and the background complement those products? Will they look more natural and comfortable sitting or standing? Will they be more appealing to your audience looking directly into the camera or slightly away from it?

Your stars' appearance should reflect their personalities, fit the image you're trying to convey, and appeal to your audience.

Lighting Considerations

Depending on where you're shooting and the lighting challenges, you'll likely need to use a semi-professional or professional lighting kit, as well as light diffusers and/or reflectors. A basic lighting kit will include three or up to five individual lights that will ultimately be positioned around your subject(s) to create even, shadow-free lighting.

If you use too much light, your videos will appear overexposed, and everything will look washed out. If there's too little light, everything will appear dark, and colors and visual details will be obscured.

Even if you're shooting outdoors, artificial light, reflectors, and/or diffusers can help create optimal lighting around your subjects. When the artificial lights aren't enough to control the lighting, a diffuser can help to eliminate unwanted shadows or glare, while a reflector redirects light onto your subjects.

For most video shoots, a basic, three-point continuous lighting system will work fine. One light is positioned in front of your main subject, while the others are to the left and right of the subject. If you access YouTube and use the search phrase "video lighting," you'll find multiple tutorials for how to best use a basic three-point lighting system.

Refer to Chapter 6, "The Equipment You'll Need," to learn more about semi-professional and professional lighting kits, reflectors, and diffusers. B&H Photo-Video (www.bhphotovideo.com), Adorama (www.adorama.com), and FJ Westcott (www.fjwestcott.com) offer a selection of affordable lighting kits that are easy to use. Thanks to technological advancements in LED lighting, you'll probably discover that LED lights are easier to work with, versatile, do not generate heat (causing your subjects to sweat), and are extremely affordable.

Don't mix different types of lighting, such as incandescent, fluorescent, and LED lights, when filming your videos. Also, make sure you adjust the camera's white balance feature when shooting with different types of artificial light. As important as the lights themselves are, another equally important consideration is the light stands you use. They should be sturdy, able to hold the weight of your lights, and be fully adjustable. You'll need to position the lights precisely where they're needed, at the best height and angle, for example.

Sound Considerations

Close your eyes and listen carefully to whatever ambient noises you hear in the background. Can you hear the fan from your computer, clocks ticking, the sound of distant traffic, airplanes flying overhead, telephones ringing, people walking and talking in neighboring rooms, or the sound of an air conditioner? If you were to start filming right now, your camera's microphone would pick up all these ambient sounds.

When you begin filming your videos, these are the distracting sounds you want to notice up front and eliminate. Chances are, the microphone that's built into your camera can't adequately achieve the high-level audio quality you'll want and need, so you'll need to attach the most appropriate type of external microphone(s) to your camera.

Different types of microphones have specialized purposes. Some are designed to pick up only the sound of people's voices or the sound that's directly in front of them, while others are designed to pick up all ambient noise in the area where you're filming.

There are also different microphone styles, such as handheld, lapel, and shotgun microphones, each of which is suitable for recording audio in different situations. You'll need to choose between wired and wireless variations of microphones, as well as specialized accessories, such as pop filters and wind screens, that can help eliminate unwanted noises.

For help making the right decision, B&H Photo-Video's website (www.bhphotovideo.com/indepth/category/tags/microphones) offers a library of tutorials about recording audio. You'll also find similar tutorials on YouTube (https://creatoracademy.youtube.com/page/education) and the FJ Westcott website (http://westcottu.com/category/lighting-tips).

Camera Preparation

Before you start shooting your videos, learn how to properly use your camera and all its functions. Then, practice using the camera, especially if it's new. This investment of time could mean the difference between shooting a clear and professional-quality video and a total mess that will require timely and potentially costly reshoots.

Be sure to begin your shoot with fully charged batteries for your camera. Ideally, you want to have two or three extra fully charged batteries on hand. If your camera uses memory cards to store your raw video content, be sure to have an ample supply on hand so you can shoot plenty of video, including multiple takes of each scene. It's not uncommon for a content producer to shoot five or ten times the amount of content they'll actually need, which will all get whittled down during the editing process. For example, you might shoot more than 60 minutes of raw video so you'll have enough content to choose from when creating an awesome five-minute video.

It's also essential that you clean your camera lens before shooting. Even the smallest speck of dust, fingerprint, or water drop on the lens can result in shooting unusable content. Use a lens-cleaning cloth—not a paper towel or your shirtsleeve—to carefully clean the lens.

Finally, practice using all the camera accessories you'll need for the shoot, including a tripod or a camera stabilizer or support rig, an on-camera monitor, and/or an external microphone.

LIGHTS, CAMERAS . . . ACTION!

Even if your goal is to create a two- to three-minute video, you'll wind up shooting a lot of extra content that you'll then edit down during post-production. The more planning

CONSIDER SHOOTING WITH MULTIPLE CAMERAS

Often, your video production will benefit if you simultaneously shoot each scene in your video using two or three cameras at once, each set at a different angle or position. Then, you can pick and choose which shot you want to use and switch between shots often to create a more visually interesting video.

Study any television show or movie. You'll notice that the same shot is rarely shown for more than five to ten seconds at a time. This technique is used to make content more visually appealing to the audience and to hold their attention. If you don't have the budget to shoot with multiple HD cameras, you can always shoot the same scene several times and position the camera differently for each take. This, too, will provide you with options when it comes to editing your videos later.

Using multiple cameras also requires added crew members. You'll also need to use video-editing software that allows you to more easily edit multi-camera shots from multiple video feeds.

For more information about how to shoot multi-camera videos, search for "shooting multi-camera videos" on YouTube for tutorials on how to use this shooting technique. For example, visit https://youtu.be/1ItW5yz9L6M to view a four-minute tutorial video.

You can also use editing techniques that allow you to use one camera for shooting, but during the editing process, fake a multi-cam shoot approach. A tutorial for how to do this can be found at https://youtu.be/1ItW5yz9L6M.

you do before you start shooting, the more efficient your shooting time will be. Because you can reorder shots using your video-editing software, there's no need to shoot your video in sequential order. In fact, you'll often find it more advantageous to shoot out of sequence.

As a video producer, you'll need to pay continuous attention to every detail during your shoot—lighting, sound, and continuity-related issues. For example, if you start shooting one day, then pick it up another day, be sure the visual is identical from one day to the next, from the appearance of the people appearing in your videos, to the lighting, the set, the position of the props, and anything else that can be seen or heard.

You'll always need to make sure that you properly present your message and call to action, and get your other key points across quickly. To make your video more visually interesting, use different shooting angles and maybe incorporate a small amount of motion into your production. Let's look at some of these important considerations.

Define, Present, and Repeat Your Message

During the pre-production phase, you should have clearly defined the message you want to get across to your audience. Now that you're shooting a video, be sure to:

- Present your core message very early in the video—within the first 10 to 15 seconds.
- Repeat your message, using different wording or a slightly different approach, several times throughout the video.
- Make sure that the message is presented in a natural and organic way that fits nicely into the overall video.
- As you're filming, put yourself in your audience's shoes. Make sure that your approach is appealing and easily understandable.
- Repeat or emphasize your core message multiple times. Try to do this every 30 seconds, if possible, without making it look forced or sound too much like an infomercial.
- Avoid taking a hard-sell, commercial-style approach. On YouTube, the soft sell almost always works better.

Take your time to make sure these important elements are in play for your videos. Always keep your audience in mind, never forgetting that you must provide them with useful value not only in your products and services but also in your video content.

Incorporate Your Call to Action (CTA)

Your productions should all have a call to action, or tell your audience exactly what you want them to do after watching your video. It might be, "For an extra savings of $100, click here to visit our website and order our new [insert product name]," or "To receive $50 off your first order, call us right now at 800-555-1234." It might also be to get the viewer to click on the "like" button, post a comment about the video on your YouTube channel page, or to share the video's link via Facebook or Twitter.

Here are some tips for presenting your call to action:

- Present your call to action near the start and end of your video, and repeat it at least once during your video. Most people won't be watching your video from start to finish, so don't wait until the very end to present your call to action.

- State the clear benefit or reward first, then explain exactly what the viewer needs to do.

- Ensure your call to action is easy to understand and straightforward. Tell the viewer exactly what to do, how to do it, and when to do it.

- Embed links or annotations in your video during post-production, as well as stating your call to action within the video, and use titles to reinforce what you're saying. You can also use text in the video's description to emphasize your call to action.

The CTA is your invitation for a follow-up action from your audience. Would you end a letter or meeting with a vague action plan? Of course not. Nor should you leave the CTA open (or not use one at all).

Get Your Key Points Across Quickly

YouTube viewers have short attention spans and are constantly bombarded with links or invitations to watch new videos. It's essential that you capture their attention within the first five seconds, so think about your opening shot very carefully.

Then, within the first 5 to 15 seconds, be sure to inform the viewer about what your video is about and exactly what they can expect from watching it. At the same time, communicate your core message and, potentially, your call to action.

Also make sure that within that first 5 to 15 seconds, a viewer can determine if your video interests them and offers a benefit they desire. Then, even if someone stops watching after 15 seconds or so, at least they were exposed to your core message.

While there is no optimal length, perfect formula, or format to follow—it depends on who your audience is, what you're trying to communicate, and what approach you're taking—you should always keep your videos short and to the point. Every shot, every visual, every word, and every sound included within every second of your video should be there for a purpose.

You're better off creating a series of shorter videos, of one to three minutes, than producing one long video. With shorter videos, it's easier to capture and keep your viewer's attention, plus create a quality interaction. You also improve the chances of someone finding your videos when doing a search on YouTube or Google, because each video will be listed separately with its own title, description, and keywords.

With more videos listed within your channel and on Google, your overall SEO rankings will improve. This increases your chances of someone finding your channel using YouTube or Google's search function.

For each of your videos, make sure you use a catchy, accurate, and informative title, description, and keywords/tags, as well as assign each to the most appropriate content category on YouTube. Then, from your YouTube channel page, link related videos into a playlist for your audience, or pre-sort and display them in appropriate categories based on their topic or content.

Use the Rule of Thirds When Shooting

Invest time learning some basic principles of cinematography. One core concept is the "Rule of Thirds." Instead of pointing your camera directly at your subject and keeping them centered in the frame, position your main subject off-center.

Envision a tic-tac-toe board is overlaid over your camera's viewfinder, with nine boxes that together make up your shooting frame. The box in the center represents the center of the shot, where most people position their subject.

Instead, line up your main subject at one of the interaction points within the grid, and pay attention to whatever is in the foreground, background, and/or to the sides of your subject within the shot as well. The goal is to move your main subject out of the center of the frame to create a more visually interesting shot.

You don't need to position your camera directly in front of your subject or head-on. Shooting from a different perspective or angle creates a much more visually compelling shot. Consider, from a creative standpoint, positioning your camera slightly above, below, or to the side of your subject, and shoot from an angle.

Using your camera's zoom lens allows you to switch between close-up, mid-length, and wide-angle shots. You can switch shots using a manual zoom as you're shooting, or stop the action, reposition, and refocus your camera, then restart shooting. Later, you can also edit in scene or shot transitions as needed.

Part of being a skilled cinematographer is to tap your own creativity and experiment. Select shots and perspectives that will be visually appealing and potentially artistic, but not distract your audience from your message. Study popular YouTube videos that take the approach or format that you intend to use.

If you plan to add a company logo, titles, or other graphics into a shot, be sure to leave room in the frame as you're shooting the core live-action footage so there's room for those post-production elements. Instead of using a close-up shot, for example, you might need to use a medium or wide shot.

Keep Your Camera Steady by Using a Tripod

While MTV and most reality TV shows use handheld cameras to create a "you are there" perspective with a lot of camera motion, you'll probably want to use a tripod or Steadicam. These allow you to hold the camera still, plus use smooth, slow camera movements to show motion without amateurish shakes and jerks.

Refer to Chapter 6, "The Equipment You'll Need," to learn more about tripod and Steadicam accessories. Especially if you're shooting people or "talking head" scenes,

CONSIDER SHOOTING IN FRONT OF A BLUE OR GREEN SCREEN

As you become more proficient using your video equipment and want to tap your creativity to produce more visually interesting videos, you can try a technique called "chroma key." This is technically a post-production special effect that's relatively easy to use with even the most basic video camera and video-editing equipment.

With chroma key, you shoot all your live-action content in front of a special blue or green background. Then, using specialized video-editing software, you can remove the background digitally, and replace it with anything you want: animated graphics, other video, or a still image. Whatever was shot in front of the blue or green screen will then be digitally superimposed over the selected background. The trick to using this effect well is to ensure proper lighting when shooting, then use the best video-editing software.

123 Video Magic (www.123videomagic.com), NCH Software (www.nchsoftware. com), Pinnacle Studio (www.pinnaclesys.com), and Magix (www.magix.com) are some of the many companies that offer video-editing software that includes the chroma key effect. The feature is also included in more advanced video-editing software packages, like Final Cut Pro X and Adobe Premier Pro, which you'll read more about in Chapter 9, "Editing Your YouTube Videos."

Here are two YouTube tutorials that showcase how to use chroma key:

1. "Green Screen Tips, Tricks and Materials—Chromakey Tutorial": www.youtube. com/user/tubetape?v=q3PZO_lCBkw

2. "Green Screen Tips, Tricks and Materials—Chromakey Tutorial": www.youtube. com/watch?v=M_WdLkaOUic

To find more videos that showcase creative ways to use chroma key, simply search for "chroma key tutorial," or visit: www.youtube.com/results?search_query=Chromakey+Tutorial.

keeping the camera steady is essential. Otherwise, you'll wind up with a video that is distracting or annoying. However, because watching a "talking head" video can become boring quickly for your viewers, use multiple camera angles or shooting perspectives, and figure out other types of shots or content you can mix in so you can more easily hold your audience's attention.

Don't Forget About Branding Your Content

Regardless of your video's purpose—be it promotional or instructional, to provide entertainment, or to demonstrate a product—make the look, sound, and overall feel of your production consistent with your other videos, your online presence, company website, and your real-world image.

To ensure you include your own branding, showcase your company logo and website URL within the video, or display your products, even if they're in the background or on someone's desk. Think about how to communicate your branding or core message visually. It can be subtle or blatant.

Also consider how to use product placement to better promote or showcase your own products, brand, or image. The person in your video can wear a T-shirt that clearly displays your company's logo, or place a computer in the shot and display the logo or photos of your products as its screensaver.

Develop strategies that will appeal to your target audience without being distracting. Remember, nobody wants to watch infomercials, but people will invest their time to watch videos that offer useful information about products or services they're interested in, as long as the viewer perceives what they're watching to be valuable, accurate, and credible. Often, taking a very subtle approach to branding within your videos works the best.

NOW, EDIT YOUR VIDEOS IN POST-PRODUCTION

Once you've shot your raw video content and have assembled any other multimedia content that will be edited into your videos, you're ready to begin post-production. Using your video-editing software, you'll edit down your raw content, and create the video production that you'll then upload and share with your audience on YouTube, your company's website, and other social media.

It's during the post-production phase that you can piece together your production, add titles, special effects, animated transitions, production credits, and animations, and insert music and sound effects. Then, once you upload your video to your YouTube channel, you can add annotations and embed links to make your video content a bit

THAT'S A WRAP! OR IS IT?

During the production process, before you wrap up your production, carefully review your raw content on a full-sized monitor or screen. Make sure the person who will be editing the video has all the shots and content needed to achieve the video's objective. One of the worst mistakes you can make is wrapping your production, and realizing several hours or days later that:

■ You forgot to shoot a specific but extremely important scene or capture an action from a certain camera angle because you didn't refer to your script or storyboard during production.

■ The lighting in one scene was handled incorrectly. Thus, it contains harsh shadows, or looks vastly different from the other scenes.

■ Someone speaking in your video mispronounced a word, incorrectly used a word, forgot a line, or somehow messed up the message they were trying to convey.

■ The cameraman didn't adjust the focus properly in one or more scenes, and the raw content is blurry.

■ The audio is unclear, or you accidently recorded unwanted ambient sounds that can't be removed during post-production.

■ For whatever reason (such as the camera's battery dying or its memory card reaching capacity), you didn't save essential content as it was being shot.

■ You discover inconsistencies in the appearance of your raw content that can't be fixed during editing, which will make the video look fragmented or unprofessional.

■ While shooting, the camera was shaken or moved in a way that ruined the shot.

These are some of the common mishaps that could happen, and can often easily be corrected if caught early, but are much harder to correct if you need to go back and reshoot. As the content producer, pay attention to detail during every step of the production process. Try to shoot every scene at least three times in a row so, hopefully, you'll have at least one good take that's usable during the editing process.

interactive. YouTube Cards, for example, are added to your videos after they've been fully edited and uploaded to YouTube, but before the videos are made public to your online audience.

Editing Your YouTube Videos

Each phase of a video's creation is important, including what happens in post-production, after the footage has been shot, and you're ready to edit and add other production elements. Post-production involves several key steps, including:

- Reviewing, cataloging, and editing the raw footage
- Adding titles, such as an opening title and end credits, if applicable
- Incorporating voice-overs, music, sound effects, and other audio elements
- Importing and adding multimedia elements, such as animated charts, graphs, tables, and/or PowerPoint slides
- Adding effects and scene transitions

- Cutting or trimming content to make it an acceptable length
- Exporting the fully produced video into an industry-standard file format
- Uploading the edited video to YouTube
- Adding a title, description, and keywords to the video; choosing a thumbnail image; and adding an End Screen or Cards to the video before publishing it on YouTube
- Embedding your videos (or adding links to your videos) within your company's web page, Facebook page, blog, electronic newsletter, and/or in social media post(s)

You'll do much of the post-production work using video-editing software on your PC or Mac. However, when it comes to editing short videos, a tablet or smartphone (in conjunction with a specialized video-editing app) can be used.

Consumer-oriented editing applications are designed for ease of use but lack a vast collection of editing and post-production tools, and range in price from free to under $50. There are also consumer-oriented applications that offer scaled-down versions of professional tools that can allow for near professional-quality results. These are typically priced around $100.

You'll also find consumer-level, online-based video-editing tools available. To use one of these services, you'd first upload your raw video footage and other content to the service, then take advantage of the online-based video-editing tools available using your web browser. This option eliminates the need to install video-editing software on your computer. Another benefit is that you can edit your videos from any compatible computer or mobile device that's connected to the internet, regardless of where you are.

WeVideo.com (www.wevideo.com) is an example of a fee-based video-editing option that's based online. You'll read more about this service shortly. As you'll discover, YouTube also offers a handful of basic video-editing tools you can use to edit and enhance your videos once they're uploaded to your YouTube channel, but before they're published and made public.

Yet another category of video-editing software is designed for semi-professional videographers and editors. These tend to be feature-packed, extremely powerful, and require a significant learning curve. They typically cost several hundred dollars to buy outright and require more advanced computer hardware. In some cases, a subscription payment model is offered to make the software more accessible if you're on a tight budget. Adobe Premier Pro (www.adobe.com/products/premiere.html) is an example of professional-level video-editing software for a PC or Mac that requires the software to be downloaded and installed onto a computer. The user then pays a monthly subscription fee of $19.99 to access and use it, so the software does not have to be purchased outright.

To create truly professional, broadcast-quality results, you'll need professional-level video-editing tools, running on a high-end computer or a specialized video-editing workstation. Plan to spend thousands on this type of setup or hire a professional editor who owns the necessary equipment. Released in late-2017, Apple's iMac Pro (www.apple.com/imac-pro) is an example of a high-end computer that can be used as a professional-level video-editing workstation.

You may be able to get by with higher-end consumer-oriented video-editing software, but for higher-quality videos, it's best to go for semi-professional video-editing software, such as Final Cut Pro X (for the Mac) or Adobe Premier Pro (for the Mac or PCs).

Depending on the video—its complexity, the amount of raw footage and multimedia elements, and the type of software you're using—plan to spend between several hours and several full days to edit each of your YouTube videos. You may also need to use other software to create production elements. For example, Microsoft PowerPoint can be used to create animated digital slides showcasing charts, graphs, tables, and lists that can be imported into your video as pre-produced multimedia content.

MOBILE VIDEO EDITING

If you shoot video footage on your mobile device or transfer video content to your mobile device, it's possible to use a specialized video-editing app to edit your raw video, handle many post-production steps, and directly upload your fully produced video to YouTube. This will work much better if you're using one of the latest model smartphones or tablets, such as the iPad Pro, which is equipped with a fast processor, plenty of internal storage, and a Retina Display.

While the quality isn't the same as that of a computer-edited video—nor will you have the same caliber of editing tools available—what is possible using a smartphone or tablet with wireless internet capabilities is adequate for many YouTube video producers.

For an Apple iOS mobile device, purchase, download, and install Apple's own iMovie app to handle many post-production steps. Additional third-party apps are also available from the App Store within the "Photo & Video" category. Among them are: Videoshop–Video Editor, Cute CUT Pro, LumaFusion, GoPro Splice, Video Editor Videorama, VidLab, Vidpro, and Video Plus.

You also may need digital audio-production software and equipment to record your own music and sound effects, as well as photo-editing software to edit and incorporate digital photos, and other software to incorporate animated elements, such as an animated company logo. Each of these elements will be imported into your video-editing software, so they can ultimately be added to your video.

WHAT VIDEO-EDITING SOFTWARE CAN AND CAN'T DO

In just the past few years, the capabilities of consumer-oriented video-editing software has dramatically improved. Once you import raw video footage into the software, then import your other multimedia elements, video-editing software allows you to transform the raw content into a slick-looking production.

While each has its own set of tools, most of the popular editing packages include the ability to:

- Add animated titles to your production, including scrolling credits
- Edit, trim, or crop footage, with control over one frame at a time
- Add professional-style, animated shot and scene transitions
- Make minor fixes to raw footage, such as shaky footage, adjust lighting, or make color adjustments
- Incorporate and mix pre-recorded music, voice-overs, and sound effects
- Add pre-produced multimedia elements
- Incorporate special effect filters
- Use optional plug-ins available from third parties that expand the video-editing tool set
- Preview your edited movies
- Export your edited/produced videos into a popular, industry-standard file format
- Upload your videos directly to your YouTube channel

To speed up the video-editing process, many consumer-oriented video-editing software packages offer pre-created themes or templates into which you can drag and drop your raw video footage and multimedia elements. Using a theme or template can dramatically reduce the time it takes to edit a video; plus, it gives you access to true professional-level video production elements, with little or no training.

Video editing is both a skill and an art form. The skill needed includes knowing how to use your computer and video-editing software. This means discovering what's possible, then learning how to use the various menus, commands, and features built into the software. You'll ultimately decide what your audience will see and hear during every second of your video, and have many tools available to transform your creative vision for the video into a finished production that caters to your target audience.

COMPUTER HARDWARE CONSIDERATIONS FOR EDITING HD-QUALITY VIDEO

The digital files associated with HD video content (especially 4K resolution video files) are massive, and most consumer-oriented editing software that runs on basic PCs, iMacs, or MacBooks can't handle long videos because of their file size. Because these basic, consumer-oriented computers don't have enough processing power, memory, or storage space, if you attempt to load a massive HD video file into a standard PC or Mac, the editing software might crash, or the computer may slow to a crawl.

To avoid this, keep your videos short, and load only 15 or so minutes of raw video at a time, especially if you're using an older computer. If you know you'll need to edit longer HD videos, consider upgrading your computer with a faster, more powerful microprocessor, along with a state-of-the-art graphics and sound card. Also, increase the amount of RAM, and use a large-capacity internal or external hard drive with a fast read/write speed.

Try to meet or exceed the hardware requirements listed by the software's developer. If you're looking to use more advanced video-editing software, such as Adobe Premiere Pro on a PC or Mac, the system requirements are rather extensive; you can find them at www.adobe.com/products/premiere/tech-specs.html.

Yet another option for editing videos is to upload your raw video footage directly to YouTube, then use its online-based video editor to edit your productions before making them public. The editing functions are limited, but for editing vlogs (a video where one person is looking directly into a camera and speaking, using a digital diary-like format) and other short videos that don't need to be polished, this is certainly a viable option, especially if you need to upload and edit a video while away from your primary computer.

What Your Software Can't Do

While some video-editing software packages offer tools that allow you to manipulate the quality of raw video, there are limits to what's possible. Especially with lower-end software, there's only so much you can do during post-production to fix video that is shot out of focus, that's extremely shaky, or that's overexposed or underexposed, for example. Before editing and adding production elements, you'll want to discover what your software is capable of and what features it offers.

CHOOSING THE RIGHT SOFTWARE

Choosing the best video-editing software will come down to a handful of decisions early on, including:

- Your budget
- Your computer knowledge and comfort using technology
- How much time and effort you want to invest in editing your videos
- How much control you want to have when editing your videos, including the selection of post-production tools you want or need to achieve your video's objectives
- The level of production quality you're striving for
- The capabilities of your computer
- The file format(s) of the raw video and multimedia content to be incorporated into your videos, and the file format(s) and data compression you'll use when you export your final productions

If you're already proficient editing or enhancing digital photos on your computer, you already have some of the core skills needed to edit video. When editing video, however, you're dealing with 24 or more individual frames per second, plus audio content, so there's a lot more to consider, and the software-based tools you'll be using are more robust.

Even if you opt to use the most user-friendly and basic video-editing software on your computer, there's still a learning curve involved when discovering how to use the software, along with its features and tools.

Should you opt to use semi-professional-level video-editing software, such as Apple's Final Cut Pro X or Adobe Premier Pro, the learning curve is much more significant because the editing tools are far more extensive and advanced. However, some Hollywood blockbusters are edited using these software packages, so you can expect top-notch results once you learn how to properly use the software.

Start with basic software that has tools to achieve the production quality you'll need to achieve your objectives and creative vision. You can always upgrade down the road.

Overview of Popular Software Packages

There are hundreds of video-editing software packages, as well as optional add-ons and plug-ins available that allow you to transform raw video footage and other multimedia elements into cohesive and professional-looking video presentations that can be published on YouTube or elsewhere.

Apple's iMovie (www.apple.com/imovie) for the Mac, for example, is a free, easy-to-use, yet powerful consumer-oriented video-editing tool that includes a nice selection of features and tools for creating decent-looking, HD-quality productions that can be published on YouTube with just a few mouse clicks.

Microsoft has discontinued support for its free Windows Movie Maker software, since so many third-party options are available. But you can still download and use this software by visiting: http://ccm.net/download/download-124-windows-movie-maker-12.

Using the Online-Based YouTube Video Editor

Another option is to upload your unedited, raw video footage directly to YouTube, then use the service's own online-based Video Editor (www.youtube.com/editor), as well as YouTube's info and settings, enhancements, audio, End Screen, Cards, and subtitles/closed captioning options (available through the Video Manager) to handle many post-production tasks.

The editing tools offered by YouTube's Video Editor can help you edit a basic video from scratch, but these tools probably aren't adequate for editing a professional-looking video aimed at representing your company, product, or service. They can be used, however, to further enhance a fully produced video that's already been uploaded to YouTube. What's nice about this editing tool set is that there's no software to download and install. The application is run directly from your favorite web browser.

The online-based YouTube Video Editor offers tools for:

- Editing and manipulating video footage that's been uploaded to your YouTube channel, including raw video that you've labeled as private. For example, you can trim your video footage to custom lengths, then merge scenes that have been shot and edited separately into one production.
- Enhancing the video footage using effects and other controls, such as "Brightness and Contrast," "Stabilize Video," and "Black and White."
- Accessing and remixing YouTube Creative Commons video content. These videos are produced and uploaded by third parties that have granted permission for anyone to use, edit, and incorporate. When you use Creative Commons video, YouTube automatically attributes the content to its creator. To learn more about using Creative Commons content within your videos via YouTube's Video Editor, visit: www.youtube.com/t/creative_commons.
- Adding music and sound effects to your videos using the "Media Picker." This grants you access to content from YouTube's vast library of free audio content.

You can't edit audio tracks using the Video Editor; you can only determine when audio (music and sound effects) starts and stops playing.

- Incorporating animated transitions between scenes or shots.
- Inserting titles into your videos.

Like many video-editing software packages, YouTube's Video Editor uses an intuitive, drag-and-drop interface. When you're done using the Video Editor, click on the "Create Video" button displayed near the upper-right corner of the browser window. Then, access the Video Manager options to adjust the various settings associated with that video. See Chapter 11, "Uploading Your Videos to YouTube," for more information about using YouTube's Video Manager options.

WHERE TO FIND ADDITIONAL ONLINE VIDEO-EDITING TOOLS

WeVideo.com (www.wevideo.com) is an online video-editing tool set that allows you to upload your raw SD or HD video footage to the WeVideo cloud-based servers, then use a handful of powerful video-editing tools to transform that raw video footage into a polished and fully produced video that's suitable for submitting to YouTube or other video-sharing services (such as your company's website or blog). All the video-editing tools offered by WeVideo are accessible from your favorite web browser. There's no software to download and install.

Individuals and small businesses can use WeVideo.com for $4.99 per month to edit small video projects at 480p or 720p resolution. Up to 30 minutes' worth of video can be edited per month, and up to 20GB of online storage space is provided. To gain full access to all the service's editing tools and be able to use them on all your HD videos (regardless of their length, resolution, or file size), you pay a $7.99 monthly fee. This Unlimited subscription plan supports up to 4K Ultra HD resolution, and offers tools so two or more people can collaborate on editing or reviewing a video project from separate locations. A free subscription plan is offered, but it only allows you to edit one video per month (up to five minutes long) using 480p resolution, and only 1GB of online storage space is provided.

As you'd expect, in addition to editing raw video and incorporating a wide range of shot and scene transitions, as well as titles and captions, for example, the WeVideo service allows users to easily add music and sound effects to video productions. WeVideo includes a library of more than 400 royalty-free music tracks that can be included within a video for free, or you can add your own music or sound effects (assuming you have obtained the rights or license to use that content). Another useful aspect of WeVideo is that the service can be used from a smartphone or tablet using a proprietary app. To learn what's possible using the mobile app, iPhone and iPad users can visit www.wevideo.com/ios, while Android-based mobile device users can visit www.wevideo.com/android.

The service supports all popular video, audio, and graphic formats, so uploading and adding any type of multimedia content to your video projects is easy. Then, once

POWERFUL, FREE EDITING SOFTWARE

There are plenty of free, open-source and shareware software packages that can be downloaded and installed on your PC or Mac. There's Wondershare Video Editor that supports dozens of popular video formats and offers hundreds of Hollywood-style effects and scene transitions you can incorporate into your productions. You can also edit and enhance your media files by trimming, cutting, splitting, merging, rotating, and fading videos, while also having the ability to adjust things like contrast, saturation, brightness, and the hue of your raw footage.

Wondershare Video Editor includes tools for inserting and editing audio tracks, plus creating and incorporating text, subtitles, and credits into your productions. What's great about this video-editing software is that it's available for free as shareware. Simply visit www.wondershare.net/ad/video-editor-win to download and install the award-winning software.

OpenShot Video Editor (www.openshot.org) is another example of a free, simple-to-use, yet powerful Windows-based video editor that supports HD video and a wide range of visual and audio effect tools.

Another shareware video-editing software package for Windows-based PCs is Ezvid VideoMaker (www.ezvid.com). This software, which works with most current versions of Microsoft Windows, is easy to use and offers a handful of tools designed for people creating YouTube videos.

For a list of other free video-editing software packages, visit:

- *Multimedia and Audio Software:* www.osalt.com/multimedia-and-audio

- *Video-Editing Software:* http://en.kioskea.net/download/video-editing-76

For PCs and Macs, you'll find a listing of editing software—some free, some not— at CNET's Download website (http://download.cnet.com) or Wikipedia (http://en.wikipedia.org/wiki/List_of_video_editing_software).

you've edited your videos using the service's online tools, transferring the finished video projects to YouTube or another video-sharing service requires just a few mouse clicks.

Once your raw video content is uploaded to your WeVideo account, it's securely stored and achieved there. You can access it only if you or your collaborators know your account login information. Storing your raw video footage, as well as your final edited videos on WeVideo (or a service like it), also allows you to conserve storage space on your computer's hard drive. As you know, HD video files can take up a lot of storage space due to their large file sizes.

COMMERCIALLY AVAILABLE VIDEO-EDITING SOFTWARE

These software packages can be purchased and downloaded directly from their respective developer's websites, and in some cases, they're also available from the Windows Store (www.microsoft.com/en-us/store/b/home) or Apple Mac App Store (accessible from your Mac by clicking on the App Store icon displayed along the Dock).

Many of the more expensive video editing applications, including Adobe Premier Pro CC and Apple's Final Cut Pro X, offer a free, 30-day trial version that can be downloaded from the developer's website. Before investing hundreds of dollars, download and use the trial versions of several packages to help you decide which work best for you.

Adobe Premiere Pro CC

Available for both PCs and Macs, Adobe Premiere Pro CC (www.adobe.com/products/premiere.html) is one of the most advanced semi-pro to professional video-editing packages available. It is offered as a stand-alone package but also integrates perfectly with the other applications in Adobe's Creative Suite, as well as with the Adobe Creative Cloud online file sharing/storage service. You can pay a monthly subscription fee of $19.99 to use this software, as opposed to buying it outright.

Adobe Premiere Pro CC supports all popular audio and video file formats and allows for HD-quality video productions to be created on a standard PC or Mac. What's great about this software is that it works seamlessly with most of Adobe's other content creation tools, like Photoshop CC, InDesign CC, After Effects CC, and Prelude CC. In fact, for a flat monthly fee, starting at $69.99 per month, per user, you can have unlimited access to virtually all of Adobe's applications.

Apple iMovie

Apple's iMovie software (www.apple.com/imovie) comes bundled with all new iMac and MacBook computers. It's a consumer-level video-editing application that's extremely

ADOBE PREMIERE ELEMENTS OFFERS SCALED-DOWN VIDEO-EDITING FEATURES

For amateur video editors, many of the most powerful and popular features built into Adobe Premiere Pro CC have also been incorporated into a more consumer-friendly version of the software called Photoshop Premiere Elements (www.adobe.com/products/premiere-elements.html). This scaled-down version of the software for PCs and Macs offers a much more intuitive drag-and-drop interface, and requires a much shorter learning curve than Adobe Premiere Pro CC. This software can be purchased for $79.99.

intuitive, thanks to its drag-and-drop interface. iMovie allows you to edit HD-quality videos, as long as they're relatively short.

This software works much better on newer Macs that are running the latest macOS operating system. If you have an older version of iMovie, there may be an upgrade fee to acquire the latest edition. What's nice about iMovie is that it works seamlessly with other Apple applications, including GarageBand, Photos, Pages, Numbers, and Keynote. It's also compatible in many ways with iMovie for iOS, which is an optional video-editing application for the iPhone and iPad.

For companies looking to define and promote their corporate image through their YouTube videos, iMovie probably doesn't offer the post-production capabilities and creative control you'll need. However, if your business would benefit from producing and showcasing animated slide shows, iMovie is a great tool for putting these types of presentations together quickly.

If you're a Mac user, this is an excellent introductory application that's also suitable for online personalities who need to create more basic, but impressive-looking videos for YouTube.

To make the video-editing process less time consuming and more intuitive, iMovie relies heavily on templates. When you begin working on a new video project, you're encouraged to select a fully customizable template, to which you can add your video footage, photos, music, sound effects, voice-over audio, and other multimedia content.

Apple's Final Cut Pro X

While iMovie is an introductory, consumer-oriented application for video editing, Apple also offers its Final Cut Pro X package (www.apple.com/finalcutpro), which features many more advanced tools designed for achieving semi-pro to professional-quality results with HD video content.

To fully use Final Cut Pro X, which is priced at $299.99, you'll need to run it on a higher-end Mac. To access the current system requirements for this software, visit: www.apple.com/final-cut-pro/specs.

Many companies that produce YouTube videos can easily take advantage of the editing and post-production capabilities that Final Cut Pro X offers. These functions are pretty much in line with what's offered by Adobe Premier Pro CC, although individual features and effects vary.

Because Final Cut Pro X offers more advanced and professional-level tools, the software requires a much more significant learning curve than iMovie, as well as a better understanding of video editing and production principles. What's nice about this software is that it gives you excellent creative control over the visual and audio aspects of your production and is compatible with a wide range of popular audio, video, and image file formats.

One of the tasks that Final Cut Pro X handles well is organizing and managing raw video content and pre-produced multimedia elements that will ultimately be incorporated into your video productions. This software is designed to help you view multiple video feeds simultaneously during the editing and post-production process. This allows you to more easily assemble and edit multi-camera projects. You can also simultaneously work with multiple audio channels and have total and independent control over each one.

Apple offers a vast library of royalty-free music and sound effects, as well as photo libraries and graphic backgrounds and textures that can be used to polish your project. A large selection of optional plug-ins and add-ons from third-party companies are also available, making this the go-to video-editing app for savvy Mac videographers and editors. A wide range of printed, as well as online training guides for Final Cut Pro X, are available to speed up the learning curve that's associated with this software. To learn more about these resources, visit www.apple.com/final-cut-pro/resources, or within YouTube's own search field, type "Final Cut Pro X tutorial."

Avid Video Editing and Production

Of all the post-production and video editing tools available to professionals, Avid's are among the most widely used when it comes to producing broadcast-quality content for TV, motion pictures, and the internet.

This suite of professional-level tools requires a tremendous learning curve, as well as a working knowledge of video production. You'll also need to operate the software tools on high-end computer equipment, especially if you'll be working with HD video.

While the editing, finishing, and post-production tools available from Avid are top-notch, they're also extremely costly. For example, the Avid Media Composer software starts at $1,299, plus has a variety of add-ons and plug-ins that are sold separately. A monthly subscription, which offers full use of the software, is also available starting at $49.99 per month. To learn more about Avid video editing and production tools, visit www.avid.com/media-composer.

The video-editing tools available from Avid are designed for professionals looking to create broadcast-quality content. It is not meant for use by amateur or even semi-professional video producers.

Video Editing Applications That Offer Specialized Functionality

Specialized video-editing applications, such as Camtasia from TechSmith, offer advanced screen recording and editing tools. Camtasia is ideal for recording software or presentations as they're being used on your computer, adding narration, and editing that content into video tutorials or software demonstration videos. It's also possible to use video and multimedia elements from other sources, including video that you shoot yourself.

Companies often use software like Camtasia to record PowerPoint slide presentations, software demos, and web pages; edit in live-action video footage or other multimedia content; and record custom voice-overs or an audio track to produce their final video productions.

Screen recording software that allows for editing and exporting into a commonly used video format has many uses to help promote online sales or promotions, showcase product demonstrations, and to adapt in-person training or workshop sessions into videos that can be watched online.

Camtasia is available for PCs and Macs and is $199. The software can be purchased and downloaded from the TechSmith website: www.camtasia.com.

Specialized Video-Editing Software for Your HD Video Camera

Many popular video cameras, including the GoPro HERO action cameras, come with free access to specialized software that's designed for editing and publishing content shot using that company's own cameras. For example, GoPro offers several different video editing mobile apps, as well as the Quik Desktop software for PCs and Macs, that can be downloaded from GoPro's website (https://shop.gopro.com/softwareandapp).

If you've acquired a camera with specialized functionality, such as a GoPro HERO, Mevo camera (https://getmevo.com), or a 360-degree camera, be sure to use the recommended video-editing software from that camera's manufacturer.

IMPORTING FOOTAGE AND OTHER PRODUCTION ELEMENTS INTO YOUR VIDEO-EDITING SOFTWARE

Whichever video-editing software you use, it's this software that provides you with the tools to edit the raw video, audio, photos, and/or multimedia content that you create and record using other equipment. For example, you'd use your camera to record raw video footage, then transfer that to your computer. It would then be imported into the video-editing software, and ultimately into a file format that's suitable for what you'd be using the video for, such as presenting it via your company's YouTube channel.

Some software will automatically facilitate the transfer of your raw footage, audio, and other multimedia content from the recording device to your computer, and ultimately into the software. Other video-editing software, however, will require you to transfer the raw footage and other content to your computer manually, store it on your computer's hard drive or an external drive, then import it manually into the software for editing.

BACK UP YOUR WORK IN THE CLOUD

Virtually all video-editing software allows you to store and/or back up your work in the cloud. However, which cloud-based services the software is compatible with will vary. Some of the more popular and low-cost cloud services that can be used to back up and archive digital video files and related content, include Microsoft OneDrive (www.onedrive.com), Apple iCloud Drive (www.apple.com/icloud), Dropbox (www.dropbox.com), Box (www.box.com), and Adobe Creative Cloud (www.adobe.com/creativecloud.html).

Before committing to a cloud-based service, make sure it's compatible with your video-editing software, then determine how much free online storage space is provided. Chances are, you'll quickly exceed the allocated free storage space, then need to pay a monthly fee for added storage space, so determine how much this will cost you as well on an ongoing basis.

You can also store your content locally on your computer's hard drive or on an external hard drive. However, if something happens to that computer, having your content stored in the cloud means you can access it from anywhere, using any computer.

START EDITING

Virtually every video you produce will require at least some level of editing and post-production, even if you're going for a grass-roots, low-budget look. Plan on spending considerable time editing and re-editing your videos until every second, scene, and shot work together to achieve your goals, adhere to your company's image, and cater to your audience.

Editing a video is a technical as well as creative process. But before you start, back up all raw footage and pre-produced elements on an external hard drive or cloud-based file sharing/storage service. Then, as you finish editing each scene, save and back up your work. Because you'll be working with extremely large files, it's not uncommon for the computer or software to periodically crash. If that happens, you don't want to lose more than a few minutes' work.

Begin by launching your editing software and importing your raw video and other multimedia assets. Write down detailed notes about what you've recorded and where each component is stored. Catalog how many times a scene was shot, or if you used multiple cameras during the shoot so when you're editing each scene, you're able to review all the footage and choose the best takes.

Use the worksheet in Figure 9–1 (on page 138) to help you more efficiently catalog your project's footage, pre-produced content, and audio components. Refer to your storyboard and shooting script as you assemble each scene and string them together. Begin to edit the raw video using the software's tools and features. You can trim sections of the video, separate footage into scenes and reorder them, and begin to shape the production. After the raw video has been edited, import and insert other multimedia elements, such as PowerPoint slides, digital photos, or graphics. Then, add video effects and filters, and insert animated transitions, as needed.

Once the main components are assembled, create an opening title sequence and any closing credits, and insert any captions or other text-based elements throughout the video. Make sure your message and call to action are clearly and cleverly incorporated, and the nearly finished product speaks to your target audience.

Video Title: _____

Scene Name: _____

Scene Number: _____

Content Details	Description/ File Name	Time Code	Storage Location	Production/ Creation Date	Edited Date	Edited Length	Notes
Raw Video (Angle/Shot #1)							
Raw Video (Angle #2)							
Raw Video (Angle #3)							
Music Track							
Music Track							
Sound Effect(s)							
Sound Effect(s)							
Digital Photo(s)							
Pre-Produced Content							
Pre-Produced Content							
Pre-Produced Content							
Other							
Other							

FIGURE 9–1. Worksheet for cataloging your raw video and pre-produced multimedia components

13 EDITING STRATEGIES FOR A MORE PROFESSIONAL PRODUCTION

1. Make sure each scene in your video flows nicely into the next, from a visual, audio, and context aspect.

2. Ensure that the overall audio levels are consistent throughout the video.

3. Avoid static images or "talking head" shots. If you use them, keep them short, and switch camera angles or shooting perspectives often.

4. If you forgot to use the Rule of Thirds when shooting your footage, use the software's cropping and editing tools to reposition your main subject off center in the frame.

5. As you're editing each scene, incorporate different shots and camera angles, but make sure you use appropriate transitions that allow the video to flow. Most editing programs have dozens or even hundreds of scene transitions that you can drag and drop into a scene to blend two video clips. A jump cut—when one scene abruptly cuts into another—is the one used most often. But alternate with animated transitions so your video isn't too choppy. Two of the most common editing mistakes are overusing elaborate transitions and using the same transition repeatedly in a relatively short video. The goal of a transition is to help one scene flow smoothly into the next—not to distract the viewer.

6. Make text-based titles, credits, and captions short and succinct so your viewers can easily read them, even on their smartphone's smaller sized screen. Likewise, keep horizontally and vertically scrolling text moving slowly and steadily.

7. Don't overuse visual effects and filters (also known as "eye candy"). While they can make your videos more visually appealing, too many can distract your audience from your core message and call to action.

8. Choose your background music wisely. It can set a mood, keep momentum going, or just be entertaining, but mostly can help convey your message— or detract from it. Think about what genre, volume, tempo, lyrics, and, of

course, specific piece of music is most appropriate, and, once you're sure there are no copyright issues, choose when and how to best incorporate it.

9. Keep production elements simple and straightforward. Your message and call to action are your video's key components, not the visual or audible bells and whistles you can throw in as eye or ear candy.

10. Remove ancillary content. You're much better off with a short, coherent video that succinctly achieves your goals than a long-form masterpiece full of the snazzy production elements that your editing software makes so easy to add.

11. Consider animated slide shows of photos or PowerPoint presentations, in addition to live-action footage. You can control how long a slide is displayed, and add animated transitions between slides as well as an audio track. One common technique included in almost all editing software packages is the "Ken Burns effect," which makes digital photos appear almost as moving video.

12. Don't be afraid to promote your company's website, Facebook page, Twitter account, blog, and other social media activities. Their URLs can be cited by the video's host, announced in a voice-over, and displayed in the credits and captions. You can also include these links on your YouTube channel page, and within a video's description. Within the videos themselves, this information can be included within Cards and End Screens. You'll learn more about Cards and End Screens in Chapter 11, "Uploading Your Videos to YouTube."

13. Once the visual elements have been edited, and you've created a rough cut of the video, start mixing in the audio components, like background music, sound effects, and voice-overs. Each audio component should be placed on a separate audio track so you can independently control and adjust each one.

Chapter 10

Keeping Your Content Fresh

IN THIS CHAPTER

- Brainstorming video ideas
- Developing a realistic production schedule moving forward
- Strategies for keeping your channel's content fresh
- Ideas to expand your audience through collaboration videos

There are two main strategies businesses can use to populate a YouTube channel with content that will appeal to its target audience. First, you can determine what content you want to feature on your channel, produce all that content at once, then publish multiple videos simultaneously, to provide your audience with a comprehensive collection of videos from day one.

This approach is ideal if you plan to use your YouTube channel to improve your customer service and technical support, for example, by offering a collection of videos that teach existing customers how to use your products. Your YouTube channel might include a handful of short videos explaining how to assemble and use your product. The channel would then only need to be updated with new content if you update the product or introduce new products.

The second approach, which is more popular, is to initially publish just one or two videos on your YouTube channel, but then commit to an ongoing production schedule, where you publish a new video several times per week, once per week, or once or twice per month, but on a consistent schedule. Based on whatever production schedule you commit to, you then need to adhere to it, to keep your viewers and subscribers happy. In other words, don't commit to a production schedule that's too ambitious. After all, you may discover that producing YouTube videos is time consuming and costly, so your initial schedule may turn out to be unrealistic based on your available resources.

Regardless of how many videos you publish on your YouTube channel, and whatever production schedule you adopt, it's important to keep your channel's content fresh, unique, and perceived as valuable by your targeted viewers and subscribers. In other words, after watching one of your videos, a viewer should feel like they got something positive out of the experience. They should never feel like they wasted their time, even if the video is only three to six minutes long. Conveying useful information or answering a question may be considered valuable. However, your audience may also consider being thoroughly entertained to be a valuable experience based on what their motivation was for watching your video in the first place.

USERS CAN EASILY MANAGE THEIR YOUTUBE ACCOUNTS

YouTube makes it very easy for users to subscribe to channels that are of interest to them, then be notified immediately when their favorite channels publish new content. It's also simple for a user to quickly access a listing of channels they've subscribed to, and determine which of that channel's recent videos they have yet to watch vs. the videos they've previously watched.

By continuously publishing new content, your subscribers will be encouraged to visit your channel more frequently, not just to watch your most recent video but perhaps to rewatch older videos.

If your subscribers notice that it's been weeks or months since you've updated your channel, they may be inclined to unsubscribe, which will make it much harder for you to reach them in the future when you publish new content.

Based on the goals of your YouTube channel, develop a plan to keep its content fresh and to periodically update the visual appearance of your channel by switching out the profile photo and channel art that's displayed, for example.

Without perceived value, people will quickly become bored with what you're offering, and seek out more interesting, relevant, timely, and unique content elsewhere—potentially from your competition.

BRAINSTORMING VIDEO IDEAS

When you brainstorm video ideas as you're establishing a YouTube channel, then moving forward as you populate your channel, maintain a comprehensive written list of your ideas—the good ones, the bad ones, and the far-fetched ones. Never discard a video idea, as you never know when that idea may help you brainstorm something better in the future. However, after defining your target audience, determine what the focus of your videos will be, and if you'll be using channel categories and/or playlists to organize your videos once they're published on your channel.

For example, you may find it beneficial to organize your channel's videos into four main categories, such as About Our Company, Product Showcase, Assembly and Setup, and Using the Product. Of course, you'll want to come up with catchier and more descriptive category titles based on your actual product(s). Using these four channel categories, Figure 10–1 (on page 144) shows examples of the types of videos you might produce within each.

To help you manage and organize your individual video ideas, use the worksheet in Figure 10–2, on page 145. You may find it easier to write details about specific video ideas on individual index cards so you can display them on a table, move them around, prioritize them, and group them together as needed. This can also be done using any project management application, such as Favro (www.favro.com) or Trello (www.trello.com).

Once you brainstorm your video ideas, analyze each of them to determine their practicality. For example, ask yourself:

- Will the video idea appeal to its target audience?
- What is the video's core message?
- What is the video's call to action?
- Is the video timely or does it have an expiration date related to how long it will be of interest to your audience? For example, if your video is timely and focuses around a holiday or event, you need to publish it on a specific date, but then remove it from your channel once the holiday or event is over. Does it make sense to use resources to produce and promote a video with a limited window during which it can be showcased online, or should the same production resources be used to create an "evergreen" video that can remain on the channel indefinitely? Making this decision will require a cost/benefit analysis.

Organize Your YouTube Channel's Video into Categories			
About Our Company	**Product Showcase**	**Assembly and Setup**	**Using the Product**
Interview with the company's founder	Product overview—features and functions	How to assemble the product—step by step	Five ways to use the product
Interview with the product's inventor	Product demonstration	Demonstration of how to use the product's key features	Lifestyle video of the product being used for specific purposes in the real world
"Behind the scenes" tour of the office and/or factory	Product comparison—your product vs. the competition (side-by-side comparison)	How to maintain the product to extend its life	How to customize the product to better meet a customer's needs
Company philosophy overview: Why we do what we do, and who we do it for	Customer testimonials	How to use the product in conjunction with other products to improve its functionality	How to use the product to achieve additional benefits that the customer might not have thought of (i.e., alternate uses for the product)
How our company is different from the competition; what sets it apart	Answers to common questions about the product; who uses it, and how users can save time, money, etc., as well as how the product solves a problem viewers may have	How to repair, return, or exchange the product if there's a problem	Unboxing video, explaining what a customer can expect once their order arrives

FIGURE 10–1. To make your channel more accessible to your audience and the information easier to find, consider dividing your content into categories.

YouTube Channel Video Idea	
Video Topic	[Write a short summary of the video and perhaps a potential title for the video here.]
Channel Category or Addition to Playlist	[List where and how this video will be used within your YouTube channel. What category will it fit into? Which playlist will it be added to?]
Proposed Production Date	____/____/____ [List when you could potentially produce this video.]
Proposed Release Date	____/____/____ [List when you'd publish this video on your channel. Based on other videos in your idea and production pipeline, where does it fit in?]
Description	[In several sentences, describe the goal for the video and the approach it will take, then summarize its content. The next step, if you plan to produce the video, would be to write a script and/or create a storyboard.]
Call to Action	[Write out the video's call to action, and explain how it could be incorporated into the video.]
Primary Message	[Write out the primary message you want to convey to your viewers within this video so it achieves its goal(s).]

FIGURE 10–2. Write down each individual video idea on an index card or use a product management application, so you can view, arrange, and display your ideas as you consider which are the most applicable and practical for your channel.

- How long will the video take to write, produce, and edit? Does this time frame fit into your overall schedule for channel content creation?
- When would the video be published on your YouTube channel?
- Based on your vision for the video, do you have the resources to create it and stay within your budget?
- Can this video be shot at the same time as other videos to save time and resources?

- Within which channel category will the video best fit?
- Will the video benefit from being made part of a playlist on the channel?
- What's the most important thing a viewer will get out of watching the video? What's the takeaway? Will the viewer perceive this to be of value to them?
- What approach will the video take? Is there an alternate approach that might work better, or be less time consuming or costly to produce, without jeopardizing the quality of the content?

Be sure you can answer these questions before diving more deeply into the process.

DEVELOPING A REALISTIC PRODUCTION SCHEDULE

Especially when you're starting out, producing quality YouTube content may take a lot of time and resources. Until you determine the overall approach you'll be taking with your videos, and actually experience how long the pre-production, production, post-production, publishing, and promotions process takes, don't commit to an overly ambitious production schedule.

If you plan to publish new content on an ongoing basis, initially commit to one new video every week, or every two weeks. You can always publish "bonus" videos or increase the number of new videos you publish once you know you can handle the production schedule (and have the budget to produce quality content on an ongoing basis).

Based on how frequently you plan to publish new content, plan out your videos and production schedule at least one month in advance so you're not scrambling on Tuesday to brainstorm and produce a new video that you promised would be live on Wednesday. Take an organized approach to pre-planning your video ideas, then determine the most time-efficient and cost-effective way to produce them. This might mean setting up your filming equipment, lights, and backdrop once per month, shooting several videos back-to-back, then editing them all at once so you always have at least a handful of completed videos ready to publish.

As you'll discover from Chapter 11, "Uploading Your Videos to YouTube," during the upload process, you can pre-schedule the date and time when you automatically want a video to go live on your channel. Thus, you can upload four or eight videos at once, then set up the channel to publish them one at a time, every Wednesday at noon (EST), for example.

Initially, plan on spending extra time on each phase of the video's production. As you become more proficient using your equipment, editing your videos, and developing high-quality content that fits nicely on your channel, less time will be required to complete each necessary task related to pre-production, production, post-production, publishing, and promotion. However, never cut corners just to get stuff done or to meet a self-imposed deadline. The quality of your content, its overall message, and ensuring that it caters to your target audience is the most important. Even if you publish just one video that offers lower production values than the others, this could have a negative impact on your audience's perception of your channel, your company's reputation, and the perceived value of your content. Remember, it's important to meet or exceed the expectations of your viewers and subscribers and provide content that they perceive as valuable. As soon as you stop doing this, you'll quickly lose your audience.

STRATEGIES FOR KEEPING YOUR CHANNEL'S CONTENT NEW AND FRESH

While keeping your overall messaging and image consistent throughout all your videos, it's important to keep your channel and its content fresh if you want your subscribers to keep visiting your channel and watching your new videos (as well as rewatching your older) videos.

At least every few months, give your YouTube channel a fresh look by updating the profile photo and channel artwork. This can be done to reflect the seasons, specific holidays, or new product launches, for example. It's also possible to alter the overall appearance of your channel by changing the thumbnail image that's displayed in conjunction with each of your video listings.

Then, based on the production schedule you commit to, it's important to publish new and original content on your channel on an ongoing basis. This might mean recreating a video you've seen elsewhere on YouTube, but giving it an original twist so it caters to your audience and helps your company achieve its objectives, or it could mean coming up with new, unique, and exclusive content on a regular basis. Keep in mind, you can also take a different approach entirely with one of your more successful and popular videos and showcase the same information, but in an entirely new way.

By updating the appearance of your channel and publishing new content to it, you'll encourage your subscribers to return often. Plus, since each video you publish is listed separately and becomes searchable (almost immediately) on YouTube and Google, the more individual videos you publish, the better your chances will be of having people in your target audience find your video(s) and your channel when they perform a relevant search. Each video should have its own unique title, description, and keywords. However, while you want to use a list of keywords that's directly relevant to each video, you also want to reuse certain keywords that describe your company, product(s), service(s), and YouTube channel, and try to incorporate some of these words into each video's title and description.

CONSIDER USING COLLABORATION VIDEOS TO GROW YOUR AUDIENCE

As you'll discover several weeks or months into producing content for your YouTube channel, eventually you're going to run out of fresh ideas, or you'll discover that the content you're creating is not allowing you to grow your channel's number of subscribers. There are several solutions to this dilemma.

First, focus more efforts on promoting your YouTube channel and its content. The focus of the last section of this book (Chapters 12 through 17) is on building your audience and subscription base using various types of online and real-world promotions, and potentially paid advertising. You will, no doubt, discover that using social media to promote your videos and YouTube channel can be a very powerful tool.

One way to come up with fresh content is to expand the cast of characters you feature in your videos. Instead of using the same company spokesperson in all your videos, introduce new people from your company to your audience. For example, when launching a new product, feature the product designer, inventor, or product manager, as opposed to the company founder or just your spokesperson in relevant videos. If you're worried about continuity between your videos, consider having your spokesperson interview other people from your company within relevant videos or introducing the additional people as occasional co-hosts.

Another approach to keeping content fresh, and at the same time, potentially build your audience, is to produce collaboration videos (also known as "collabs") with other YouTube channel operators. For example, pinpoint other companies or YouTubers that are targeting the same audience as you, but do not have competing products or services. Produce videos together that can be cross-promoted on both your channels. After collaborating on the production of one or more videos, you and your collaborators can benefit from each other's resources and established audiences when it comes to promoting those videos, which is a faster and more cost-effective way to build your subscription base and audience than many other methods available to you.

You can also hire a well-established YouTuber (online personality) to star in some of your videos, or feature your products/services, or your own company spokesperson, within their videos. Depending on the popularity of the YouTuber, they may agree to work with you in exchange for free products or if you're willing to offer the subscribers of the YouTuber's channel a discount on your products/services. You also have the option to pay them a product placement fee, or hire them as a paid spokesperson for your company. Whichever option winds up working, you'll benefit because the YouTuber's established audience (which may be thousands or even millions of subscribers) will quickly be exposed to your company, its products/services, and your YouTube channel. This approach is covered within Chapter 17, "Using Paid Product Placement in Videos as a Promotional Tool."

CONSIDER EXPANDING YOUR TARGET AUDIENCE

At some point in the future, once you've populated your channel with many videos, all targeted to the same audience, it might make sense for your company to expand the target audience for its YouTube Channel and to start also producing content for this expanded audience. For example, you may already have a secondary audience in mind that your products/services appeal to.

Once you believe you have enough content on your channel to appeal to your target audience and that content provides them with the information and resources they need, while at the same time, your content is achieving your company's goals using those videos, consider slowly introducing videos that will appeal to a broader or secondary target audience.

Using YouTube's free Analytics tools (as well as third-party tools that are described in Chapter 14, "Promoting Your YouTube Videos"), you will be able to see trends related to your channel's traffic. If over time, you see the channel's growth slowing down, despite your continued efforts to promote it, this may be a good time to broaden your target audience and the focus of your content in future videos so the content appeals to this broader audience. Exactly when and how to do this will be unique to your company and its YouTube channel, but in the future, this may be necessary to maintain your channel's growth and popularity. For example, if your company releases a new product or service that caters to a slightly different audience than your original products/ services, this would be the perfect time to simultaneously broaden the target audience for your YouTube channel and its content.

MEET DUSTIN MATHEWS, CHANNEL HOST OF SPEAKING EMPIRE

YouTube Channel URL: www.youtube.com/user/speakingempire

Dustin Mathews trains speakers to better deliver their message. While he operates a YouTube channel, he uses it to follow up with perspective clients, as opposed to using it as a method for attracting new clients.

"When we receive a new lead, for example, someone visits our website and requests more information. What we do is provide links to videos that were designed to build a relationship, provide value and education, and ultimately get that prospect to act. I have uploaded a collection of videos onto YouTube and shared emails with perspective clients that make reference to the videos. These videos take them on a journey through my auto-responder sequence. Of course, the YouTube channel has also amassed subscribers who watch new videos as they're published, but I look at that as a side benefit," says Mathews.

The content Mathews has published on YouTube is a combination of videos he's produced specifically for YouTube, as well as compilations of clips from presentations he's personally given. He's also created videos during which he's interviewed his clients discussing their own success stories. These tend to be shot during one of his national conferences. His channel is also populated with videos that offer case studies and testimonials. "Once in a while, I will also get in front of a camera and deliver a video that answers questions from my audience that were posted on social media, for example," says Mathews, who has most recently been experimenting with live broadcasts using the YouTube Live service.

In terms of appealing to his audience, Mathews admits he hasn't discovered a secret formula for YouTube videos that guarantees views. "Some people like high production value videos, while others better appreciate storytelling videos that feature less production. What works for me is that I use a variety of different styles and approaches when producing content for YouTube, all with the goal of providing valuable content to my audience. For my audience, the videos need to be 10 minutes or shorter for storytelling and Q&A videos, and less than five minutes for the more highly produced videos. When I do a Q&A video, for example, I use a white board to draw things and make it more visual. This is more visually entertaining than just a talking-head video that's shot from a single camera angle," says Mathews.

Another way Mathews has used YouTube is to create a series of 15- to 30-second videos that he pays to have shown as video ads prior to other YouTube videos that are also designed to appeal to his target audience. "This is a way for me to capture people in my target audience when they're about to watch someone else's video. This approach has worked very well and has been the most successful way we've spent our online advertising budget. We have very successfully used these short, ad-based videos to promote events, for example," says Mathews.

As for promoting his other YouTube content, each time Mathews publishes new content on his channel, he sends out a targeted email to his list. "This is a way for me to more frequently engage with the people on my email list. It allows me to build better relationships with clients and prospects," he says.

Like everyone else who has attempted to use YouTube, Mathews has made mistakes that he's learned from. "Early on, I did not put a lot of emphasis on good lighting or sound quality, and that was a huge mistake. If people can't hear you, that kills the deal for someone watching your videos. Having the right equipment is important. I spent countless hours early on trying to learn how to produce quality videos myself.

"Ultimately, I hired some professionals to come in and help me achieve the level of quality I was striving for to uphold my professional reputation and meet the expectations and demands of my viewers. If you're on a tight budget, you can produce your own videos, and really focus on quality content, as opposed to top-level production. However, your viewers need to be able to see and hear you. As long as your information is perceived as valuable, your audience will typically forgive a low-budget production. When you can afford it, upgrade, and hire a professional video production crew.

"The second important mistake I made was trying to cram too much information into a single video and allowing it to drag on for too long. 'Less is more' is the mantra I learned when it comes to video length and how much information to include within a video," says Mathews.

Mathews believes that every video you publish on YouTube should contain a call to action. "The call to action does not have to be an advertising message, but it should be something you want your audience to do after watching your video. Encourage them to take some type of an action. There are many ways to include a call to action in a video itself or using the post-production tools offered by YouTube.

"My biggest piece of advice to would-be content creators is to provide value within your content. If you take a strong sales approach within your videos, you'll wind up turning people off. If you provided good content within your video, I believe you have the right at the end to ask your viewers to visit your website, subscribe to your YouTube channel, sign up for your email list, or pursue some other action that you request. You just need to be very clear when telling people what you want them to do and when they should do it," says Mathew.

Especially if you're new to creating YouTube content, ask some co-workers or close friends to watch your videos before you publish them. Solicit their honest feedback. "What I have found is that people like organization and systems, so when you present information within your videos, do it in an organized and easy-to-follow way. Don't just turn on the camera and start to ramble. Come up with three to five points that you want to get across within a video, then stick to those points. In between each point, tell a short story, offer a case study, or include a statistic to help make the information relevant," adds Mathews.

Before creating new videos, do your research. Mathews states, "Explore all aspects of social media and see what people are interested in when it comes to your area of expertise or topic. If you understand what already interests people, you'll have an easier time creating content and providing information that they'll want to watch. My goal with YouTube is to drive traffic to my web page, so instead of encouraging people to subscribe to my YouTube channel, I typically encourage them to visit my website, and I provide links to the website within the videos and within each video's description, for example."

Because Mathews engages with so many people in person, he relies on their feedback, as opposed to using YouTube Analytics, to better understand his YouTube viewership. As for how often he publishes content, he does not follow a strict schedule. Instead, he publishes new content only when he's inspired to do so.

"If you want to play the YouTube game well, focus on all aspects of it. Take advantage of the post-production tools offered by YouTube, invest the time to come up with catchy video titles, create strong lists of relevant keywords, choose attention-getting thumbnails, pay attention to the feedback you receive from viewers, and use YouTube Analytics. Also," concludes Mathews, "drive as much traffic to each new video as possible, within the first 24 hours after it's published."

Chapter 11

Uploading Your Videos to YouTube

IN THIS CHAPTER

- Preparing your video for uploading and choosing the right file format
- Length limitations for YouTube videos vs. length recommendations
- How to upload your videos
- Using Video Manager tools to enhance your videos

You've already learned all about what it takes to shoot and edit a professional-quality video. Once the video is ready to be shared, you'll need to upload it to your YouTube channel, customize settings related to the video, perhaps add optional Cards or an End Screen to the video, and present it to the public via your channel.

YouTube offers a handful of methods for uploading one or more videos at a time to your channel. In addition, however, you can also record "live" video using your computer's webcam, then use YouTube's online editing tools to edit and publish that content. Another option is to use YouTube Live to present a live online broadcast that can also be recorded, potentially edited, and later offered as recorded video on YouTube. See Chapter 16, "Go Live with Your Broadcasts," for more information about broadcasting live from your YouTube channel.

HOW TO UPLOAD LONGER VIDEOS

To upload videos to YouTube that are longer than 15 minutes, you must go through additional steps to verify your account. More information about how to verify your account and upload longer length videos can be found at: https://support.google.com/youtube/answer/71673?hl=en. To go through the channel verification process, visit: www.youtube.com/my_videos_upload_verify. This needs to be done only once per channel, not each time you upload a video. Note that if you turn on the YouTube Live feature for your channel, this, too, unlocks the ability to upload longer length videos.

In this chapter, you'll learn how to upload videos from your computer using your favorite internet web browser. Keep in mind, by default, you can upload videos that are up to 15 minutes or use a file size up to 128GB (when using the latest versions of most web browsers). If you're using an older web browser, the maximum file size you can upload is 20GB.

PREPARING YOUR VIDEO FILES

YouTube is compatible with a wide range of popular video file formats such as .MOV, .MPEG4, .MP4, .AVI, .WMV, .MPEGPS, .FLV, 3GPP, and WebM. If your video-editing software does not allow you to export your edited video into one of these popular file formats, take advantage of YouTube's online-based file format converter (https://support.google.com/youtube/troubleshooter/2888402).

Typically, after editing your video, you'd use your editing software's built-in "Share" feature or its "Save As" or "Export" command to convert the file into one of YouTube's compatible file formats. If you attempt to upload a video file to YouTube, but receive an error message that says "Failed (Invalid File Format)," this means you'll need to convert the video file into a compatible file format before uploading it.

Always upload your videos at the highest resolution possible and in the video's original quality. If given the option, save the video file using a 16 to 9 aspect ratio, with the highest bitrate possible. Also, do not change the frame rate of the video. If the video was captured at 24 or 30 frames per second, which is standard, keep it at that frame rate when exporting the files from your video-editing software, then uploading them to YouTube.

Many video-editing software packages, including iMovie for the Mac, have a built-in "Share" option. This feature allows you to upload your edited videos, and adjust its YouTube-related settings, directly from your computer while using the video-editing software. If your video-editing software doesn't have a Share or Publish to YouTube feature, save the video file(s) on your computer's internal or external hard drive, then follow the steps outlined in the next section of this chapter to upload your video to your YouTube channel.

Video files captured on your smartphone or tablet can also be uploaded to YouTube via an app that comes bundled with your mobile device or a specialized third-party app. For the iPhone and iPad, the iMovie app, available from the App Store, offers powerful tools for editing, viewing, and sharing video footage, including an option to upload files to your YouTube channel.

As your video is being uploaded and processed, the YouTube service determines if its content violates any copyrights. If it does, the video will be blocked from being posted. Meanwhile, if you suspect that someone has violated your copyright in their videos, file a complaint online with YouTube by visiting: http://support.google.com/youtube/bin/answer.py?hl=en&answer=140536.

How to Upload Videos from Your Computer

When you're ready to upload a video to your YouTube channel from your computer, follow these steps:

1. Log into YouTube (www.youtube.com) with the Google account information that was used to create your YouTube channel.

2. From the main YouTube home page, click on the Upload icon that's displayed near the upper-right corner of the browser window. It's located to the immediate left of your profile photo and/or username.

3. When the "Select Files to Upload" window appears (shown in Figure 11–1 on page 156), click on the Privacy Setting pull-down menu that's displayed, and choose whether you want the video to be Public (the default option), Unlisted, Private, or Scheduled. It's also possible to adjust this setting during the upload process, or any time later.

4. Either select the video file you want to upload from your computer, then drag and drop the file into the Select Files to Upload window, or click on the upload icon that's displayed in the center of the window, then select the file from the location where it's stored locally on your computer.

5. The uploading process will begin automatically. Depending on how large the HD video file is and the speed of your internet connection, the upload process

FIGURE 11-1. The Select File to Upload window.

WHAT THE PRIVACY SETTINGS MEAN

When adjusting a video's Privacy settings, choose "Public" if you want the video to be published online and made public immediately after it's been uploaded and processed. Choose the "Unlisted" option if you want to make the video available online, but only to people who are given its unique URL address. Select the "Private" option to lock the video so it's only accessible to you (and nobody else). Choose the "Scheduled" option if you want to select the exact date and time you want the video to be unlocked and made public.

could take anywhere from a few minutes to several hours. Along the top of the uploading window, a progress timer and approximate time remaining for the upload process is displayed. During this time, you'll need to enter the video's title, description, and tags, plus adjust various settings (shown in Figure 11-2 on page 157). To access these fields, click on the default "Basic Info" option.

6. Within the "Title" field, type the title for the video. This title will be displayed in conjunction with the video's listing and become searchable when someone uses the YouTube or Google search field.

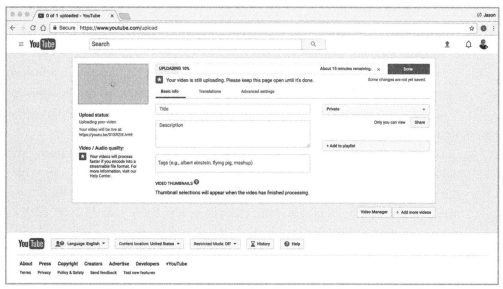

FIGURE 11–2. While the video file is uploading, enter details about the video, including its title, description, and tags.

7. Within the "Description" field, type a text-based description of your video. This should include a summary of what's included within the video, who it will appeal to, and what the viewer will get out of watching the video.

8. Within the "Tags" field, create a list of keywords that accurately describe your video. Separate each tag with a comma.

9. To the right of the "Title" field, click on the "Privacy" pull-down menu if you want to change the privacy setting for the video, which will go into effect as soon as the video is uploaded and processed by YouTube.

10. If you want to add the video that's uploading to an established playlist or create a new playlist that includes the video that's uploading, click on the "+Add to Playlist" option.

EVERY VIDEO RECEIVES ITS OWN WEBSITE ADDRESS

In addition to your YouTube channel having its own, unique website address (URL), each video you upload also automatically receives its own URL. During the uploading process, what will become the video's unique URL is displayed immediately below the video thumbnail box when you select the Basic Info tab.

11. When the video is finished uploading and has been processed, return to the Basic Info window, if necessary, and select the video thumbnail that will be displayed in conjunction with the video's listing.

12. Once the requested information has been provided in the Basic Info window, either click on the "Done" button to save your information, or click on the "Translations" tab or "Advanced Settings" tab to continue customizing the settings associated with the video being uploaded.

13. Click on the "Translations" tab to display the Translations window during the upload process (shown in Figure 11–3). From here, select the "Original Language" the video is produced in, and if you want, select the "Translate Info" pull-down menu to choose a language you want the video's text-based information (such as the description) to be translated into.

14. Click on the "Advanced Settings" tab to access the "Advanced Settings" menu (shown in Figure 11–4 on page 160). From here, you can adjust specific settings related to the video. How to use each of these options is discussed later in this chapter.

15. After the video is uploaded and has been processed, return to the Basic Info screen and select the "Video Thumbnail" you want to display in conjunction with the video's listing. The thumbnail you choose should be attention-getting and represent visually what the video is all about. Keep in mind, once your YouTube channel has been verified, you're able to create a custom video

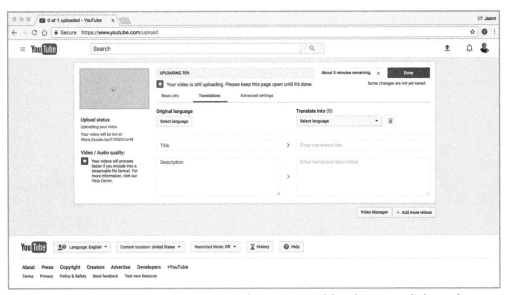

FIGURE 11–3. The "Translations" window is accessible when you click on the "Translations" tab as your video is being uploaded.

HOW TO CUSTOMIZE EACH VIDEO'S METADATA

The title, description, tags, and thumbnail image that you provide for each video become part of that video's metadata. This is information that becomes public and searchable once your video's privacy setting is set to Public and the video becomes accessible to anyone.

Within the "Title" field, enter the title of your video. As you create the title, remember your goal is to entice potential viewers to watch it, so choose something that's catchy, descriptive, accurate, succinct, and targeted to your audience. The video's title will be displayed on YouTube, along with your description and other information, and is separate from whatever titles you incorporated in the video itself when shooting or editing it.

Within the "Description" field, enter a few sentences that describe your video and why someone should watch it. This is your video's marketing tool, so use as many tags in the text as possible to increase the probability that someone will find your video when performing a keyword search.

The "Tags" field is used to compile a list of keywords or phrases that best describe your video. Separate each tag with a comma, and include as many relevant keywords or phrases as you can think of to improve its discoverability during a potential viewer's keyword search.

There are a variety of online tools available to help you compile an appropriate and highly targeted list of applicable keywords or tags. The following are links to some of these free and fee-based tools:

- *Google AdWords:* https://adwords.google.com/KeywordPlanner

- *MOZ:* https://moz.com/mozpro/lander/keyword-research

- *Semrush:* https://landing.semrush.com/keyword-research-tool-3/usa.html

- *SEOBook:* http://tools.seobook.com/keyword-list/generator.php

- *WordStream:* www.wordstream.com/ad-text-generator

After your video has processed, YouTube will automatically select and pull three thumbnail images from your video. Click on the video thumbnail you want to accompany your video's title and description within its listing. Choose the thumbnail you believe will capture the most attention and visually communicates the most about the content of your video. Once your YouTube channel has been verified, you'll have the ability to create a custom thumbnail for your video.

FIGURE 11–4. From the "Advanced Settings" menu, you can adjust a wide range of options related to your video and how it will be accessible from your YouTube channel.

thumbnail for each of your videos, as opposed to selecting a still image from the video itself.

16. Click on the "Done" option to save your work, and if you selected the "Public" privacy-related option, to allow your video to be published and go live on your YouTube channel.

17. At any time in the future, you can edit any of the video's customizable settings by accessing your YouTube channel's Video Manager, then selecting the video's listing. When viewing the listings for your videos (shown in Figure 11–5 on page 161), click on the "Edit" button associated with the video you want to work with.

18. Using the Video Manager, you can adjust the video's "Info & Settings," take advantage of YouTube's online-based video editing tools to further enhance

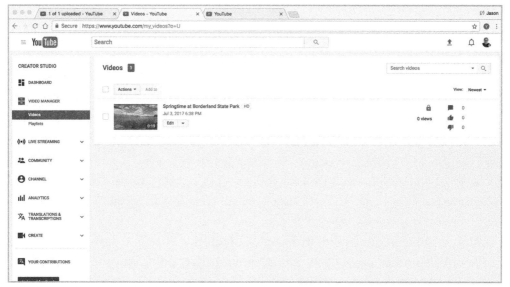

FIGURE 11–5. From the Video Manager's video listing, select the video you want to work with, and click on the "Edit" button associated with it.

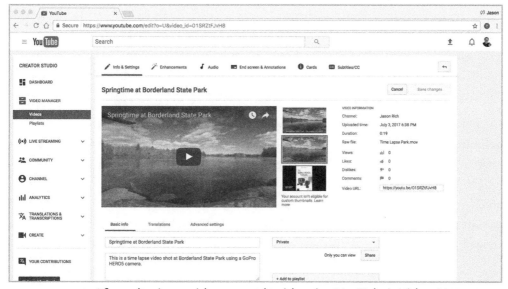

FIGURE 11–6. After selecting a video to work with using YouTube's Video Manager, you have access to a wide range of additional tools, including the ability to further edit the video, add an End Card, or incorporate up to five interactive Cards.

your video before making it public, or incorporate Cards and/or an End Screen (shown in Figure 11-6).

Overcoming Uploading Problems

Here's what to do if you experience a recurring problem using the YouTube uploader:

- Make sure you're using the latest version of your web browser.
- Try using another web browser, such as:
  - *Microsoft Edge (PC):* www.microsoft.com/en-us/windows/microsoft-edge
  - *Safari (Mac):* www.apple.com/safari
  - *Google Chrome (PC/Mac):* www.google.com/chrome/index.html
  - *Firefox (PC/Mac):* www.mozilla.org/en-US/firefox/new
- Point your web browser to: www.youtube.com/upload_classic. This will give you access to YouTube's Basic Uploader, which is more widely compatible with various web browsers.
- One common cause of recurring upload problems is the anti-spyware, anti-virus, or VPN (virtual private network) software that's running on your computer. Try temporarily deactivating that software, but don't forget to reactivate it after the video uploads to YouTube.
- Another common cause of video upload problems is a poor wifi signal. If this is the case, try moving your computer closer to the wireless router so the signal improves. or try connecting your computer directly to the router using an Ethernet cable. If you're using a 4G LTE cellular data network to access the internet, move to where the signal is stronger, and retry the upload. A slower 3G or 4G cellular data connection will also work to upload your videos, but the upload process will take a lot longer.

Once a video file is uploaded, it will take time to process. Videos shot in high definition (1080p or 4K) resolution will take longer to process than videos shot at a lower resolution. When uploading a large HD video file to YouTube, if processing takes longer than eight hours or so, a problem could have arisen. Access the Video Manager, and select the "Videos" option for your channel. See if the video is listed. You may need to start the upload process again if you don't see the video listed or if you notice that the upload progress meter appears to have frozen for more than a few minutes.

PROVIDING ADDITIONAL DETAILS ABOUT YOUR VIDEO

In addition to the Basic Information you're prompted to provide during the upload process, when the uploading and processing of the video is completed, be sure to access the Video Manager, select the newly uploaded video listing, click on its "Edit" button, then click on the "End Screen & Annotations" tab, the "Cards" tab, or the "Subtitles/CC" (closed captioning) tab to add additional information or interactive elements to your video before allowing it to go live on your channel. If you want to fine-tune the video's editing using YouTube's online-based editing tools, click on the "Enhancements" tab.

There are also a wide range of important customizable options available from the "Advanced Settings" menu. The more detailed the information you add and the more customization you do when accessing the Basic and Advanced Settings menus, the more likely people will find and view your video.

ADJUSTING THE ADVANCED SETTINGS FOR YOUR VIDEO

From the "Advanced Settings" menu offered by the YouTube Video Manager, be sure to click on the "Category" pull-down menu and choose which YouTube category your video fits the best into. As you can see in Figure 11–7, options include:

- Film & Animation
- Autos & Vehicles
- Music
- Pets & Animals
- Sports
- Travel & Events
- Gaming
- People & Blogs

FIGURE 11–7. Choose the most suitable YouTube category for each video.

- Comedy
- Entertainment
- News & Politics
- How To & Style
- Education
- Science & Technology
- Nonprofits & Activism

Keep in mind, you might not always be able to choose a category that matches perfectly, so choose the most relevant option. Your selection will now be displayed in the "Categories" field. If your YouTube channel has multiple videos, each video can be placed into a separate category.

Click on the "License and Rights Ownership" pull-down menu if you want to change the default setting, which is "Standard YouTube License." The alternative is to choose the "Creative Commons—Attribution" option. Here's what each means:

- *Standard YouTube License*: Within YouTube's "Terms of Use" document, which can be found online (www.youtube.com/t/terms), you'll find information pertaining to publishing videos on the service. It explains what content can (and cannot) be used in a video.
- *Creative Commons—Attribution*: If you activate this feature, you give other people the right to take clips from your video and incorporate them in their own videos without violating any copyrights. You can only choose this option if you own the rights to 100 percent of your video's content, including the rights to the visuals, sound effects, content, and music.

After you update the information related to the "Advanced Settings" menu options, be sure to click on the "Save Changes" button that appears in the top-right and bottom-right corner of the browser window. Located near the "Save Changes" button in the lower-right corner of the screen, if you see a message that says, "Some changes are not saved," do not exit from this browser window until after you've clicked on the "Save Changes" button.

One of the other options available from the "Advanced Settings" menu is labeled "Comments" (shown in Figure 11–8 on page 165). This option has multiple checkboxes and a pull-down menu associated with it. These options include:

- *Allow Comments*. Check this box to allow viewers to post comments about the video and, from the pull-down menu that's displayed below this option, choose "All" or "Approved." By selecting "All," all comments that are submitted will be displayed with the video. If you select the "Approved" option, you can read and

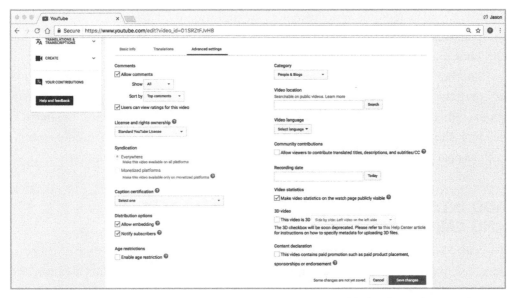

FIGURE 11–8. The "Advanced Settings" menu is accessible by first selecting the Video Manager option, then clicking on the "Edit" button associated with a specific video's listing.

approve each comment before it's published and made public. If you have a new YouTube channel, choose the "Approved" option, and be sure to moderate the comments that your viewers post.

■ *Allow Users to View a Video's Ratings.* While anyone who views a video can rate it, you can choose whether others will be able to see those like or dislike ratings.

From below the "Distribution Options" heading, you can choose to *Allow Embedding.* By adding a checkmark to this option, you allow others to embed your video within their website, blog, Facebook page, etc., so your video can be viewed without accessing your YouTube channel page. You'll also be able to embed your own video into your own website or blog. If you remove the checkmark from this option, users will need to access the video directly from YouTube to view it.

Within the *Video Location* field, manually enter where your video was shot. You can be as specific here as you'd like. For example, you can enter an exact address, or simply cite a country, city, or state. A Google Map of the location will be created and displayed with the video listing, and people will be able to find your video using a geographic search.

Within the *Recording Date* field, you're able to manually enter the date your video was recorded. This is useful if the date is relevant to the content or if you want people to be able to search for your video based on a specific date.

If your video contains content that's not appropriate for all ages, to avoid having complaints issued against the video and your channel, be sure to add a checkmark to the checkbox that's associated with the "Enable Age Restrictions" option.

Another important piece of information you need to share with your viewers is whether the video contains paid promotion or paid product placement, has been sponsored, or includes a product endorsement. Under the "Content Declaration" heading, check the box that's associated with the "This video contains paid promotion, such as paid product placement, sponsorships, or endorsements" option.

ADD INTERACTIVE ELEMENTS USING END SCREENS AND CARDS

The Video Manager offers several of what it refers to as "view engagement tools" that can be added to a video after it's been uploaded to YouTube, but before the video is made public. End Screens, Cards, subtitles, and closed captioning are among these tools. An End Screen is used within your video (that's more than 25 seconds long) to help direct your viewers to a related video or another YouTube channel, for example. It can also be used to promote your social media links and/or company website.

To add an End Screen to your video, access the Video Manager, open the video you want to work with, and then click on the "End Screen & Annotations" tab. You're then able to pinpoint the exact location (time code) within the video where you want an End Screen element to appear. Up to five End Screen elements can be added to a video. Use the time slider to pinpoint a location, then click on the "Use Template" button to select a template that makes formatting the element much easier.

Other interactive elements that can be added to an End Screen are similar to what's possible using Cards. Since this feature continues to expand and evolve, be sure to visit YouTube's Help section to learn what's currently possible. For more information about

MAKE SUBSCRIBING TO YOUR CHANNEL AN END SCREEN ELEMENT

Several of the End Screen templates allow you to showcase your profile photo, along with a message that encourages viewers to subscribe to your channel as they're watching your video. At the same time, a separate End Screen element can direct viewers to another video or playlist, for example.

YOUTUBE ANNOTATIONS ARE A THING OF THE PAST

Up until May 2, 2017, Annotations could be used to add interactive elements to a video. However, for a variety of reasons, including that they didn't work when YouTube was accessed using a mobile device (which represents more than 50 percent of the people watching YouTube videos), this feature has been discontinued and replaced by Cards.

If a video published prior to May 2, 2017, contains annotations, they will continue to function, but they can no longer be edited. For newly uploaded videos, annotations are no longer offered.

using an End Screen within your videos, visit https://support.google.com/youtube/answer/6388789.

A Card can be used within a video to direct viewers to a website, once your YouTube channel has been verified. YouTube offers several different types of Cards, including:

- *Channel.* Directs viewers to another YouTube channel that you're willing to promote; for example, if you've produced a collaboration video, and you want to promote your collaborator's YouTube channel
- *Donation.* Solicits a donation for a recognized nonprofit organization
- *Link.* Directs your viewers to a specific website link, such as your company's website, blog, or social media accounts
- *Poll.* Creates an interactive poll for your viewers within a video
- *Video or Playlist.* Directs viewers to a specific video or a playlist that's offered by your channel

To access the Card selection and customization tool, launch the Video Manager, select the video you want to add Cards to, click on the Cards tab that's displayed near the top of the browser window, then click on the "Add Card" button that's displayed to the right of the video player window. To learn more about Cards, visit: https://support.google.com/youtube/answer/6140493.

YOUTUBE'S VIDEO ENHANCEMENT FEATURES

After you've uploaded an already edited video to YouTube, from the Video Manager it's possible to tweak the video and make it look even better using the optional Enhancement

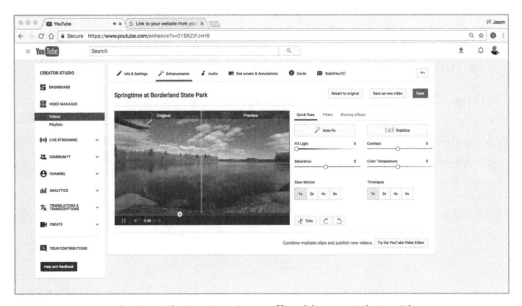

FIGURE 11–9. The "Quick Fixes" options offered by YouTube's Video Manager.

tools. To access this functionality, access the Video Manager, open the video you want to work with, then click on the Enhancements tab that's displayed near the top of the browser window.

YouTube's Enhancement tools are divided into three categories, which are accessible by clicking on the "Quick Fixes," "Filters," or "Blurring Effects" tabs that are displayed to the right of the video player windows (shown in Figure 11–9).

To access YouTube's Video Editor, which offers a more comprehensive collection of online-based video-editing tools, visit: www.youtube.com/editor.

Using the Quick Fixes Tools

Click on the "Quick Fixes" tab to access the "Auto Fix" and "Stabilize" buttons. Clicking on the "Auto Fix" button once allows YouTube to automatically analyze the video and make light, contrast, saturation, and color temperature adjustments it deems necessary to improve the appearance of your video. Clicking on the "Stabilize" button allows YouTube to analyze your video and remove some of the subtle shaking or movement within the video that may have been caused by holding the camera in your hands while shooting, or using the camera while inside of a car, boat, or train, where there was a constant vibration, for example.

Using the sliders displayed once the "Quick Fixes" option is selected, it's possible to adjust the "Fill Light," "Contrast," "Saturation," and/or "Color Temperature" within the video. Keep in mind, these sliders are sensitive, so the slightest movement left or right can have a major impact on the video's appearance. Use these tools to brighten a video and make the colors appear more vibrant, for example.

If you want to display a video in slow motion, from below the "Slow Motion" tab, click on the 1x, 2x, 4x, or 8x button to determine the playback speed that the viewer will experience. To transform a standard video into what looks like a time-lapse video (to condense the amount of time is takes to watch a long video sequence, such as a sunrise or sunset), click on the 1x, 2x, 4x, or 6x button that's displayed below the "Time Lapse" heading.

To trim a video clip, and either clip off content from the beginning and/or end of the video, click on the "Trim" tool, then choose the portion(s) of the video you want to remove. To rotate the video 90 degrees per click, either clockwise or counterclockwise, click on either of the "Rotation" icons that are displayed to the immediate right of the "Trim" button.

Once you make any changes to the video using the tools offered by the "Quick Fixes" menu, be sure to click on either the "Save as New Video" or "Save" button. If you want to remove all the edits you've made to the video using the "Quick Fixes" tools, click on the "Revert to Original" button.

Using the Filters Tool

Again, once a video has been uploaded to YouTube, but before it's been made public, the "Filters" tool is available from the Video Manager. This tool offers 29 one-click, special effects filters that you can add to your video to alter or enhance its appearance (shown in Figure 11–10 on page 170). Click on the "Filters" tab, then click on the "Filter" thumbnail that you want to add to the video. If you like the impact the filter has, click on the "Save as New Video" or "Save" button. To remove the filter, click on the "Revert to Original" button.

Using the Blurring Effects

By clicking on the "Blurring Effects" tab, the Video Manager offers two different effects that blur content within your video (shown in Figure 11–11 on page 170). The "Blur Faces" option works automatically when you click on the "Apply" button. This feature automatically identifies people's faces within a video and blurs them so the people can't be identified.

The Custom Blurring tool can be used to manually add a blur effect over specific objects, items, or people within a video. For example, if there's a product logo or sign that doesn't belong to your company that you don't want the viewer to easily identify when watching your video, you could blur out that content.

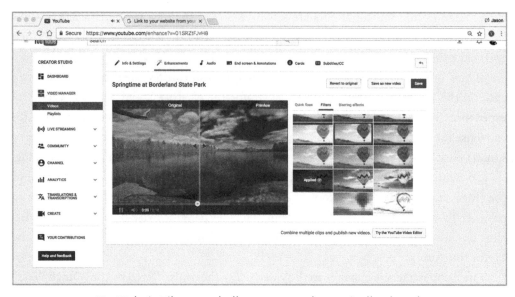

FIGURE 11–10. YouTube's Filters tool allows you to dramatically alter the appearance of a video (or video clip) with a single mouse click.

FIGURE 11–11. YouTube's Video Manager offers two different but related blur tools.

Once again, after using either of the blur tools, be sure to click on the "Save as New Video" or "Save" button, or to remove the blur effect from the video, click on the "Revert to Original" button.

YOUR VIDEO'S WORLDWIDE PREMIERE

As soon as you've uploaded your video and made it public, it will be displayed on your YouTube channel page and made available for anyone to view. Notice that below the video, your viewer can access the "Thumbs Up," "Thumbs Down," "Add To," "Share," and ". . . More" options.

If the viewer scrolls down, depending on how you (the content publisher) have adjusted the video's settings, they may also be able to post a comment about the video and/or read comments posted by other viewers. By clicking on the ". . . More" menu, viewers are given the option to Report the video if they believe it violates the content policies of YouTube, for example.

If viewers want to tell the public about your video, they can click on the "Share" button that's displayed below the video, then choose an option to share a link to the video on Facebook, Twitter, or Google+, for example. A pop-up window will appear, allowing viewers to compose a message to their online friends and followers that will be accompanied by a direct link to your video (or the message will have the video embedded within it).

The focus of Chapter 13, "Interacting with Viewers and Subscribers," discusses ways to entice your viewers and subscribers to help you promote your videos by clicking on the "Share" option. If this is one of your video's goals, it should be included within the video's call to action.

Chapter 12

Monetizing YouTube: Getting Paid for Your Video Views

Online advertising is a big business, which is something the folks at Google and YouTube understand extremely well. To encourage YouTube content creators to display online-based ads in conjunction with their videos, YouTube has not only made accepting and displaying ads an easy and automated process, but also a potentially lucrative one for its participating YouTube Channel operators. However, as a business operator using a YouTube channel to promote your own business, becoming a YouTube Partner, then displaying third-party ads before and during your videos, as well as around the video player window while your content is being watched, may not make a whole lot of sense.

If you're setting up a YouTube channel for your own business and branding it accordingly, you probably do *not* want third-party ads displayed. After all, based on the title, description, and tags associated with your YouTube channel and your individual videos, YouTube and

Google will match up advertising that will appeal to the same audience—in other words, potentially display ads from your direct competition.

Thus, in this situation, becoming a YouTube Partner and displaying ads in conjunction with your company's videos is probably not advantageous. However, you can use Google AdWords and Google AdWords for Video to run paid ads (as an advertiser) to promote your own videos and YouTube channel. In this case, instead of becoming a YouTube Partner (who gets paid), you'd become a paying YouTube advertiser. Refer to Chapter 14, "Promoting Your YouTube Videos," for more information about using paid, online-based ads to promote your videos.

WHEN BECOMING A YOUTUBE PARTNER CAN BE ADVANTAGEOUS

The concept behind the YouTube Partner program is simple. You create and publish content on your YouTube Channel, then do what's necessary to build an audience for your videos. Each time someone views one of your videos, some type of Google/YouTube selected ad will be displayed in the form of a video ad before your video or as a display advertisement surrounding your video's player window.

There are also opportunities for content creators to insert short video ads within the videos (like a commercial break in a television show) to boost their revenue opportunities. In recent years, the format, duration, and location where ads can be displayed within a YouTube channel, and in conjunction with individual videos, has expanded.

Each time someone views, clicks on, or watches a video-based ad on your YouTube Channel, you earn a little bit of revenue. How much you earn depends on a variety of factors, including the type of ad that's seen or responded to by the viewer. So, if you want

ADDING ADS DURING YOUR VIDEO IS AT YOUR SOLE DISCRETION

Note that if you opt to insert one or more video-based ads in the middle of your content, this is at your discretion, and you run the risk of your viewer exiting out of your video before they've finished watching it to the end. Use this option only if you're confident your viewers will stick around, watch the "commercial break" in your video, then continue watching your video.

to earn significant and ongoing revenues from YouTube (as a YouTube Partner), you'll need to consistently generate thousands or, better yet, tens of thousands (or more) video views every month.

Millions of individual people (YouTubers) and independent business professionals (freelancers, experts in their field who are not representing a specific employer, or consultants who operate their own YouTube channel) have launched YouTube-based careers as full-time or part-time endeavors and generate a respectable income from it. In fact, the annual YouTube-derived income for some popular YouTubers is now in the millions.

However, achieving this objective not only takes a lot of creativity to produce videos that are popular, but you also need to work hard to promote your videos and YouTube channel to generate ongoing video views, plus cater to your channel's subscribers. Building a sizable enough audience of viewers and subscribers so your videos generate decent revenue from ad views typically takes several years of producing continuously good content. For most YouTube channel operators, this is not a get-rich-quick scheme.

Becoming a YouTube Partner costs nothing and is totally optional. Anyone who creates and operates their own YouTube channel can sign up to become a YouTube Partner and potentially begin generating revenues from their content. When you apply to become a YouTube Partner (so that you can display online ads in conjunction with your videos), you'll also need to set up a Google AdSense account (which is also free) so you can get paid. This requires linking your Google AdSense account (which gets tied to your Google Account) with your established bank account. You'll discover how to do this shortly.

One of the biggest benefits to becoming a YouTube Partner is that Google handles the advertising placement, revenue collections, and your payments. Once you become part of the program, Google matches your videos with advertisers, decides what ads will appear, and keeps track of all traffic (views), as well as ad responses. YouTube then pays you accordingly for your participation in the YouTube Partner program. There is no need for you to find, solicit, or manage the advertisers. For you, this becomes an automated process.

Once you become a YouTube Partner, you can only earn revenue from videos that contain all original content and adhere to YouTube's Terms of Service and Community Guidelines. Videos that violate copyrights, for example, do not qualify for this program. It is possible to become a YouTube Partner, then enable or disable advertising for each individual video added to your YouTube channel. So, if you have at least one video published on your channel that has advertising enabled (after you join the YouTube Partner program), you're good to go.

HOW TO JOIN AND PARTICIPATE IN THE YOUTUBE PARTNER PROGRAM

If you want to generate money from your videos' views, first establish and customize your YouTube channel. Then populate the channel with original content. When you're ready, turn on the YouTube Partner functionality for your account using the directions offered later in this chapter, and make sure at least one of your videos has advertising (referred to as "Monetization") enabled.

Next, set up a Google AdSense account using the same Google Account you used to set up your YouTube channel. Upon doing this, you will need to provide the bank account details and tax information that is requested. (Yes, you will need to pay taxes on the revenue you earn from YouTube/Google AdSense.)

Remember, your AdSense account must be associated with your YouTube account for you to get paid. It's also essential that you set all this up before your video(s) are heavily promoted and/or go viral, which results in their popularity. The content of your videos must also be "advertiser friendly."

After you join the YouTube Partner program, remember that only videos that contain original content can display ads that allow you to earn revenue. For example, if your video contains copyrighted music that you do not own or visual content that does not belong to you, the video is not eligible.

You can use content, however, that is royalty-free or Creative Commons content, as long as the license agreement grants you the right to use that material commercially. YouTube/Google will automatically analyze each video you make part of the YouTube Partner program, determine what type of content it contains, as well as its subject matter (based on the video's title, description, tags/keywords, and category), then match up ads that will appeal to that same audience. As a YouTube Partner, you have no say in terms of what types of ads are displayed, nor can you choose which advertisers can have ads displayed in conjunction with your content.

So, if you sign up for the YouTube Partner program to generate revenue from people viewing your videos, you could wind up having your competitors advertise in conjunction with your video content. This, obviously, can be detrimental.

However, if you're a YouTuber, online performer (such as a musician), independent consultant, freelancer, or an expert in your field (who is not affiliated with a specific employer), becoming a YouTube Partner can help to supplement your income, as long as you are not concerned about competing companies advertising on your YouTube channel or in conjunction with your videos.

Whether the revenue-generation business model offered by becoming a YouTube Partner works for you is a matter of personal preference, based on your overall goals. If you don't want to run the risk of promoting ads from competing products/services in

AT LEAST 10,000 CHANNEL VIEWS ARE REQUIRED

As of April 6, 2017, before you can get approved to be a YouTube Partner, the videos on your channel must have at least 10,000 combined views. In other words, if you have five published videos, between all of them, the total view count needs to be at least 10,000. However, you can complete the YouTube Partner and AdSense application process any time.

conjunction with your content, don't become a YouTube Partner. Instead, to boost your company's popularity or expand your channel's viewership, consider becoming a paid advertiser on YouTube and have your ads displayed in conjunction with other videos and YouTube channels.

HOW TO SIGN UP FOR THE YOUTUBE PARTNER PROGRAM

Registering to be a YouTube Partner is something you need to do just once—after your YouTube channel has been established. To add YouTube Partner functionality to your YouTube channel, access YouTube, and sign in using the same Google account information that was used to create the YouTube channel. Then, follow these steps:

1. Near the upper-right corner of the browser window, click on your username or profile picture.
2. When the YouTube menu appears, also near the top-right corner of the browser window, click on the "Creator Studio" button (shown in Figure 12–1 on page 178).
3. When the "Dashboard" for the YouTube Creator Studio screen is displayed (shown in Figure 12–2 on page 178), click on the "Channel" option that's displayed along the left margin of the browser window.
4. From the "Status and Features" window, click on the "Enable" button that's associated with the "Monetization" option (shown in Figure 12–3 on page 179).
5. From the Monetization screen, to begin the application process, click on the "Start" button that's associated with YouTube Partner Program Terms (shown in Figure 12–4 on page 179). You'll discover that this application process is divided into four sections. The interactive application will guide you through each step of the application process, so follow the on-screen prompts.

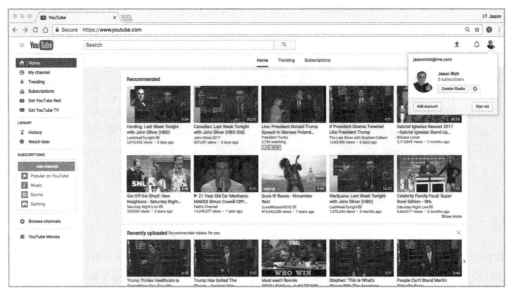

FIGURE 12–1. Click on the "Creator Studio" button to proceed to the dashboard that's associated with your channel's Creator Studio.

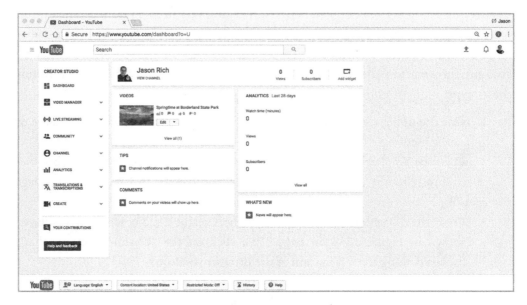

FIGURE 12–2. Click on the "Channel" option, found along the left margin of the browser window.

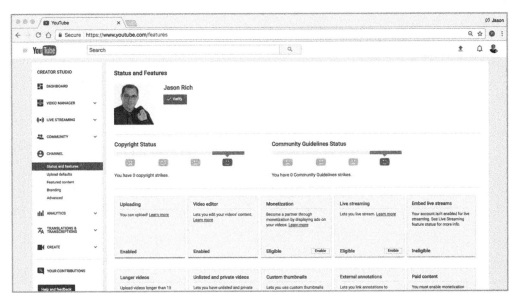

FIGURE 12–3. Scroll to the "Monetization" option and click on the "Enable" button.

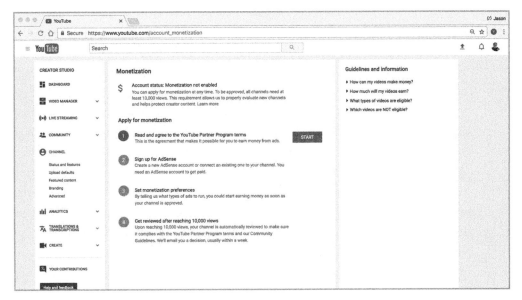

FIGURE 12–4. Click on the "Start" button to begin the YouTube Partner
application process.

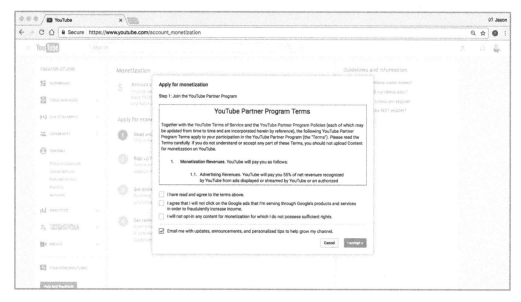

FIGURE 12–5. Accept the terms displayed within this Partner Program Terms screen.

6. When the YouTube Partner Program Terms screen is displayed, read this information carefully, then check the three boxes that are displayed near the bottom of the window (shown in Figure 12–5). Checking the fourth box grants YouTube permission to send you promotional emails. Click on the "I Accept" button to continue.

7. The second section of the application process requires you to set up an AdSense account. Click on the "Start" button to proceed (shown in Figure 12–6 on page 181). Follow the on-screen prompts, and click on the "Next" button to proceed as directed. At this point, you will be prompted to sign into your existing Google Account or create a new Google Account through which AdSense will be managed. Click on either the "Sign In" or "Create Account" button. If you already have an approved and active AdSense account for yourself or your company, you can link it to your YouTube channel using the directions provided. Only one AdSense account can be linked with a Google Account and/or YouTube channel.

8. Assuming you opted to sign in to your existing Google account (the same one used to establish your YouTube channel) and create an AdSense account, you'll be prompted to select your home country, time zone, and account type (Individual or Company), and provide your mailing address. From this same screen, you'll be asked to choose your AdSense-related email preferences. Click on the "Submit My Application" button to continue.

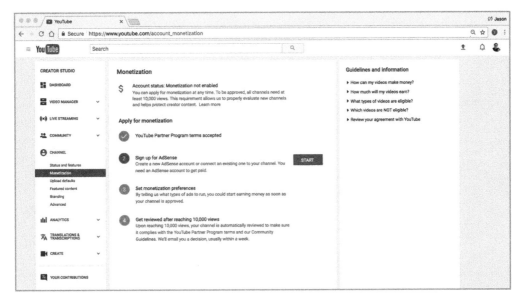

FIGURE 12–6. Set up your AdSense account.

9. At the bottom of the AdSense Terms and Conditions window, check the box associated with the "Yes, I have read and accept the agreement" option, then click on the "Accept" button.

10. The third step in the application process involves setting up the monetization preferences. Click on the "Start" button to continue.

11. The Set Monetization Preferences window (shown in Figure 12–7 on page 182) allows you to choose the format of the ads that will be displayed in conjunction with your video(s) and on your channel page. Choose all four of the available options to increase your revenue earning potential. Check the appropriate boxes, and click on the "Save" button to continue. (You can change your preferences any time in the future.) Ad format options include:

  ■ *Display ads.* These are graphic (banner) ads that will be displayed when viewers use a computer's web browser to access YouTube and watch your videos.

  ■ *Overlay ads.* These are graphic (banner) ads that get superimposed over the YouTube video player window, when a viewer is using a computer's web browser to watch your videos. The drawback to this option is that the bottom portion of what's displayed in your own content (seen within the video player window) will be covered while the ad is displays.

  ■ *Sponsored cards.* These are ads that appear to the right of the YouTube player window, regardless of whether the viewer is using a computer's web browser or a YouTube mobile app to watch your videos.

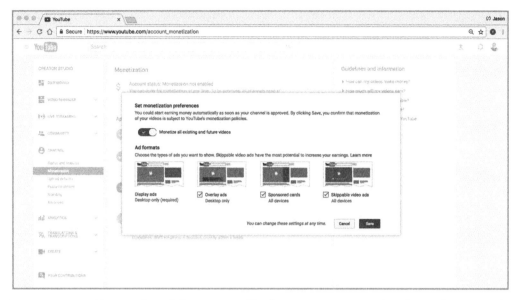

FIGURE 12–7. Choose the ad formats you'll allow on your YouTube channel page and that can be displayed in conjunction with your individual videos.

- *Skippable video ads.* This are video-based ads that will be played before your video, which a viewer can typically exit out of (to proceed directly to your video) after a few seconds. These video ads can be very short (less than 15 seconds) or 30 seconds, for example. The more of each ad viewers watch, the more you get paid. Likewise, you get paid more if viewers click on the link embedded within the ad.

12. The final step in this process is to accrue at least 10,000 video views on your YouTube channel. YouTube will automatically keep track of your channel's traffic and process the YouTube Partner application once you achieve this required milestone. A progress meter is displayed at the bottom of the Monetization screen that shows the total number of video views your channel has.

13. While you're waiting for your channel to earn the required 10,000 views, you can learn more about the YouTube Partner program and invest some time promoting your YouTube channel and its content.

Shortly after your channel is approved as a YouTube Partner, and you turn on the Monetization option for one or more of your individual videos, ads will automatically begin appearing in conjunction with your videos and on your YouTube channel page.

Again, the ads that are displayed are often directly relevant to the content within your videos or channel, based on the titles, descriptions, and tags you've associated with

HOW MUCH YOU CAN EARN FROM VIDEO VIEWS

According to YouTube, how much you'll earn by participating in the YouTube Partner program varies dramatically, based on a variety of factors. Two key factors are the type of ads that are displayed in conjunction with your content and how much the advertisers have paid YouTube to run those ads. AdSense prices ads based on an auction model for its advertisers.

To learn more about AdSense Auctions and how pricing works, visit: https://support.google.com/adsense/answer/160525. To learn more about the YouTube Partner program, visit: https://support.google.com/youtube/answer/72851.

Once your channel is approved to be a YouTube Partner, you will have access to a customized Ad Rates Report from YouTube, which outlines how much you will earn based on specific actions taken by your viewers who see and/or respond to the ads. For more information about how to access and understand this report, visit: https://support.google.com/youtube/answer/2423005.

To determine approximately how much other YouTube channels or individual YouTubers are earning as a YouTube Partner, take advantage of the Social Blade service (which is not affiliated with YouTube). Visit www.socialblade.com, and within the Search field, enter the YouTube channel name (or account username) you're interested in learning more about.

Figure 12–8 on page 184 shows a video-based ad being played before a selected YouTube video. Notice the "Skip Ad" button that's displayed in the bottom-right corner of the video player window, and the ad's timer that's displayed in the bottom-left corner of the video player window. Based on this timer and the content of the ad, a viewer can opt to watch the entire ad, or exit out of it and proceed directly to watching the video they selected. Displayed within the top-right corner of the browser window is an example of a Display Ad.

each video file, as well as the description of your YouTube channel. In some cases, public service announcements (PSAs) are shown or displayed.

As a YouTube Partner, you cannot control which advertisers' ads appear in conjunction with your videos or on your channel's page, nor do you have any say over the advertisers' ad message or content. This is all done at the discretion of

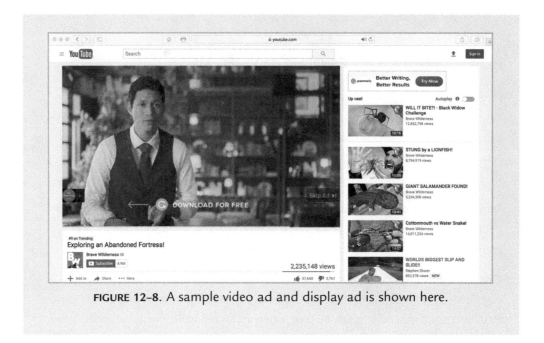

FIGURE 12–8. A sample video ad and display ad is shown here.

Google. What you can choose is whether specific videos featured on your channel will have ads associated with them (once your channel has been approved as a YouTube Partner). You always have the option to turn off ads for specific videos featured on your channel.

Be Sure to Activate the Ad Features for Your Individual Videos

Once you turn on the YouTube Partner functionality for your channel and get accepted as a YouTube Partner (by earning at least 10,000 video views on your channel), it's then necessary to turn on Monetization for individual videos already featured on your YouTube channel, as well as any new videos you add to your channel.

TRACK YOUR EARNINGS IN REAL TIME WITH YOUTUBE ANALYTICS

Once everything is set up correctly, at any time, you can visit your YouTube channel's Analytics page to see detailed information about your videos, and determine the number of views, likes, dislikes, and comments it's received. You can also see how many people have shared and/or favorited each of your videos, and how many people have subscribed to your YouTube channel.

To access your YouTube channel's Analytics page, log in to your YouTube account, access the menu near the top-right corner of the browser window (by clicking on your username or profile photo), then click on the "Creator Studio" option.

From the Creator Studio Dashboard, click on the "Analytics" option that's displayed along the left margin of the screen. Notice there are 21 different Analytics reports you can view, one at a time (shown in Figure 12–9). These are all listed below the "Analytics" heading. Each report offers detailed information pertaining to some aspect of your YouTube channel's performance or the performance of specific videos that populate your channel.

Keep in mind, Google pays its YouTube Partners monthly. However, you need to earn a specific amount of money each month to receive a payment. Otherwise, your earnings keep getting rolled over to the following month, until the preset earning threshold is reached. The information reported through Analytics is displayed in real time and, unless otherwise noted, is updated every ten seconds.

HOW TO MONETIZE YOUR INDIVIDUAL VIDEOS

As you're filming your videos, you can opt to accept money and/or products from companies, then highlight those products within your video in exchange for a paid endorsement. This is considered a paid product placement or a sponsored video, and is yet another way you can earn money with your YouTube videos.

FIGURE 12–9. Access almost two dozen different reports that allow you to keep real-time tabs on how your channel and individual videos are performing.

As a business operator, however, you can also pay other YouTubers and YouTube Channel operators to incorporate your product placements into their videos, or somehow showcase or talk about your products. Some YouTubers will do this for free, in exchange for free product samples. Others will seek financial compensation, but you wind up with an endorsement by an online personality who potentially has a vast and dedicated following.

According to Google, "Paid product placements are defined as pieces of content that are created specifically for a sponsor, and where that sponsor's brand, message, or product is integrated directly into the content. A typical example of a paid product placement is one in which a marketer pays a partner to specifically mention their product or brand in what would normally be the editorial part of the content."

To incorporate paid product placements into your videos, you must be a YouTube Partner in good standing, and you must notify YouTube when you upload this type of video. (Simply check the "Content Declaration" option that's found within the "Advanced Settings" menu. To access it, launch the Video Manager, select the appropriate video, and then click on the "Advanced Settings" tab.)

You are also responsible for working directly with the company that is paying to sponsor your videos, to determine the terms of the arrangement and to collect your own fees. How much you charge is negotiated directly between you and the company placing the products.

As you'll discover from Chapter 17, "Using Product Placement in Videos as a Promotional Tool," there are independent marketing and advertising agencies that specialize in working with YouTubers and companies to facilitate product placements and video sponsorships.

Other Options for Generating Revenue in Conjunction with Your Videos

Many YouTubers, performers, bands, clubs, organizations, charities, and some types of small businesses are also able to earn additional income by designing and selling T-shirts, hoodies, hats, wristbands, posters, mouse pads, mugs, digital downloads, and other merchandise with their name, YouTube channel name, likeness, and/or logo. This business model works well if you begin to establish a large and dedicated following through your YouTube channel.

You can create and sell merchandise on your own or by using a third-party company that handles merchandise sales for YouTube channel operators. Many companies allow you to design, promote, and sell custom products that the company then manufactures and drop ships to your customers. Thus, you have no upfront or inventory costs. In exchange, the company you hire to handle your merchandise takes a percentage of the sales.

Depending on what types of merchandise you're looking to sell, some of the companies you may opt to work with include:

- *CafePress:* www.cafepress.com
- *District Lines:* www.districtlines.com/youtube
- *Short Run Posters:* www.shortrunposters.com
- *Sticker Mule (Stickers and Buttons):* www.stickermule.com
- *TeeChip Custom T-Shirts:* https://teechip.com
- *UberPrints Custom T-Shirts:* www.uberprints.com
- *Zazzle:* www.zazzle.com

For a more extensive list of YouTube-approved merchandise manufacturing and drop-ship companies, visit: https://support.google.com/youtube/answer/6083754.

FOCUS ON YOUR OBJECTIVES

Before you commit to displaying ads from other companies in conjunction with your videos and on your YouTube channel page, think carefully about what your objectives are for using YouTube and creating videos, and determine if displaying ads is truly beneficial to your overall goals. Also, make sure you realize that unless you have a significant number of viewers seeing your videos (and the related ads), you won't generate a lot of money.

Google has created detailed how-to guides for its YouTube Partners to help them produce the best possible videos, and use the tools at their disposal to promote them and build an audience. Check out YouTube Creator Academy's "Make Money with YouTube" section by visiting: https://creatoracademy.youtube.com/page/course/earn-money.

Another way to become skilled at generating revenue from your YouTube channel is to interact with content creators who are already successful. AKT Enterprises is a convention producer that sponsors Playlist Live events where top YouTubers and content creators gather. In the United States, these three-day gatherings are typically held throughout the year in Los Angeles, Washington, DC, and Orlando. For more information, visit: www.playlist-live.com.

Chapter 13

Interacting with Viewers and Subscribers

IN THIS CHAPTER

- How to build an ongoing rapport with your viewers, fans, and channel subscribers
- Ways to interact with your viewers
- Strategies for expanding your online following
- Safety and privacy considerations

According to Pixability (www.pixability.com/industry-insights/top-100-global-brands-youtube-2016), in 2016, the top 100 global brands hosted more than 3,000 YouTube channels, which were populated by more than 10,000 separate videos. These channels combined are subscribed to by a total of more than 104 million viewers, and the videos on these channels received a combined total of more than 63.4 billion views. This represents a 58 percent growth in popularity for these channels within a one-year period.

Companies like Apple, Microsoft, AT&T, Visa, Verizon, McDonald's, Disney, Google, Amazon.com, Samsung, Coca-Cola, Honda, Toyota, Nike, and Nintendo have each discovered how useful YouTube marketing can be, and a growing number of these companies have managed to cost-effectively reach millions of viewers on their respective channels. As a small-business operator, even if you just reach 500 to 1,000 potential new customers in a year, for virtually no cost using YouTube, that could provide a tremendous boost to your company's growth.

From this chapter, you'll learn ways to solidify your YouTube marketing strategy by developing interesting, effective, and unique ways to interact with your audience. To continuously build your YouTube channel's subscriber base and cater to your content's viewers, you'll need to develop efficient ways to interact with these people in a manner that seems highly personal—but without you investing the time and resources to communicate directly with individuals (which is obviously a time-consuming and ultimately costly endeavor).

When you publish a video on YouTube, it's a form of one-way communication. People simply watch your videos. Encouraging people to post comments, like, and/or favorite or share your videos and provide feedback directly on your YouTube Channel, however, helps create an informal and interactive online community, based around your content.

You can opt to make comments on your videos public or private via the "Advanced Settings" menu offered by the Video Manager. It's also possible to choose whether you'll have the opportunity to read and approve all comments before they're published on your YouTube channel page; this is a feature that you should turn on so you can moderate the comments. You also have the option to allow users to rate the comments, then view each video's and comment's ratings.

If you notice your videos, or the comments related to them, are receiving a lot of dislikes (by people clicking on the thumbs down icon), you should reassess your approach, and determine why you're not positively connecting with your viewers. When a video receives a lot of dislikes early on, this will cause potential viewers to avoid watching it, because they can easily determine that a lot of other people didn't like your content. This can also hurt the search result rankings for your videos. Thus, if you see this negative trend, it's important to fix it quickly.

The more active you become on YouTube, the more important it is that you integrate your YouTube channel with all your other online activity, including your company web page, blog, Facebook page, Twitter and Instagram feed, and/or your other social media activities. These other online services offer much more robust tool sets for interacting with people, and all can be cross-promoted through your YouTube channel and individual videos. The focus of Chapter 15, "Using Social Media to Build and Interact with Your Audience," is how to use social media as a powerful marketing tool for your YouTube channel, individual YouTube videos, and your company.

To help expand your audience, be sure to encourage your viewers and subscribers to share links to your videos with their online friends, using any of the poplar social networking platforms. When someone clicks on the "Share" button associated with one of your videos,

VIEWERS VS. SUBSCRIBERS

Anyone can visit your YouTube channel to watch one or more of your videos. They may learn about a video from your own marketing or promotion, receive a referral for the video from one of their online friends, or stumble upon your video after performing a Google or YouTube search.

Viewers can watch your content as often as they'd like on demand. They simply need to return to your YouTube channel, or reclick on the link to a specific video. However, a subscriber is someone who likes your content and opts to click on the "Subscribe" button that's associated with your channel. This allows that person to be notified whenever you publish new content and view a listing for your channel whenever they access YouTube from their account.

Subscribers can become very loyal to your channel (and your company) if you treat them appropriately and continue to provide content on your channel that appeals to them. Subscribing to a YouTube channel is free for a viewer. However, once someone subscribes to your channel, this makes it much easier for you to communicate with them in the future, and get them to revisit your channel to watch your newest content, and potentially rewatch older content.

One of the key ways a YouTube channel's popularity is measured is based on the number of subscribers it accumulates.

this helps you build your audience through word-of-mouth advertising, which is highly effective and free. The easiest way to do this is to display "Share" buttons in conjunction with each of your YouTube videos. Also, within a video's call to action, ask your audience to share the video with their online friends by clicking on the "Share" button.

ALWAYS CONSIDER YOUR TARGET AUDIENCE

Just as you did when planning your YouTube channel, before interacting with your audience on an ongoing basis, you need to understand their wants, expectations, and needs by having a good understanding of your audience's demographics.

As you know, the demographics of your audience can be categorized by their age, sex, geographic location, income, education level, race, religion, political party affiliation, interests, hobbies, career, employment status, sexual orientation, what computer or technology they use, what type of car they drive, what TV shows they watch, their favorite books or magazines, or by a wide range of other factors that you determine to be important. By figuring out how you can best describe your target demographic, you can then determine the best approaches to take on YouTube and in your videos to best cater to the wants and needs of that audience.

For example, you may determine that your target audience comprises single men who are between the ages of 18 and 24, in college or graduate school, and enjoy playing or watching football. Alternatively, you may determine that your ideal customer and the people you want to target on YouTube are women who are between the ages of 24 and 49, are college graduates, live within a major city, who are employed full time, and who have an annual income over $45,000.

You can use any combination of the previously mentioned criteria or traits, or develop your own list that you believe allows you to accurately describe your target audience. The more you know about your audience and the more clearly you can define this group of people, the easier it will be to produce videos that will appeal to them so you can promote your videos to this group in the most cost-effective way.

In addition to determining your audience's basic demographics, think about exactly who makes up your YouTube audience:

- Are they technologically savvy?
- What computer equipment do they use?
- When and where do they typically watch YouTube videos?
- Why do they watch YouTube videos?
- Are they active on other social media services?
- What are some of the best ways to communicate with your audience outside You-Tube?
- Is real-time or direct communication important to your audience? How could your company benefit from real-time communication or interaction with your viewers and subscribers?

Once your videos are published online and available for the public to watch, you can then determine exactly who is watching them—and how to better target that audience—by using YouTube's free Analytics tools. In addition to helping you plan your next videos, the information provided by Analytics can help you more efficiently interact with subscribers and viewers. It can also tell you if your viewers' demographics are slightly different than you had anticipated, and if you need to adapt your video planning and communication strategies.

You may discover when using Analytics that your target audience and actual audience are not the same. If you discover this, it means you need to:

- Refocus your content to target the audience you're actually reaching, as opposed to the audience you planned to reach.
- Adapt your content to better appeal to your original target audience (and potentially lose the audience you're already reaching).
- Develop content to appeal to your target audience *and* the secondary audience your videos are already appealing to.

Which option to choose is a matter of what the goals are for your company, and whether the actual audience your content is appealing to is also interested in the products or services your company offers.

When it comes to expanding your audience, the Analytics tools can help you in several ways. You can use these tools to determine who is already appreciating your content. You can also determine what days and times your content is most frequently accessed, where the content is being accessed from, and very specifically who your actual audience is.

Analytics data is also useful when trying to determine ways to improve your content, because you can determine exactly how long people are watching your videos, at what point they're clicking out of your videos (if they're not watching them to the end), and what actions the viewers are taking in response to your videos. Thus, you can easily see if your call to actions are working, if your content is running too long, or if you're losing your audience's attention at a certain point in each video.

This information can be used to help you create more targeted content and more effectively promote your content in the future. By studying your Analytics data on an ongoing basis, you may discover a vast and dedicated audience for your content (and your company) that you've been overlooking, because you didn't know it existed.

RECAP: HOW TO ACCESS YOUTUBE ANALYTICS

To access YouTube Analytics for your YouTube channel, sign in to YouTube using the username and password used to create your channel. Click on your username or profile photo that's displayed in the top-right corner of the browser window. Click on the "Creator Studio" button (also displayed in the top-right corner of the browser window). From the Creator Studio Dashboard, click on the "Analytics" option that's displayed along the left margin of the browser window. Click on the YouTube Analytics report you want to view.

HOW TO DEVELOP AN ONGOING RAPPORT WITH YOUR VIEWERS, FANS, AND SUBSCRIBERS

Once you get people to watch just one of your videos, make it easy for them to watch your other videos as well. This can be done within the videos themselves, on your YouTube channel's page, via email announcements of new videos, and by using announcements on Facebook, Twitter, and other social media.

Remember, within every video you produce, it should contain some type of call to action—a request that your viewers immediately do something. This call to action should be accompanied by a reward. For example, say something like, "To save $50 on your first order, click here to visit our website."

Some of the popular ways to use or promote a call to action within your content includes:

- Add a message inviting people to watch the other videos on your channel.
- Embed links to your other videos within each of your videos.
- Encourage your viewers to like and rate your videos.
- Make it easy for people to share your videos via social media or email by enabling the "Share" function.
- Ask viewers for ideas for future video topics so they feel like they're part of the creative process.
- Pose questions to your viewers and encourage them to post their responses in the comments section associated with the video. You can also ask survey questions or solicit feedback. For example, if you're using a YouTube video to demonstrate a new product, ask people to post their thoughts about the product or their own ideas about how they'd use it.
- Ask viewers, customers, potential customers, or subscribers to send you questions via email, social media, or the comments section of your videos, then answer the most common questions in future videos. When you do this, be sure to credit the person who posed each question. For example, begin with, "[Insert YouTube username], asked . . ."
- Encourage people to visit your web page, read your blog, and follow you or your company on social media.

If you're using YouTube videos to communicate with your potential or existing customers, it's essential that you publish your company's contact information in conjunction with your videos. However, only do this within your videos and/or on your YouTube channel's page if you intend to respond quickly and, potentially, personally. Otherwise, simply ask your viewers and subscribers to post comments related to your videos through YouTube (or other social media), and make it clear that you read them all.

YouTube Videos Can Teach You How to Interact with Your Audience

Just as YouTube can be a learning tool for your audience, it can also be a learning tool for you as a content creator and channel operator. When it comes to learning how to interact with your YouTube viewers and subscribers, you can find numerous videos that offer how-to information, as well as valuable advice. Within the YouTube search field, enter something like, "How to interact with YouTube viewers" to find a collection of instructional videos.

For example, Video School Online's YouTube channel (www.youtube.com/user/VideoSchoolOnline) publishes weekly videos designed to help YouTube content creators and channel operators produce better content. One of this channel's videos discusses "best practices" for interacting with your viewers and subscribers. You can watch this video by pointing your web browser to: www.youtube.com/watch?v=CupliHXaRkM.

Meanwhile YouTube's own Creator Academy offers a video titled, "Connect with Your Community," which provides valuable tips for developing positive dialogue with your YouTube audience. You can find this video at: https://creatoracademy.youtube.com/page/lesson/invite-conversation.

Hold an Interactive Conversation within the Comments Section

Once your viewers post a comment in conjunction with one or more of your videos, you can reply to that person within the comments section of your video. If you've set up the comments to be public, your video's viewers can read all comments, then respond to them. Then, comment responses can be responded to, and you and your audience can establish an ongoing dialogue—that's either between you and that person, or that all of your viewers can participate in.

Assuming you moderate this dialogue and invest the time to interact with your audience by posting text-based responses to their comments, this can be a powerful way to address questions, comments, and concerns, while at the same time building your online reputation and audience loyalty. You can also learn from the feedback your viewers provide.

Make sure someone within your company is assigned the responsibility of moderating and responding to video comments on YouTube on a daily basis and that you establish strict guidelines about what is permissible within their responses. For example, you never want to embarrass, talk down to, insult, or be rude to a viewer or subscriber. Likewise, you want to avoid sharing too much personal information about yourself, spokesperson, or other company employees.

If questions or comments pertaining to your company philosophy or its products/services will be addressed, make sure the person responding on behalf of your company understands what should and should not be discussed based on information your company deems to be proprietary. The person interacting with your YouTube audience should always stay on message and promote the company in a positive way to enhance, not tarnish, its reputation. In other words, the role of the person responding to YouTube comments and viewer interaction is as important as the people creating, publishing, and promoting the content.

Once you opt to allow for comments from your viewers and subscribers, or if you solicit specific information from your audience, be sure to respond to all comments in a timely manner. While everyone would appreciate a personalized response, if the number of comments you need to respond to becomes overwhelming, either cut and paste pre-written responses to common questions, or refer commenters to a FAQ (frequently asked questions) document you've posted on your website.

Finally, if you do solicit comments and feedback from your audience, thank them for their participation, loyalty, honesty, and time. Show your gratitude as the content provider, and make it clear that you value your viewers, subscribers, customers, and/or clients.

How to Deal with Hate

One thing to avoid when interacting with your YouTube audience is engaging "haters" or "trolls"—people who continuously post negative or hateful comments related to you, your company, or your videos. Responding to these people in either a public or private forum often leads to escalation of their behavior. If you determine someone is simply trying to be a nuisance by posting negative information, delete their comments and do not respond to them. These people are typically looking for a reaction. By providing no reaction, they'll often get bored quickly and go away.

Obviously, if one of your viewers, customers, or potential customers has a legitimate gripe, address that on a one-on-one basis by phone or email. But be aware that there are many "haters" on YouTube that simply make a habit of posting negative and potentially reputation-damaging comments on the service for no good reason.

Determine Who in Your Audience Has Influence

Using online-based third-party tools, such as Klout (www.klout.com) or Social Blade (www.socialblade.com), or simply by reviewing the number of friends your viewers or subscribers have in conjunction with their social media accounts, you can see firsthand how much influence each person has over others in cyberspace.

As you're working to promote your videos and YouTube Channel, analyze your audience, figure out who the influencers are, and try to cater to them through direct contact. At the same time, figure out who is producing videos that are similar in focus or content to yours, as well as YouTube channels that are catering to the same target audience, even if their content is vastly different from what you're offering.

In addition to reviewing the competing video content, and paying careful attention to the production quality and approach that's been taken by other content producers, try to determine how competing videos and channels are being promoted, what keywords are being used, and who the audience is for that content.

HOW TO CONTINUOUSLY EXPAND YOUR ONLINE FOLLOWING

There are also many ways of generating more video views and for increasing viewer/subscriber loyalty. Many of these activities will require time to manage but are free or inexpensive to use.

Include Accurate and Relevant Keywords in Your Video's Title, Description, and Tags

As you're uploading and publishing each new video, compose a creative, well-thought-out, informative, and captivating title for each video, as well as a detailed description that's short, direct, and enticing. Equally important are the tags you associate with your videos.

Every word in a video's title, description, or tag(s) becomes keyword searchable—not just on YouTube but through search engines like Google. Ideally, if someone is interested in a topic that's related to one or more of your videos (or your YouTube channel), they should be able to discover your content easily by entering appropriate keywords or a relevant search phrase into the YouTube or Google search field.

You'll be pleasantly surprised by the number of views you can achieve based on random people using a keyword search to find your content. Thus, it's essential that you incorporate as many keywords as possible within a video's title and description and you also associate relevant keywords as tags. This is all done when you upload your video, but it can also be updated at any time via your YouTube channel's Video Manager menu. Even after a video is published, you can add or revise a video's title, description, and/or tags to reach a broader audience. Refer to Chapter 11, "Uploading Your Videos to YouTube," for more information on how to do this.

Take Advantage of Social Media

Social media can become a powerful and free (or inexpensive) tool to promote your company, products/services, and your YouTube channel (and its content). Social media also provides another informal way to interact with your viewers and subscribers.

The focus of Chapter 15, "Using Social Media to Build and Interact with Your Audience," is on how to use services like Facebook, Twitter, Instagram, Pinterest, and LinkedIn to expand and communicate with your YouTube audience, as well as promote your brand.

In today's business world, it's essential for companies to have a presence on social media. This can be accomplished for free. However, managing various social media accounts (including your YouTube channel) can get time consuming. You can also use paid advertising on many social media platforms to quickly reach a highly targeted audience relatively inexpensively. This is a popular way for companies to quickly grow their YouTube channel audience, for example.

If you have a budget to promote your videos, consider using keyword advertising on Facebook. These ads are inexpensive, highly targeted, flexible, and easy to create and launch. You can begin advertising on Facebook for as little as $50 and begin reaching potential viewers in just minutes. You'll learn more about advertising on Facebook (and other online services, like Google and Yahoo!) to promote your videos in Chapter 14, "Promoting Your YouTube Videos."

Post Comments about Videos Produced by Others

Yet another way to promote your videos is to find the most influential people who are also targeting your audience and become active on their respective YouTube channels, Facebook pages, and other social media feeds. This can be done by posting your own comments to their videos and by engaging in online conversations. Comments you post to other videos and channels can help boost your online popularity, assuming the comments you post are constructive and insightful. Never be negative, unprofessional, or rude within the public comments you post that relate to content created by others.

Another powerful tool YouTube offers for promoting your channel is to create and publish video responses to popular videos on other channels. Doing this essentially allows you to ride on the coattails of an already popular and relevant video, and potentially reach a broader audience. However, be careful. If your video responses appear too promotional, they could be labeled as spam, which will result in your account being blocked. So, if you plan to use video responses, be creative, subtle, and not overly aggressive.

Host Live, Interactive Real-Time Video Chats

Another way to interact with your viewers and subscribers is to occasionally host live video chats or video conferences and invite your target YouTube audience to participate. This can easily be done using YouTube Live functionality (which is the focus of Chapter 16, "Go Live with Your Broadcasts"), or you can use a third-party service, such as YouNow (www.younow.com), Twitch.tv (www.twitch.tv), or GoToMeeting (www. gotomeeting.com), that allows you to host free or low-cost live video conferences, or to broadcast live—to an audience comprised of a handful of people to thousands of viewers. You can then publish recordings of the live conference or chat on your YouTube Channel so other people can access this content on an on-demand basis.

Keep in mind, Google owns both YouTube and the Google+ service. Thus, the company has made it easy to host a live Google+ Hangout (live conference), then quickly record and publish it on your YouTube Channel.

A live video broadcast gives your viewers and subscribers a chance to interact with you in a real-time and safe online environment. Many businesses and successful YouTube personalities host weekly or monthly live broadcasts to interact more directly with people who share an interest in them, their company, or their products or services.

During a live broadcast, a text-based chat allows people to pose questions to you, the host, which you can respond to. Some live broadcast services also allow you to "guest" people watching your broadcasts. Using their webcam and computer or mobile device, they can be seen and heard using a split-screen video format so the guest can see and hear you, you can see and hear them, and your entire audience can see and hear both you and your guest.

Hosting live (streaming) broadcasts requires a slightly different skill set than recording, editing, publishing, and promoting YouTube videos, because there is no delay and no chance to edit your content. When you host a live broadcast, it's essentially public speaking, because you're communicating with a live audience. Thus, while you probably won't want to script your broadcast word for word, you will want to prepare a detailed outline for what you'll discuss or cover within your "program," then rehearse your presentation before going live.

Keep in mind, there is no time limit for live broadcasts. However, you will want to monitor your audience in real-time, and based on whether the audience is growing, stagnant, or shrinking (because people stop watching the live broadcast), make an educated decision about when to end it. Some YouTubers and YouTube channel operators promote an ongoing schedule about when they'll host live broadcasts, so their viewers and subscribers can plan to attend. Others go live at random days and times, based on their availability, or when they have something to say. Which option you choose should be based on the preference of your target audience.

Organize Your Channel with Playlists and Categories

By organizing groups of relevant videos into playlists, you'll encourage viewers to watch multiple videos back to back in the order you determine is most beneficial to both you

GOALS FOR YOUR VIEWERS

In terms of promoting your YouTube channel and content, and helping your channel grow in popularity, five goals (and potentially calls to action) for your viewers should be to:

1. Encourage viewers to watch multiple videos—your new content, as well as relevant older content, for example.

2. "Like" the video they're watching.

3. Subscribe to your channel so they get alerted when you post new content.

4. Share a link to your video with their online friends by clicking on the video's Share button.

5. Leave a positive comment about the video.

Be creative when asking people to "like" your videos (which means they simply click on the thumbs up icon that's associated with the video). For example, while you could simply ask your viewers to "like" the video by saying something like, "If you enjoyed this video, please click the 'thumbs up' icon," you could also say something like, "If you agree with what I'm saying, click the 'like' button," or "If you'd like to see more videos like this on our channel, click the 'like' button."

and them. At the same time, by organizing your videos into clearly labeled categories that are relevant to your audience this allows you to group together and display videos with similar types of content or that relate to the same topic, for example.

Using Cards and an End Screen within your videos, as well as links to other content within the descriptions for your videos, you're easily able to promote other relevant content that your channel offers. Encourage viewers to watch multiple videos during each channel visit.

SAFETY AND PRIVACY CONSIDERATIONS

Online popularity, even if you're a company that develops videos that ultimately become popular on YouTube, can become a double-edged sword. Thus, for the company spokespeople appearing in your videos, it may become important to maintain some level of privacy in their lives. Remember, total strangers from all over the world will potentially have access to your videos. Over time, your audience will feel as if they're getting to know you or your spokespeople—which can be a great thing.

However, as an online personality or the spokesperson for a business, you'll want to separate your online popularity from real life, or you could wind up with some of your more motivated viewers turning into unwanted stalkers. When it comes to maintaining your online safety and privacy, use common sense. Here are a few strategies you might want to incorporate from the start:

- Never disclose your home address. You can simply refer to home as being within the closest major city to where you live.
- Don't disclose too much detail about your family, especially your kids. If you're a business operator, be careful about how much personal information you share about your co-workers or employees.
- Avoid revealing anything that could help unwanted stalkers discover where you live.
- Create a separate email address that you can share online with your audience. Keep it separate from your personal or work email. Set up a free Gmail email account (http://mail.google.com), for example.

If you want to give out a mailing address, rent a P.O. box from your local post office branch. This can be done online (www.usps.com/manage/po-boxes.htm) or at any post office for an annual fee. Be aware, however, that a P.O. box will only accept U.S. mail deliveries, not packages sent through other couriers, such as UPS or FedEx.

Another option is to rent a mailbox from a company like The UPS Store (www.theupsstore.com/mailboxes). Packages from all carriers will be accepted, and you can arrange for mail forwarding.

Once you disclose information online, it's out there in cyberspace forever, even if you attempt to delete it later. Be very careful about what personal information you disclose in your videos, as well as in your video descriptions and when communicating with your audience via YouTube or any form of social media.

Within your actual videos, don't include content that may reveal your home's location or personal information, such as a house number, street sign, or vehicle license plate. This is all content that can easily be blurred out in your videos using YouTube's blur tools, which were discussed in Chapter 11, "Uploading Your Videos to YouTube."

Promoting Your YouTube Videos

Creating a branded YouTube channel, then producing attention-grabbing content to populate that channel (so that it appeals to your target audience) are two important steps. However, a third step in the quest to build a successful YouTube presence is to continuously promote your YouTube channel and its content. If you want to build a growing audience for your videos, you'll need to implement a multifaceted and ongoing approach to how you promote them. In fact, as soon as you stop promoting your content, chances are you'll see a sharp decline in viewership.

Based on your goals for your YouTube channel and its content, success can be measured in several ways, including:

- The number of people who place an online or telephone order for your product or service after watching your video(s)

- How many views each video receives
- The number of new subscribers a video attracts to your YouTube channel
- The quality of engagement your viewers experience (For example, do viewers watch the entire video, or click out of it before it's over?)
- The number of positive (or negative) comments a video receives
- How many people "like" the video vs. how many people "dislike" it, compared to those who watch it and don't click on either the "like" (thumbs up) or "dislike" (thumbs down) icon
- The number of people who favorite a video
- The number of people who share a video (or a link to the video) with their online friends via email or social media
- The number of people who respond to your video's call to action
- The number of people who watch your video on YouTube, then use one of the links offered within the video (or within a video's description, for example) to access your company's website, blog, Facebook page, etc.

Receiving between 100 and 500 video views that ultimately result in additional sales of your product or service may be deemed a huge success by your company. However, if you're looking to extend your brand awareness across a targeted demographic, throughout a region, or an entire country, your goal may be to achieve thousands or tens of thousands of views for each of your YouTube videos.

Whether you're trying to attract 100, 1,000, 10,000, 100,000, or a million views for each of your videos, you'll need a well-thought-out, ongoing, multifaceted, and creative plan to promote your channel and its content—both online and in the real world—that's specifically targeted to the audience you're attempting to reach. Even if you create awesome videos that perfectly target your audience, if you don't properly promote them, people are not going to find and see your content. You can't simply rely on people stumbling across your videos after performing a YouTube or Google search, as this will result in a slow trickle of new viewers to your channel at best.

This chapter focuses on the promotional aspect of building an audience for your YouTube content, and includes a handful of no-cost or low-cost strategies you can either implement yourself, or pursue using third parties. Chapter 15, "Using Social Media to Build and Interact with Your Audience," focuses exclusively on how to use services like Facebook, Twitter, Instagram, LinkedIn, and Google+ as a promotional tool for your YouTube Channel and your company.

Properly promoting a YouTube channel and its content (on an ongoing basis) will require time and resources. So once again, before you begin any promotional or paid advertising efforts, define your overall objectives. Based on the goal for your YouTube channel and the content you've published on that channel, consider:

- Who do you want to see your videos?
- How many views would you like to attract?
- What do you want your audience to do after watching your video(s)?
- How will your company measure the success of its YouTube efforts?
- How much time, money, and other resources are at your disposal to promote individual videos and your company's YouTube channel?

Promoting individual YouTube videos and your YouTube channel is the only way to continuously build and sustain an audience. However, once you develop a dedicated audience for your first few videos, and those people become subscribers to your channel, getting them to watch future videos will be much easier. When you reach this point, your goals then include retaining your existing subscribers, while continuously seeking out new viewers and subscribers.

Most of your promotional efforts will take time to work. Be patient! Don't expect to publish your first video and generate hundreds or thousands of views in the first few days. Have realistic expectations. It takes time to build a YouTube audience. In fact, most YouTube channels that have tens of thousands or millions of subscribers have been active on YouTube for at least five years—publishing new content and promoting it on an ongoing basis. Alternatively, the content producer has invested a fortune in paid advertising and promotions to quickly build an audience.

Once you have defined your objectives, consider using at least several of the strategies outlined in this chapter to achieve them. In other words, adopt a multifaceted approach to these activities. Your promotional/advertising effort should include the following three components:

1. *It should be highly targeted.* Figure out how to best reach your target audience online and in the real world. If you want a specific demographic to watch your videos, you need to reach those people and inform them of your YouTube channel's existence, as well as how and where to find and access it.

2. *It should be ongoing.* If you want to maintain a steady flow of viewers and expand your subscriber base, you need to continuously promote your content and channel.

3. *It should be multifaceted.* Don't just rely on one promotional or advertising activity to build and maintain an audience for your content, even if you notice a single approach is initially working. Over the long term, you're much better off simultaneously pursuing at least three or more different promotional and/or advertising opportunities to drive a steady flow of new viewers to your channel and get subscribers to revisit your channel.

Using Analytics and other third-party tools, be sure to track the results of your promotional and advertising efforts as carefully and accurately as possible so you can determine what's working, what's not working, and what efforts need to be fine-tuned to achieve better results. Ultimately, your goal when it comes to promoting/advertising your YouTube videos and channel should be to dedicate as little time, money, and resources as possible to generate the desired results and to make sure you're generating the best results possible based on your actions and the resources you allocate.

TRACK YOUR PROGRESS: BE SURE TO USE YOUTUBE ANALYTICS

As you know, in conjunction with your YouTube channel, YouTube and Google offer a free, online tool set called YouTube Analytics. These tools can help you track, in real time, information about who is watching your videos. In some cases, more powerful traffic and viewership tracking tools are offered by third parties for a fee or are provided when you take advantage of online paid advertising to promote your videos.

The data provided by YouTube Analytics can help you plan and execute successful video-marketing strategies. Google is constantly upgrading these free tools and adding new functionality. For example, in addition to quickly determining who is watching your videos, where they're from, and how they're engaging with your videos, you can now track their quality of engagement, and see if people are clicking out of your videos before they're over, and if so, exactly when. Knowing this, you can go back and fine-tune your content to prevent people from exiting early.

Social Blade (www.socialblade.com) is an online-based service that compiles data from YouTube, Twitter, Twitch, and Instagram, and uses the data it collects to help content creators track their progress and growth when it comes to current traffic, projected viewership, and estimated earnings, for example. In addition to the tools the service offers, the company's blog (https://socialblade.com/blog) is continuously updated with articles and news of interest to content creators, helping them stay on top of evolving trends and ways to better use YouTube and other social media services.

Based on YouTube's current revenue sharing formulas for YouTube Partners, Social Blade offers a free online tool to help channel operators calculate potential earnings by displaying ads within their videos and on their channel's page. This tool can be found at: https://socialblade.com/youtube/youtube-money-calculator.

Another free service offered by Social Blade is a free subscriber counter, which updates in real time and displays your current number of YouTube channel subscribers. You can customize this tool at https://socialblade.com/youtube/realtime. Plus, the company offers a personalized consulting service, designed to help content creators maximize the impact of its YouTube channel and content. To learn more about this fee-based service, visit: https://socialblade.com/grow-and-brand-your-youtube-channel.

If you don't want to invest further time tracking your efforts and figuring out what worked and what didn't, there are companies you can hire to assist with these tasks. For example, a service called Adobe Advertising Cloud (https://blogs.adobe.com/digitalmarketing/advertising/introducing-adobe-advertising-cloud), which was formerly called TubeMogul, is operated by Adobe, and offers fee-based tools that go beyond what YouTube Analytics offers and can help you measure things like brand awareness, message recall, favorability, and purchase intent when it comes to implementing an online advertising campaign simultaneously across several platforms.

Other online-based alternatives to YouTube Analytics, some of which include tools for promoting a YouTube channel or YouTube videos, in addition to monitoring channel traffic, include:

WHAT IS INFLUENCER MARKETING?

Out of all your subscribers, viewers, customers, and/or clients, you should be able to identify a handful of people who are considered "influencers." These are people with a large social media following, who could potentially help you promote your YouTube channel, content, company, products, and/or services, simply by referencing your company within their social media posts, or by sharing links to your videos with their followers.

For example, if one of your customers or subscribers has 1,000 or more followers on Twitter, Facebook, and/or Instagram, just one mention within a tweet or Facebook post from that person could potentially generate a bunch of extra views for one of your YouTube videos. Seeking out these influencers and enticing them to help you promote your content is what "influencer marketing" is all about.

Visit *AdWeek*'s website (www.adweek.com/digital/10-reasons-why-influencer-marketing-is-the-next-big-thing) to read an article about why influencer marketing is becoming so popular. *Entrepreneur* magazine also published an article titled, "How to Create a Successful Influencer Marketing Campaign," which you can read for free online (www.entrepreneur.com/article/290745).

Then, for help developing your influencer marketing campaign, visit the Influencer Marketing Hub website (https://influencermarketinghub.com).

- *ChannelMeter* (www.channelmeter.com/analytics). This service offers tools for simultaneously tracking all of a company's social media efforts, including a YouTube channel.

- *StatFire* (www.statfire.com). This service publishes lists of the most popular YouTube channels, based on specific categories and time frames. For example, you can view a comprehensive list of the most popular YouTube channels of all time, in the past 30 days or the past 7 days, plus view the most popular channels based on YouTube's categories (Autos & Vehicles, Comedy, Education, Entertainment, Film & Animation, How-To & Style, Movies, Music, News & Politics, etc.).

- *Traackr.com* (www.traackr.com). Use this tool to handle "influencer marketing" related to your company, YouTube channel, and other social media activities. According to the company, "Influencer marketing is the process of identifying, researching, engaging, and supporting the people who create high-impact conversations with customers about your brand, products, or services." To learn more about how this process works, visit: www.traackr.com/influencer-marketing.

- *VidStatsX* (http://vidstatsx.com). Use this tool for researching current popular YouTube channels, based on Most Subscribed, Most Viewed, Top Gainers, and Top Losses. This information will help you see how other channels are successfully targeting the same audience you're striving to reach with your content and quickly analyze what they are doing right, or wrong. You can also access analytics pertaining to your own channel and see how it is performing, compared to other channels.

START PROMOTING ON YOUTUBE AND BEYOND

It can't be emphasized enough how important it is to properly title your videos, add an accurate description to them, and associate highly relevant keywords with them. This information will allow people who access YouTube to more easily find your videos, even

---

READ SOCIAL MEDIA-RELATED NEWS ONLINE

AdWeek, an industry-oriented publication that covers advertising, publishes the online-based *Social Pro Daily* (www.adweek.com/category/social-pro-daily), which includes articles targeted to content producers that relate to all aspects of social media and content creation.

if they don't have the direct link to them or details about your YouTube channel's page. This information is also shared (usually very quickly) with Google's search engine. Thus, potential viewers will be able to find your video by entering relevant keywords into the search field of YouTube or Google, as well as other search engines you list the video's link on.

EMBED YOUR VIDEOS IN YOUR WEBSITE

In addition to using the tools available on YouTube, you can feature your videos on your company's website, Facebook page, blog, and through other online social networking services. If you've built an opt-in email list of your customers, clients, or other individuals, be sure to share a link to your latest videos with those people via email. However, avoid using spam (unsolicited email) as a promotional tool.

If you opt to feature your videos on your company's website or blog, for example, allow YouTube to host them and simply embed the videos using the HTML coding that's supplied by YouTube. While it will be obvious the video is linked to YouTube,

GET HELP CREATING KEYWORDS TO ASSOCIATE WITH VIDEO LISTINGS AND ADS

For assistance with creating a comprehensive list of keywords to use in conjunction with each of your video's online listings (as well as within your video titles, descriptions, and advertising to promote your content), there are a variety of free and fee-based tools to help you.

For example, Google AdWords offers a free Keyword Planner (https://adwords.google.com/KeywordPlanner). Also for free, you can access the Keyword Tool (http://keywordtool.io/youtube) from Key Tools, Ltd. Starting at $99 per month, there's the Semrush service (www.semrush.com). Meanwhile, companies pay upward of $300 per month to use WordStream software (www.wordstream.com).

In addition to recommending keywords related to your YouTube channel content, many of these tools and services help you choose keywords based on their popularity. In other words, you're able to accurately determine how many people type a specific keyword into the search field of YouTube (or a search engine) to find what they're looking for.

every view it receives from your website or blog will help boost your YouTube channel and video traffic statistics. The other benefit to allowing YouTube to host the videos that you showcase on your website or blog is that the storage space and bandwidth needed is provided by YouTube for free.

To embed one of your YouTube videos in a website, visit the Video Manager area of YouTube after logging in to your YouTube channel. Select the video you want to embed, then click on the "Share" option, followed by the "Embed" option. Within a window, the HTML code needed to embed the video into your website will automatically be created and displayed. Copy the HTML code exactly as it appears and paste it into the appropriate place within the HTML code for your website or blog. Information about how to do this, and how to embed a YouTube playlist within your webpage or blog can be found online at: https://support.google.com/youtube/answer/171780.

In addition to encouraging your viewers to "like" your videos, post comments, and share your videos, you should allow (and even encourage) your videos to be embedded within other websites and blogs, because this will help boost their exposure and accessibility.

One of your responsibilities as you evaluate your audience data is to listen. Pay attention to what your viewers are saying in their comments. Also pay attention to the number of likes your video receives. These are indicators of how your content is being received by your audience, which you can use to fine-tune your message and create future videos to reach a broader audience. You can also go back and re-edit or rework your existing videos to increase their effectiveness and appeal, based on your audience-related data from Analytics.

Also, while you can encourage comments, initially keep them private—viewable only by you. You want to be sure that the consensus among your targeted audience is positive. Your initial efforts will involve a bit of a learning curve as you get to know how to fully use YouTube and become acquainted with your target audience's viewing habits. Keep in mind that negative comments and "dislikes" will quickly tarnish your online reputation and make it difficult for your subsequent videos to gain traction and popularity.

TAKE ADVANTAGE OF SEARCH ENGINE OPTIMIZATION TO PROMOTE YOUR VIDEOS

Because many web surfers decide what websites they'll visit or which YouTube videos they'll watch based on results given to them by their favorite search engine (such as Google or Yahoo!), one way to promote your videos is to get them listed on the popular search engines. Then use search engine optimization (SEO) techniques to help ensure a link to one of your videos is one of the first results someone sees when performing a keyword search using a popular search engine.

Using SEO is a specialized skill unto itself. It requires that you stay up to date on how the popular search engines work. When you publish a new video on YouTube, it becomes searchable via Google rather quickly. How effective your Google listing is at attracting viewers will depend on several factors, including the title, description, and keywords that are associated with the video itself. Thus, if you have 10 or more separate videos on your YouTube channel, and each is listed on Google using the same or related keywords, for example, this dramatically increases your company's ability to be found on Google by your potential customers. Instead of having just one listing on Google for your company's main website, you'll now have multiple Google listings, which will improve your SEO rankings. Then, from your YouTube channel, you can link videos together as a playlist, for example, so your audience will be able to watch more of your content easily once they've accessed your channel.

While you can learn to implement SEO strategies yourself, it requires a considerable learning curve. You may be much better off hiring a legitimate company or independent consultant who specializes in SEO. The investment could increase your chances of success, plus speed up the time it takes for your highly ranked search engine listings to appear.

The Google Webmasters website (www.google.com/webmasters) offers a collection of free tools, tutorials, and resources to help companies use SEO, as well as other techniques to promote a company and its online-based content. The Google Business Solutions website (www.google.com/services) also offers a collection of useful tools that can help a business promote itself online.

Keep in mind, even if you do everything related to achieving top search results using cutting-edge SEO techniques, this will be a time-consuming, and often costly, process. Because your YouTube content automatically (and quickly) gets listed on Google (and YouTube) when it's published, if you have limited resources, focus on creating the best video title, description, and keyword list possible to ensure your content will be easily found when someone uses the Google or YouTube Search tool, then focus your resources on other promotional and advertising opportunities that can increase your viewership quickly, such as paid online advertising.

ADVERTISE YOUR VIDEOS: IT COSTS MONEY BUT WORKS FAST

If you have the budget, seriously consider using paid search advertising (also referred to as keyword advertising) to promote your YouTube videos. This online advertising opportunity works quickly and is highly targeted and relatively inexpensive, plus you can measure the results in real time and then tweak your ad campaigns as needed to maximize the results.

Each of the popular social media services and internet search engines offer advertising opportunities. To learn more about how to create and launch an ad campaign on each service, visit:

YOUTUBE OFFERS ITS OWN ADVERTISING OPPORTUNITIES

As a YouTube content creator who produces and publishes video content on You-Tube, it certainly makes sense to promote that content to a highly targeted group of existing YouTube users. This is easily accomplished using video- and banner-based ads that can be purchased and displayed on YouTube (www.youtube.com/yt/advertise).

You'll discover that YouTube's video ads are cost-effective to run and can be targeted to a precise demographic (based on age, gender, interests, location, etc.). It's also possible to display YouTube ads exclusively to people accessing YouTube via their computer or a mobile device (each group represents about 50 percent of YouTube's overall audience).

Depending on the length of the video ad, in many cases, you pay for a view only if someone watches at least 30 seconds of the ad, or the entire ad. How much you spend producing the video ad, however, is entirely up to you, based on the production quality you want to showcase.

YouTube offers ten ad formats you can choose from, which include a combination of display ads and video-based ads of varying lengths. For example, a video ad can be 30 seconds long, or you can use what YouTube refers as "bumper ads," which are six seconds (or less) and can be used to quickly communicate a video-based message to a highly targeted audience. You can learn more about bumper ads by visiting: https://support.google.com/adwords/answer/7159363.

However, to learn more about each ad format available on YouTube and how each can best be used, visit: https://support.google.com/displayspecs. All YouTube adver-tising is managed by Google AdWords.

- *Bing*: https://advertise.bingads.microsoft.com
- *Facebook*: www.facebook.com/business/products/ads
- *Google and YouTube*: www.google.com/intl/en/ads
- *Instagram*: https://business.instagram.com/advertising
- *Twitter*: https://ads.twitter.com
- *Yahoo!*: https://advertising.yahoo.com/solutions

Depending on the ad platform, it's possible to create ads in a variety of formats that include a direct link to one of your videos or your YouTube channel page. Using these paid advertising opportunities, your ad(s) will be seen at the exact moment someone is searching for content based on a keyword or search phrase that matches keywords associated with your video content or channel.

These services typically work on a pay-per-click (PPC) basis, which means you pay only when someone clicks on the link featured within your ad. While thousands of people may see the ad, if only 100 of those people click on the ad's link, you only pay for those 100 clicks, not the thousands of views. For you, the advertiser, this is a very economical and risk-free way to promote your content and YouTube channel.

How much you wind up paying per click will vary greatly based on the popularity of keywords you select to associate with your ad and the ad format you choose, along with a handful of other factors. How much you pay per click is referred to as the cost per click. Other benefits to this type of advertising are that you can set your daily ad spending budget in advance, monitor the results in real time, and quickly edit your ads to improve the results being generated.

For example, if you know the cost per click is 50 cents, and you have a $100 per week budget, you know that in your best-case scenario, your ad will generate 200 responses per week. You also know that the people responding to your ad are well-qualified and part of your target demographic. This method works best when your cost per click is very low, but the click-through rate (the number of people who click on the link in your ad vs. the number of people who see the ad) is very high.

A Google AdWords ad, for example, includes a short headline, a web link (URL), and two short lines of text. When you advertise on Facebook, you're also allowed to incorporate a logo or thumbnail graphic within your ad. A Google Video Ad includes a short video, which you produce (that could link to your website or YouTube channel). This video will ultimately be seen before a viewer watches another YouTuber's video, which features related content.

What's not seen by the people viewing your ad, but that you as the advertiser need to create, is a list of highly specific keywords or tags related to whatever it is you're promoting. These keywords (along with the content within your ad), combined with a few other factors, will determine who sees your ad, where, and how often. The keywords you select are as important as the content of the ad itself.

Every character, word, and line within this type of ad should have a purpose, plus help to convey your message. The ad's goal is to attract attention and get someone to click on the provided link, potentially to immediately access a specific video, YouTube channel page, or your website that has your YouTube video embedded in it.

When establishing this type of ad campaign, it's possible to create, launch, and see the results from your ads within hours of launching a new campaign. It's also possible to easily run and track multiple campaigns simultaneously, on just one platform (such as Google), or separately, across multiple platforms (including Google, Yahoo!, Bing, and Facebook), each using a slightly different ad message or a different (but related) assortment of keywords.

REACH A LOCAL AUDIENCE IN A SPECIFIC GEOGRAPHIC AREA WITH GOOGLE ADWORDS EXPRESS

If your goal is to reach a local audience, Google has developed AdWords Express (www.google.com/adwords/express), which allows small businesses to reach potential customers within a specific (and local) geographic radius. This service takes advantage of the latest wireless mobile technologies to help you reach your audience at precisely the right moment, based on their location. Using AdWords Express, all you need to do is select a business category, write a two-line ad, and set your budget. Unlike traditional AdWords ads, there are no keywords to choose. AdWords Express ads also appear in conjunction with Google Maps, as well as other map-related apps used with smartphones and tablets.

When you run ads with AdWords Express to promote a video, for example, only people who do a search in your geographic area for a relevant topic will see your ad(s). AdWords Express ads can lead people directly to a video's URL, your YouTube channel, a company website, or a Google+ page (which is provided for free). Like AdWords, when you use AdWords Express, you only pay for clicks, you can start and end a campaign at any time, you control your spending, and you're given access to tracking and reporting tools for measuring an ad's results in real-time.

To learn more about pricing for this type of ad campaign, visit: www.google.com/adwords/express/pricing.

Keyword or search-based advertising is one of the most cost-effective ways small businesses can promote their company, product, service, or YouTube content online. Because Google AdWords is so closely related to YouTube, this is probably the best service to begin advertising with. However, getting back to the multifaceted approach concept, ultimately you may want to run ad campaigns using two or more of these services simultaneously to reach web surfers when and where they're looking for your product or service (or content that's related to your videos). Use paid online advertising in conjunction with the free promotional opportunities you have available by actively participating on social media (which is the focus of the next chapter).

SEEK THIRD-PARTY HELP

There's an entire industry of YouTube video marketing companies selling their services to promote and create audiences for YouTube videos. Some even have video production expertise and serve as a complete turnkey solution to creating high-quality videos, targeting a specific audience, managing a company's YouTube channel, and promoting videos to the company's target audience. The cost can range from several hundred dollars to tens of thousands of dollars per month.

One way to find low-cost help from YouTube video marketing experts is to seek out experienced freelancers using a service like Upwork (www.upwork.com). YouTube publishes a comprehensive Creator Services Directory, which can help you find companies that specialize in all aspects of channel management, branding, content creation, and content promotion/advertising. To access this free directory, visit: https://servicesdirectory.withyoutube.com.

Keep in mind, unless you have very specific needs that require the people you work with to be available to you in-person, you may find top-notch resources you can hire on a freelance or consulting basis located elsewhere in the country or in another country. For this type of work, focus on a company's capabilities, accomplishments, and pricing, as opposed to its geographic location.

Obviously, you need to review a company's portfolio or resume, evaluate its experience, ask to see samples of their successes, as well as obtain references from past clients. Ensure the person or company you plan to hire has expertise and experience working for a company in your industry, or truly understands your business and its unique needs.

You Can Buy Video Views, But Why?

There are many companies that simply sell video views at a specific cost. Be very careful before hiring one of these services, because many of them use fake YouTube accounts and other tools to generate artificial views. While the view counter associated with your video goes up, a human, much less someone from your target audience, never actually sees your content.

Plus, if you get caught generating fake views for your videos by YouTube, your video may be taken offline, or your YouTube channel could be suspended. In addition, most of these services will not help to improve your overall quality of engagement scores, which is now how YouTube gauges the quality, popularity, and success of a video.

When a company offers to sell you YouTube video views, such as 10,000 views for a flat-rate price, chances are you're being offered some type of scam. You're much better off hiring a company that will guarantee that the viewers they drive to your YouTube channel will be human, fall into your target demographic, and will actually watch your video(s). This can only be done by using proven video marketing and promotional techniques that you could do yourself, if you have the wherewithal, knowledge, and time to handle it.

To hire a company to handle your YouTube video marketing, and do it well, you'll pay a premium, but you're apt to see better results faster than doing it yourself, if you're inexperienced at managing YouTube video promotions.

Among the independent companies that offer legitimate services for helping to boost the popularity of a YouTube video (or YouTube channel) are: YouTubeBuzz (www.youtubebuzz.com), Virool (www.virool.com), Taboola (www.taboola.com), and Promolta (www.promolta.com), although you'll find many more listed within the YouTube Creator Services Directory.

20 PROVEN STRATEGIES FOR PROMOTING YOUTUBE VIDEOS

When it comes to marketing and promoting YouTube videos, your YouTube channel, and expanding your viewership, follow these 20 basic strategies:

1. Start by using the tools available through YouTube. For example, provide a detailed and accurate title and description for each of your videos and associate tags (keywords) that are directly relevant.

2. When creating a new listing or a video on YouTube, choose an attention-getting thumbnail image to accompany it. This is the graphic that people see in conjunction with a video's title and description when seeking out content on YouTube to watch. Instead of using a selected frame from your video, it's also possible to create a graphic from scratch to use as a thumbnail. To learn more about how to use video thumbnails as a promotional tool, read Vlog Nation's article, "How to Get More YouTube Views with Custom Thumbnail Images" (www.vlognation.com/custom-youtube-thumbnail-images). YouTube's Creator Academy also offers an informative video on this topic (https://creatoracademy.

youtube.com/page/lesson/thumbnails).

3. Use a call to action within your videos to encourage people to like, comment on, and share your videos, plus subscribe to your YouTube channel.

4. Begin by promoting your videos to the people you know, including your real-life friends, relatives, customers, and clients. Ask these people to watch your video(s) and share them with their online friends. Come up with a way to thank and reward people who share your videos.

5. Take advantage of the power and capabilities of the social media to promote your videos. Assign a spokesperson from your company, for example, to become active on Facebook, Twitter, and Instagram, as well as other relevant services. Be sure to create an online presence for your business on Facebook (www.facebook.com/business/learn/set-up-facebook-page), and then use that presence to promote your videos.

6. Incorporate (embed) your videos in your company's website and blog.

7. Share links to your videos with your existing customers or clients via opt-in email, and add an email signature that contains a link to your YouTube channel within the signature of all outgoing emails from your company.

8. Use public relations techniques and press releases to contact editors, reporters, and TV/radio producers to generate free media coverage for your videos in mainstream media, as well as in blogs that cater to your target audience.

9. Get bloggers to discuss or feature your videos or YouTube channel, or promote your channel by offering to be a guest contributor to a well-established blog that caters to your audience. To pinpoint influential and appropriate bloggers to contact, use an online-based blog directory, such as Blog Top Sites (www.blogtopsites.com), Best of the Web Blogs (https://blogs.botw.org), Blog Directory (http://blog-directory.org), BlogLog (www.bloglog.com), or Blog Search Engine (www.blogsearchengine.com).

10. Get your videos (and your YouTube Channel) listed with the major search engines, including Google, Yahoo!, and Bing, then focus on SEO strategies to get the best possible listing placements.

11. Try to collaborate on videos with other companies that are already using YouTube effectively and targeting the same audience but are not in direct competition with you. This will allow you to capture the attention of your collaborator's viewers and subscribers. There are also opportunities to pay for product placements or sponsor the videos of popular YouTubers to generate hype for your content, company, products, and/or services.

12. Start promoting your YouTube channel within your company's printed catalogs, on your company letterhead and business cards, and in your brochures, printed

and digital sales materials, and traditional advertising. Your channel should also be promoted in your product manuals, especially if you offer how-to videos for assembling and/or using your product(s).

13. Consider paying for advertising on YouTube, Google, Yahoo!, Bing, Facebook, Twitter, and/or Instagram to quickly generate views for your videos.

14. If you have the budget, hire a YouTube video marketing company to help you plan and implement a promotional campaign for your videos.

15. Give away free T-shirts (or other items) that promote your YouTube channel. When people wear the shirt in public, they become a walking promotional billboard. Encourage your employees to wear the shirt, and send them (for free) to your most loyal customers/clients.

16. Become active on other YouTube channels (as a commenter), Facebook pages, blogs, and online forums that cater to your target audience. Position yourself as a friendly expert in your field, answer other people's questions, and share valuable advice or knowledge. In the process, mention your YouTube channel (or a specific video on your channel) as a free, relevant, and informative resource.

17. Focus on creating high-quality and targeted content, not necessarily a large quantity of content, on your channel.

18. Within your videos, take advantage of Cards and End Screens to promote your website, as well as other (related) videos on your YouTube channel.

19. Create Playlists that include a collection of related videos, in a specific order, for your viewers to watch. This encourages viewers to watch several of your videos back-to-back, and makes it easier for them to find content on your channel that's relevant to what they're looking for.

20. Organize the content of your channel into categories with accurate and descriptive category headings, especially once your channel is populated with many individual videos. This makes it easier for people to find content they're looking for, plus it makes the appearance of your YouTube channel page look less cluttered and easier to navigate.

Are these 20 steps a bit time-consuming? Yes. Are they worth it? Absolutely. Follow the adage on "Measure twice, cut once" in this case and make the time for these 20 tricks.

MEET PERRY MARSHALL, AUTHOR OF *ULTIMATE GUIDE TO GOOGLE ADWORDS FOR BUSINESS*

As an expert in online advertising, Marshall uses YouTube as part of his virtual auto-responder and remarketing activities. In this interview, Marshsall focuses a lot on "remarketing," using YouTube as an advertising strategy.

If you're not familiar with remarketing, it can be used in many ways, such as when people visit your website. These visitors are then tracked. As those same people later watch YouTube videos as part of their ongoing online activities, your short (15- to 30-second) paid, video-based ads appear prior to certain videos that your audience watches.

"My point of view as a Google AdWords guy is that YouTube is generally a lot less competitive than Google AdWords for search. As an advertiser, when you use AdWords, most keywords are bid on and prices can get high. If you want to get some traction with your online ads, there's a great opportunity on YouTube right now. The easiest way to do it is to use remarketing via YouTube," says Marshall.

"'Remarketing' is when someone visits your website, they get 'cookied,' and ads for your company, products, or services start following them around as they surf the web and/or watch YouTube videos. Consumers sometimes find this annoying when it's too noticeable, but this is when remarketing is typically being done badly by the advertiser. I believe this is one of the best advertising approaches you can do online.

"Someone who visits your website is more likely to buy something from you than someone who has never been to your website," says Marshall. "So, using remarketing, you track who's been to your website, and ads for your products or services then appear elsewhere on the web, including on YouTube, based on your visitor's activities. I have found that the money you spend on remarketing will probably have a two to four times better return on investment than other forms of online advertising. I believe if you're new to online advertising, on YouTube or elsewhere, the safest place to start is with remarketing.

"In many cases, a consumer will need to be exposed to your website or message multiple times before making a purchase," continues Marshall. "Remarketing allows people who visit your website once to later see your ad/message multiple times in the future, as they go about their web surfing and YouTube video-watching activities.

"To best use remarketing on YouTube, you want to produce attention-getting pre-roll ads for YouTube viewers who have previously been to your website," recommends Marshall." [These are also referred to as bumper ads.] You also want listings for your full-length sponsored YouTube videos to show up on someone's page when they're watching YouTube.

"Generally, as the advertiser, you can determine how long after someone visits your website they'll continue seeing your ads elsewhere. In general, several days tends to work well," he adds. "I would not recommend going longer than a week or two to achieve the best results. Three days is generally an ideal time. Also, if you're using YouTube videos as a remarketing tool, use a variety of videos. Don't keep showing the same video, with the same offer, to the same viewer."

To learn more about YouTube advertising formats and how they're best used, visit: https://support.google.com/youtube/answer/2467968. More information can be found online within the YouTube Creator Academy (https://creatoracademy.youtube.com/page/lesson/ad-types).

For companies that are trying to build a large lead generation email list, paid pre-roll ads on YouTube can be useful and cost effective. Meanwhile, to drive traffic to your YouTube channel, you can also use the Google Display Network [https://support.google.com/adwords/answer/2404190?hl=en] to pay for ads that promote your individual videos or your channel.

As a YouTube channel host, whether or not you should monetize your channel and display ads from third parties in conjunction with your content, Marshall believes it all depends on what type of channel you've created and what the goals are for it. "If your channel receives a lot of traffic, but it's not targeted, and you're not trying to sell something yourself, it's probably to your advantage to monetize your YouTube channel, because it does not dilute your brand," explains Marshall. "On the other hand, if you are an authority or brand, and have a highly targeted or niche YouTube audience, it's probably to your disadvantage to accept third-party ads on your channel, because you will make more money marketing your own products or services to your audience."

Once you start advertising using Google AdWords or YouTube advertising, sales representatives from Google will start to call and email you consistently about expanding your paid ad campaign. "These people are not your friends," says Marshall. "If you choose to work with an independent ad agency to help you create, launch, and manage your online ad campaign, do your homework first.

"Do not give Google reps or independent agencies the benefit of the doubt, especially when they start making grandiose promises about the success your paid ad campaign could have," says Marshall. "There is no substitute for learning how online advertising works. I recommend you learn how to use Google AdWords or YouTube advertising yourself successfully, before you outsource the work to someone else. If someone is going to work on your account, ask that person to prove they've successfully made Google AdWords or YouTube advertising profitable on their own dime. Ask to see their stats."

To learn more about remarketing to YouTube viewers, visit: https://support. google.com/youtube/answer/2545661. Additional information about remarketing in conjunction with Google AdWords can be found at https://support.google. com/adwords/answer/2453998 and https://support.google.com/adwords/ answer/3124536. WordStream (www.wordstream.com/google-remarketing) also explains how remarketing works on its website, plus offers tools to help small businesses adopt this type of advertising strategy.

Chapter 15

Using Social Media to Build and Interact with Your Audience

IN THIS CHAPTER

- Ways social media can help you promote your channel
- Using social media to interact with your viewers and subscribers
- Overview of Facebook, Twitter, Instagram, and Reddit

As a business operator, at the very least, it's become important to have a presence on Facebook, then use a branded Facebook page to promote your business, interact informally with current customers/clients, and simultaneously reach potential new customers/clients with your content and online activities. Operating a Facebook page for your company is free. In addition to Facebook, many businesses have begun successfully using Twitter and/or Instagram, as well as other social media services for similar purposes.

When using social media on behalf of your business, think synergy! Your overall branding, messaging, target audience, and approach should remain consistent across your website, social media accounts, blog, electronic newsletter, direct emails with customers, during any other online interactions, and on your YouTube channel page.

In terms of promoting your YouTube channel, several main tasks can be handled using social media, including:

- Promote your latest YouTube videos by posting a link to the video within social media messages or posts. Viewers will follow the link and watch your content by visiting your YouTube channel page.
- Embed your latest YouTube videos directly onto your Facebook page, for example, so people can watch the content without leaving Facebook.
- Informally interact with your viewers and subscribers using social media, as opposed to within the comments section of each YouTube video.
- Attract new viewers to your YouTube channel.

If your business doesn't have a Facebook page, Twitter account, or other social media presence, set up separate accounts for your business. In other words, don't use personal social media accounts to handle business-related activities.

TAKE ADVANTAGE OF A FACEBOOK PAGE FOR YOUR BUSINESS

According to YouTube, more than 500 years' worth of YouTube video content is watched on Facebook every day, and 40 percent of people who watch these videos share video links with their online friends. You'll discover it's easy to promote your YouTube channel and its content by announcing new YouTube videos on your Facebook page and providing a link that leads to your YouTube channel. Alternately, you can embed your latest YouTube videos in your Facebook page so they can be watched on Facebook. At the same time, it's possible to use paid Facebook advertising to attract new viewers to your YouTube channel (or a specific video) and simultaneously boost your following on Facebook.

Creating a Facebook page for your business is free. To create a branded Facebook page for your business, follow the step-by-step process that's outlined when you visit: www.facebook.com/business/products/pages.

What's great about Facebook is you can:

- Customize the appearance of the page and include customized banner art and your company logo.
- Link the Facebook page with all your other online activities, including your company's website and YouTube channel.
- Tap into Facebook's more than two billion active users worldwide, yet cater to a highly targeted audience.
- Create an online community in which you can interact informally with your customers and potential customers, while these people can interact with each other in moderated conversations based around your products/services.

■ Take advantage of paid Facebook advertising to attract followers to your Facebook page, while simultaneously promoting your YouTube channel content, thus quickly building your following and viewership.

A Facebook page allows you to communicate with your audience using text, graphics, photos, videos, audio, and other multimedia content, yet requires no programming or graphic design skill to set up and operate. In fact, the operation of a business-oriented Facebook page is much like a personal Facebook page, but with a few additional options and features. There's even an official Facebook mobile app, called Facebook Pages Manager, that can be used to manage your company's Facebook page from anywhere, using an internet-connected smartphone or tablet. From a computer, you can set up and manage a company Facebook page using any web browser and by visiting www.facebook.com.

You can use a Facebook page to tell your company's story and humanize your business; showcase its products/services; interact with existing customers/clients; use it as a soft-sell and promotional tool to attract new customers/clients; share information; promote sales; and build customer loyalty around your company, its brand, and its products/services. The best way to use Facebook is to focus on building an interactive community, as opposed to just posting messages and content that your followers simply read or watch.

However, before establishing a Facebook page for your business, visit the Facebook pages of other businesses to see how each has formatted its page, discover what it's primarily being used for, and to determine how other companies are interacting with their Facebook page's followers and visitors. Learn what's possible. Then, just as you did for your YouTube channel, devise a specific plan for how you'll use your company's Facebook page. Develop an overall set of goals for the page and a plan for how you'll achieve those objectives.

Make sure your Facebook page is branded in a way that's consistent with your website, YouTube channel, and other online presence, and be sure to include your company's contact information prominently. Then, once the page is established, cross-promote your Facebook page with your website, YouTube channel, Twitter feed, Instagram feed, and other social media accounts. While some content can (and should) overlap, provide at least some unique content on each platform, giving visitors a reason to follow your business on multiple social media services.

Keep in mind, operating a company-oriented Facebook page takes time. You'll need time to set up, establish, and customize your presence on Facebook, then invest time on an ongoing basis to update the page with new content, moderate public comments and posts created by others, and interact with your Facebook followers. This interaction will help you build loyalty, but will likely be the most time-consuming, since timely and personalized responses to questions and comments will be expected.

Don't just establish a free Facebook page and abandon it, allowing your followers and visitors to interact freely, in an unmoderated forum. Not only will this give the people who access your Facebook page the impression that you don't care about them or your content, but it could quickly lead to misinformation or negative information being published about your company and its products/services. People visiting the page will potentially post information that may or may not be correct, and there won't be anyone from your company correcting or moderating what's being said in this public forum.

Keep in mind that just about everything published on a Facebook page, and within the profile that's associated with a Facebook page, becomes searchable. So, if someone does a Facebook or Google search about your company or its products/services, they could easily come across negative posts that have been published on your Facebook page if no one from your company is moderating the content.

BECOME ACTIVE ON OTHER FACEBOOK PAGES

Facebook hosts thousands and thousands of independent Facebook pages that focus on specific topics and/or that cater to niche audiences. Using Facebook's search tool, find existing pages that cater to the same target audience that you're trying to reach and become active on those pages.

As an active participant, position yourself as an expert in your field, or someone who is knowledgeable about a specific topic, and post relevant messages that share valuable information, plus answer other peoples' questions in public forums. When explaining how to do something or conveying a relevant piece of information, subtly work a mention of your YouTube channel, a specific YouTube video, or your company into the message, and state that the provided link offers additional information that the reader will find helpful.

Each Facebook page is independently operated by a person, organization, or company and has its own etiquette in terms of the types of content that people can post, so be sure to follow these guidelines. When people start seeing your name and messages repeatedly on a Facebook page that they frequent, they're more apt to follow links you recommend that lead to your YouTube channel or specific YouTube videos.

How to Publish a YouTube Video on a Facebook Page

One of the great things about operating a Facebook page is that YouTube videos from your channel can be embedded in the page very easily. Then, someone can view your video(s) without leaving Facebook, yet YouTube tracks all the video views and interactions, just as it does when someone watches videos from your YouTube channel.

To embed a YouTube video on a Facebook page, follow these steps:

1. Log in to your YouTube channel, and select the video you want to share.
2. Click on the "Share" button associated with the video.
3. From the Share menu, select the "Facebook" option.
4. Click on the "Share on Your Timeline" pull-down menu, and choose the "Share on a Page You Manage" option.
5. From the Share on Facebook window, make sure your company's Facebook page is selected, then choose the person the video will be posted by from the "Posting As" pull-down menu.
6. Within the "Say Something About This..." field, type a text-based message that will appear on Facebook, in conjunction with the video. For example, say something like, "Please watch our latest YouTube video, which discusses . . ." Keep the message short and simple so that it entices someone to watch the video.
7. Click on the "Post to Facebook" button to publish your video on your company's Facebook page as a new, separate, and searchable public post.

In addition to promoting your newest YouTube videos on your Facebook page, you can also use this as a platform to promote older videos that your Facebook followers might have missed. For example, in conjunction with an older video, post a message that says, "Back in [insert date], we published this video, which explains [insert topic]. If you missed it, be sure to watch it now. It provides [list benefits to the viewer]."

USE TWITTER AS A YOUTUBE PROMOTIONAL TOOL

In addition to Facebook, one of the more popular social media platforms is Twitter. Thus, it's a good idea to create a dedicated Twitter account for your business that includes your company's name as its unique Twitter username (@YourCompanyName).

To set up a free Twitter account for your business, from any computer's web browser, visit www.twitter.com and click on the "Sign Up" button that's displayed in the top-right corner of the browser window. Be sure to brand your Twitter account by using your company logo as the account's profile image, and use a custom graphic as the header photo. This can be done by customizing your profile. Also within the profile, be sure to include a short but attention-grabbing description of your company. A Twitter profile also allows you to include one website URL. Use this for your company's website, then within the bio field, include your YouTube channel's URL as part of the 180-character sentence you use to describe your company and what it offers.

When publishing individual tweets (outgoing and public messages), you're limited to 280 characters of text, but you can also embed a website URL, photo, video clip, animated GIF, poll, and/or your exact location. Thus, you're able to compose just one short sentence to get your message across to your followers and the general public.

Companies have gotten very creative when devising innovative ways to share information on Twitter. For example, some companies publish online-only sales or promotions on a regular basis. These are sales/promotions that can only be found within a company's Twitter feed—not on its website or Facebook page, for example.

When it comes to promoting YouTube content on Twitter, some of the things you can do include:

- Publish a tweet (a public Twitter message) that promotes each new video on your YouTube channel, and embed a link to the video within the message.
- Include a specially edited, five- to ten-second "preview" of the YouTube video within the tweet to entice people to watch it.
- Post relevant hashtags (#keyword) within the tweet, allowing people who are not already following you on Twitter to easily find the tweet that promotes your video. Based on the number of characters remaining in your tweet, add as many relevant hashtags as possible.
- Ask your Twitter followers to send you questions via Twitter if you're planning to produce a question-and-answer-format video. The questions should be related to your company, product/service, or any related topic that they'd like you to answer. Instruct them to use a specific hashtag within the message and address it to your company's Twitter account (using the @username format).
- Ask people to retweet your tweets that promote your new video(s). This basically serves as word-of-mouth advertising. If you have influencers following you on Twitter, and they opt to retweet one or more of your tweets, your message(s) could immediately be seen by thousands of people (or more).
- Allow people to respond to your YouTube videos on Twitter by encouraging them to post their feedback, by addressing it to your company (using the @username format), or by including a specific hashtag within their messages.
- Take advantage of paid Twitter advertising (https://ads.twitter.com) to promote the tweet(s) that include links to your YouTube videos. This is a quick and inexpensive way to quickly increase video views and build your company's Twitter following. You can also use Twitter Business, which for a flat monthly fee of $99

makes it easy to automatically promote your tweets. (For more information, visit: https://business.twitter.com/en/a/amplify-your-message-automatically.html.)

In addition to using Twitter to promote your YouTube videos, the best way to attract and retain Twitter followers is to use this platform to share short tidbits of information that your audience will find interesting and valuable. If a viewer knows that exclusive sales will be listed each week and being a Twitter follower is the only way they can benefit from these sales, this is a huge incentive for them to follow your company on Twitter. Use this as a forum to share content that's exclusive to Twitter. In other words, don't always publish the same messages on Facebook, Twitter, Instagram, and on your other social media accounts, or there will be no reason for people to follow your company on all these services.

USE INSTAGRAM AS A PROMOTIONAL TOOL

In many ways, Instagram and Twitter are very similar. However, while Twitter focuses on each tweet's 280-character text-based message (that can include a photo or video clip, for example), the focus of Instagram is on showcasing photos or video clips that can be accompanied by a short, text-based caption or message. Instagram is also designed to be accessed primarily from a smartphone or tablet (using the official Instagram mobile app), although it can also be accessed using a computer's web browser.

Facebook owns and operates Instagram, but has thus far kept it an independent social media service. It's possible, however, to link your company's Instagram account to your Facebook account so when you publish something on Instagram, it simultaneously and automatically also gets published on Facebook (and if you choose, Twitter and Tumblr as well).

The easiest way to set up and manage an Instagram account is to download and install the official Instagram app on your mobile device, launch the app, and choose the "Sign Up" option. Follow the account setup process, and be sure to customize and brand your account by creating a unique username that incorporates your company name, then use your company logo as your account's profile photo. For simplicity's sake, try to use the same username for all your company's social media accounts.

Once your account is set up, access your account settings by clicking on the "Profile" icon, then tap on the "Edit Profile" button. Just as with Twitter, your profile can include one website URL; however, you can also add a second URL for your YouTube channel within the Info field that's used to describe yourself or your business. Be sure to click on the "Try Instagram Business Tools" option to learn about how you can further customize your Instagram account and gain access to analytics tools to help you build and manage your company's Instagram following. Similar information can be found using any web browser, by visiting: https://business.instagram.com.

Because Instagram puts an emphasis on displaying photos and video clips, this can be used to your advantage when promoting your YouTube channel and its content. For example, when promoting a new YouTube video, an Instagram message can showcase the same thumbnail image from your new video and include a text-based message that encourages people to check out your latest video. The message should also include a hyperlink (URL address) to the video. Of course, you can also create postings that promote your company's YouTube channel and include a link to the channel's main page or to a specific playlist, as opposed to a specific video.

USE PRIVATE MESSAGING TO INTERACT WITH INDIVIDUAL PEOPLE

Facebook, Twitter, and Instagram, for example, all provide an option to publish content that's public. In other words, it can be seen by everyone and is searchable, so even people who don't follow you on a specific social media platform could stumble on your account and its contents by using a keyword or hashtag search.

In addition, these and other social media services allow for private messages to be exchanged between two parties. This provides an opportunity to communicate directly with individual people. Keep in mind, if you opt to use this functionality, your company spokesperson should understand that they're representing your company with each message they send or respond to. Make it clear what types of customer relations and/or technical support issues your company spokesperson should handle via private messages on social media, and instruct the spokesperson to maintain a professional demeanor at all times, just as they would when communicating with a customer or potential customer in person, by telephone, or via direct email.

If you opt to communicate with people via private messaging, those who contact you will expect a prompt and personalized response. So, unless you're able and willing to provide this type of interaction via social media, encourage your followers to contact you by calling your company's phone number or by sending an email message instead. Social media provides a powerful forum for interacting with large groups of people at once (publicly) or on a one-to-one basis (publicly or privately). However, it's important to offer the information and attention to your audience that they want, need, and expect, or your social media presence could wind up becoming detrimental to your company.

Another option is to create a short video clip (a preview of your YouTube video) and include that clip within an Instagram posting to promote a newly published video. Then, if you have the budget, consider using paid Instagram advertising to promote your YouTube content and Instagram account. To learn more about Instagram advertising opportunities, visit: https://business.instagram.com/advertising. For example, a video-based Instagram ad can be up to 60 seconds long and used to preview YouTube content.

To build and maintain an Instagram following for your business account, consider using Instagram as a tool to share photos and video clips related to your company, as well as its products/services. As with any social media presence, you want to provide content that will be considered valuable and of interest to your target audience.

Since this platform focuses on sharing photos and videos, you can use it to humanize your company by offering behind-the-scenes photos taken at your offices or manufacturing facility, and to introduce your followers to key personnel from your company in an informal way. You can also use posts to share details about your products/services, to solicit feedback from your audience, and to answer questions or interact with your customers and perspective customers as a group. To encourage people to follow your Instagram account, in addition to your other social media accounts, try to develop and publish content that's exclusive to Instagram.

Except for optional paid advertising, creating and managing an Instagram account for your company is free. The only requirement is a time commitment to create and manage the account, develop unique content, and interact with your followers. Again, be sure to adopt a synergistic approach to the appearance, branding, and messaging that you convey on Instagram, so it's in line with your other online activities and meets the expectations of your target audience.

USE REDDIT AS A PROMOTIONAL TOOL FOR YOUR VIDEOS

Reddit (www.reddit.com) is an interactive online forum that allows people to share articles, information, news stories, and videos that they believe will appeal to other people. The entire Reddit platform is based around three core activities—share, vote, and discuss.

Anyone can share an article, video, or news story, for example, and showcase it within one of Reddit's topic-related online communities (also known as "subreddits").

Other Reddit users can then vote on the story (or content) if it's something they like or find interesting, plus share their own ideas, comments, and feedback. The more positive votes, feedback, and interaction a posting receives, the more prominence it gets on the Reddit platform and the more exposure it ultimately receives. The trick is to target your content to a specific audience on Reddit that will find it interesting and rate it positively.

Before posting content on Reddit that represents your company or YouTube channel, be sure to spend time exploring this service to learn its unique etiquette, as well as the types of content that Reddit users are interested in. For example, unless you're paying for advertising, this platform is not meant to be used to publish content with a strong sales approach. It's more for disseminating information that readers will find informative, educational, or entertaining, for example.

In addition to posting a message about a new YouTube video, it's possible to embed the video in a Reddit posting. To learn how to do this, visit: https://about.reddit.com/embed_infographic.pdf.

Once you set up a free Reddit account, posting new content is quick and easy. To learn more about how to publish content on Reddit and have it gain traction with a potentially large audience, visit: https://about.reddit.com/publishers.

OPPORTUNITIES OFFERED BY OTHER SOCIAL MEDIA SERVICES

The internet is chock full of online forums and social media services that cater to specialized audiences or that focus on distributing specific types of content. While Facebook, Twitter, and Instagram continue to be among the most popular social media services around the world, others tend to become trendy for months at a time, or launch and quickly gain popularity among specific types of people.

Each time a company chooses to establish a presence on a social media platform, this requires time and resources on an ongoing basis. Unless you have one or more full-time employees dedicated to managing your company's social media presence across multiple platforms, pick which service(s) offer the most potential for reaching the largest group of people within your target audience, and offer the tools and features your company will find useful for achieving its unique goals.

Keep in mind, each social media service offers something that's unique to its users or presents specific types of content in a unique way. Take advantage of this to share compelling, creative, engaging, entertaining, and/or informative content that will appeal to your target audience by using the strength(s) of the social media platform you're using.

Maintaining a presence on some social media platforms will require more time to manage than others. Also, the more interaction you opt to have with your online followers, the more time commitment will be required.

Don't overextend your resources by attempting to manage an online presence on all popular social media services at once. Instead, create and build a presence on one of the more popular services, such as Facebook or Twitter. Then once it's up and running and attracting a growing following, consider expanding your company's presence onto additional services. At no point should the quality of your content or the engagement with your online followers become compromised due to limited time or resources.

Depending on what your goals are and the audience you'd like to reach, other popular social media services you might want your company to become active on include:

- *Google+* (http://plus.google.com). This robust online platform (somewhat similar to Facebook) offers many different ways for a company to interact with an audience using a company account and branded Google+ page, for example. At the same time you create a YouTube channel using a Google account, a Google+ account is automatically set up for you. Invest the time to customize and brand the account, even if all you use it for is to tell people about your company's YouTube channel.

- *LinkedIn* (www.linkedin.com). This popular social media platform is designed for business professionals to be a networking and information exchange tool.

- *Pinterest* (www.pinterest.com). Used to share groups of related photos and video clips, Pinterest's core user base is primarily adult women looking for visual inspiration pertaining to specific topics.

- *SnapChat* (www.snapchat.com). Targeted more to young adults, this service is used for sharing photos, video clips, and text messages via a mobile device. The content "self-destructs" after the recipient has viewed it.

- *Tumblr* (www.tumblr.com). This easy-to-use blogging tool has its own vast online community. Creating a customized Tumblr page requires no programming, graphic design skill, or even formatting to share text, photos, videos, and other content. In fact, if you know how to operate a word processor and surf the web, you have the skill set needed to create and manage a presence on Tumblr.

YouTube's Creator Academy discusses how to use social media to promote your YouTube content. To watch this instructional video, visit: https://creatoracademy. youtube.com/page/lesson/reach-beyond.

MEET KIM WALSH PHILLIPS, CEO OF ELITE DIGITAL GROUP

Personal Website: http://kimwalshphillips.com
Company Website: https://elitedigitalgroup.com

In addition to being an award-winning speaker and author, Kim Walsh Phillips is the CEO of Elite Digital Group (https://elitedigitalgroup.com), a high-end, direct-response social media agency that works primarily with multimillion-dollar companies and high-profile clients. In addition to being an expert on all things social media, Walsh Phillips has extensive experience assisting her clients in fully using YouTube.

"Everything we do for our clients is measurable. When it comes to YouTube, we always want to determine who we're trying to reach, exactly what we want to accomplish, and what we want the viewers to do. We use YouTube to deliver content in a video format, because we have found that video can be used to quickly build trust, authority, and credibility," explains Walsh Phillips. "When it comes to building trust, authority, and credibility, using video is second only to meeting people in person."

She adds, "The first step, however, is to define a clear goal about what you want to accomplish. Next, consider carefully how you can best leverage video-based content to accomplish the specific goal. Then build content based around that one big idea. Each video, however, should focus on just one aspect of that big idea or topic. There are many types of video content that can be used on a YouTube channel, but for us, it always focuses on that one big idea. The biggest mistake I see businesses make when they opt to use video and YouTube is they begin creating content and populating their YouTube channel, but they don't have a clear idea about what they're trying to accomplish."

As a small-business operator or entrepreneur, consider using your YouTube channel to build and showcase your expertise. "As soon as you try to incorporate too many ideas into a single video, you're going to quickly lose your audience," states Walsh Phillips. "At the end of each video, always, always, always include a call to action. I personally believe the call to actions should include a link to go somewhere else, because I believe it's important to drive your audience to a media platform that you own and fully control, like your website, blog, or opt-in email list. Do this as quickly and succinctly as you can, and within your video, give viewers a definite and enticing reason why they should follow through and complete your call to action."

For companies working with a tight budget, Walsh Phillips believes a company can use low-cost technologies to create compelling video content, without hiring an expensive video production team or agency. "Use the free and low-cost tools that are available, as long as that makes sense for you and your business. When you start having disposable income, then you can hire a production crew. However, just because you're creating your own video content, does not mean that your videos can look or sound like garbage.

"The appearance and audio quality of your videos need to be professional, and you must have your thoughts and ideas mapped out ahead of time so your videos flow well and have a defined strategy," says Walsh Phillips "If you need help with video editing, there are a lot of low-cost resources online, like Upwork [www.upwork.com], HireMyMom [www.hiremymom.com], or Thumbtack [www.thumbtack.com], where you can find and hire freelance content creators, videographers, and video editors, for example."

When it comes to creating your YouTube content, you never want to guess about what your target audience wants. Walsh Phillips explains, "Content should be based on what you know your audience wants, and there are some great ways to find this out. For example, you can ask your customers or clients in person. You can conduct an online survey, or you can solicit information about peoples' interest via social media.

"One site I really love is called Answer the Public [www.answerthepublic.com]," says Walsh Phillips. "You can enter any topic and instantly see a list of questions that people are asking online about your topic, based on real-time Google and other search engine searches. Another great tool is Buzzsumo [http://buzzsumo.com], which can be used to determine the most popular posts across all social media and help you determine what people are really interested in. If you're at a loss for content or video topic ideas, simply determine what your audience wants to know about in regard to your topic or area of expertise, then answer their most commonly asked questions."

One thing Walsh Phillips recommends against is creating content, then trying to find an audience for it. "Instead, figure out what your audience wants to know and incorporate that into your content. In terms of video length, test out what works for your audience, based on the type of content you're creating. We have some clients that do very well by producing long-length video content and publishing it on YouTube. We have other clients, however, where the maximum length of their videos is less than three minutes before interest and engagement diminishes," said Walsh Phillips.

As you develop titles, descriptions, and keywords for your YouTube videos, again you should focus on what people are currently searching for. "Use a title that describes what your video is all about," says Walsh Phillips. "People want to know that what they're interested in will be addressed or answered within your video. Refrain from using click-bait or clever titles, because that approach does not help you build a trusting relationship with your audience."

If you want your videos to be found organically when people are doing searches on YouTube or Google, the level of engagement your videos receives is essential. In this case, "likes," comments, and channel subscribers are critical. "I have discovered that if you want to continue building your channel over time, it's important to publish new content on your channel at least once per week, or more often, if possible," says Walsh Phillips. "The most important thing, however, is to be consistent with your channel and in the quality and type of content you provide.

"Find out what your target audience wants, create great content, and publish the content on a consistent basis," she adds. "I love the idea of branding videos and a YouTube channel, especially if you're trying to draw in potential customers and clients, or attempting to build relationships. Once your YouTube channel is operational, track the results of your activities on an ongoing basis."

One final piece of advice Walsh Phillips offers regarding YouTube is to develop partnerships to help build your audience. "Seek out others who are in your industry or serve your market, but are not direct competitors. Team up with these people and develop and cross-promote YouTube content with them," says Walsh Phillips. "For example, if you're an insurance agent, find an accountant or attorney in your area who you can interview in one or more of your videos, then have those people help promote the videos using their respective social media activities. Perhaps you could also appear as an expert in their videos, on their YouTube channel. Leverage these partnerships to reach more people and build stronger relationships. This is a strategy that I have been using very successfully for years."

Go Live with Your Broadcasts

There are countless ways you can use recorded YouTube videos to communicate and convey information to your target audience by populating your YouTube channel with a plethora of quality and unique content. To retain the attention of your audience, keeping your recorded videos short (under six minutes) is key. This requires you to plan your videos, figure out the most efficient way to communicate information, record your content, then edit your productions so they flow smoothly and look professional.

The pre-production, production, post-production, publishing, and promotion for each of your videos is going to take time and resources. Yet what you'll discover is that the videos themselves are a passive form of media. In other words, your audience simply watches the content on their screen. Any interaction between the viewer and your content happens if the viewer opts to like or share the video, or leave a comment. As you know, the comments section of a video can become a dialog between you and your viewers, and/or between groups of your viewers, when comments are published, then replied to.

Yet another approach to sharing content with your audience is to stream live broadcasts. As the name implies, a live broadcast happens in real time. There's no delay, editing, or redos. Anything you say or do on camera is transmitted via the internet and is seen by your audience as it happens.

Hosting a live broadcast has several potential advantages, including:

- A live broadcast can be any length.
- You can have real-time interaction with audience members.
- There's no post-production (editing) unless you opt to record the live broadcast and then edit it before you publish it on your YouTube channel for people to watch lateron an on-demand basis.

More and more companies are utilizing live broadcasts to share special events, press conferences, seminars, live question and answer sessions, or product launches, for example, with an audience.

LIVE BROADCAST CONSIDERATIONS

Until relatively recently, before YouTube Live and similar services were introduced, hosting a live broadcast via the internet was a costly endeavor. Today, you need little more than a computer or mobile device that's equipped with a camera and a high-speed internet connection. Very little additional equipment is required. However, just like when recording YouTube videos, your lighting, sound quality, and background continue to be important considerations.

From a lighting standpoint, use the same type of lighting setup you'd use to record a video. Whomever and whatever is being shown in the broadcast should be well and evenly lit and not hindered by unwanted shadows.

In terms of sound, the people who will be speaking during your live broadcast need to be heard clearly. However, any ambient or background noise where you'll be broadcasting from should not be heard at all. Thus, it's necessary to choose the right type of microphone(s), which typically means that you do not rely on the microphone that's built into your computer or mobile device. Refer to Chapter 6, "The Equipment You'll Need," for more information on lighting and sound equipment.

As for the camera to be used for a live broadcast, most computers and mobile devices are now equipped with an HD-quality camera, or you can easily connect an HD webcam to your computer. In most situations, this will be adequate, as long as you're able to connect external microphones as needed. However, to improve the quality of your broadcast, you might consider connecting a higher-resolution and more powerful camera to your computer.

A SPECIALTY CAMERA MIGHT BE USEFUL FOR LIVE BROADCASTS

There are a handful of specialty cameras on the market that connect directly to your computer (or even a mobile device) but provide added functionality that's useful when hosting a live broadcast. For example, there's the Mevo camera ($399 to $599, www.getmevo.com).

This highly portable, battery-powered camera offers 4K resolution (at 30 frames per second) for recording, and 1080p resolution (at up to 30 frames per second) for streaming. The camera specializes in producing live streaming broadcasts, because it simulates shooting with multiple cameras, and via a proprietary mobile app, allows a "director" to instantly switch between shots. To view sample videos and live broadcasts shot with this camera, visit: https://getmevo.com/videoexamples.

If you're broadcasting from a special event, consider using both a regular camera, as well as a 360-degree camera, to provide your viewers with a truly immersive experience, as if they were at the event live. Refer to Chapter 7, "Selecting the Right Video Camera," for more information on choosing the most appropriate cameras to use for live broadcasts and when shooting recorded content.

CHOOSING A SERVICE TO HOST YOUR LIVE BROADCASTS

When it comes to broadcasting live via the internet, if you already have a YouTube channel and a following on YouTube, using the YouTube Live service probably makes the most sense. It's free and tied directly to your YouTube channel. However, Facebook, Twitter, and Instagram have all introduced live broadcasting capabilities, plus a handful of independent online services make hosting live broadcasts via the internet a straightforward process that can be done from virtually anywhere.

Just some of the specialized services that can be used to host live streaming broadcasts include:

- *Cisco WebEx:* www.webex.com
- *GoToMeeting:* www.gotomeeting.com
- *Live.me:* www.live.me (www.twitch.tv)
- *LiveSteam:* www.livestream.com

- *Periscope:* www.periscope.tv
- *YouNow:* www.younow.com

Some specialized services used to host live-streaming broadcasts are designed to work from almost any PC or Mac and require no specialized software. Everything is done from your web browser. The consumer-oriented services tend to be free for broadcasters and viewers alike, while some of the higher-end and business-oriented service are fee-based for the broadcasters. You'll also discover some services were designed to host broadcasts using an internet-connected smartphone or tablet, in conjunction with a proprietary mobile app.

PRE-BROADCAST CONSIDERATIONS

In addition to lighting and sound considerations, and making sure the available internet connection is both high-speed and stable, be sure to choose an appropriate location to broadcast from.

Whatever is in the background should not be distracting. Plus, you want to be able to control the lighting and ambient sound in that location during the broadcast. Just like when shooting a video, airplanes flying overhead, people talking in the background, sounds from an air conditioner or machinery, or traffic from outside could all generate noise that will be distracting to your audience.

HIGH-SPEED INTERNET IS ABSOLUTELY REQUIRED

To host a successful live broadcast via the internet, the computer or mobile device you're using to broadcast must have a stable and high-speed internet connection. Otherwise, your live stream will likely be glitchy, the connection will drop in and out, and your audience will quickly become frustrated and leave.

When hosting a broadcast related to your business from any location, do not rely on a public wifi hotspot or a cellular data connection (3G, 4G, or LTE). These types of internet connections typically can't handle the bandwidth required for a live video broadcast.

Before hosting any live broadcast, always test your internet connection, as well as the lighting and sound, to make sure everything is working properly.

Consider your live broadcasts to be like giving a live presentation or public speaking in front of a large group. Preparation is essential. Don't just wing it. Unless you're skilled at using a teleprompter and reading a speech word for word in a manner that seems natural, develop an outline for what you want to cover during the broadcast, as well as a timeline. This should be written out in advance, and everyone appearing in the broadcast (and working behind the scenes) should be well-rehearsed and familiar with the plan.

For example, if you're planning a 30-minute live broadcast to introduce a new product to your audience, Figure 16–1 shows what a timeline for the broadcast might look like. When promoting your broadcast, and at the beginning of it, be sure to explain:

- What exactly will be covered. Set expectations, but make sure you can live up to them.
- Why your audience should not miss the live broadcast. What's in it for them? Focus on the benefits to your audience.
- How long the broadcast is scheduled to last.
- How your audience can interact during and after the broadcast.

Also plan to include a call to action several times during your live broadcast based on what you want your audience to do while either watching it or immediately after the broadcast. If you want them to place an order for your new product, give them an

Time	Description
0:00 – 0:03	Welcome message from the host and introduction of the company CEO and product manager
0:03 – 10:00	Opening remarks from CEO
10:00 – 13:00	Product manager introduces the new product
13:00 – 22:00	Product demonstration
22:00 – 24:00	Product pricing and release schedule revealed
24:00 – 29:00	Q&A
29:00 – 30:00	Thank audience and promote call to action

FIGURE 16–1. Plan your live broadcast minute by minute.

incentive to do this immediately (such as a discount and/or free shipping on orders placed within one hour of the broadcast).

Provide your audience with specific, yet easy to follow, directions on how to place their order. For example, state, "To receive a 20 percent discount on your order, within the next 60 minutes, be sure to call our toll-free number at (800) 555-5555, or visit our website at www.[YourCompanyName].com, and use promotion code: [insert code] at checkout."

When planning your live broadcasts, unless the host (you or your company spokesperson) is comfortable looking directly into a camera and speaking with a virtual audience, consider including a co-host. This allows two people to interact with each other, as well as the virtual audience, which typically makes the hosts come across more naturally.

During your pre-planning, plan on some viewers arriving late to the broadcast. Without disrupting the flow or being overly repetitive, devise a way to offer a few recaps during the broadcast, so latecomers can quickly get up to speed on what's transpiring and being covered.

Also, prior to promoting or hosting a live broadcast, compose a compelling, attention-getting title and description, and come up with an eye-catching image thumbnail that will be used to promote the broadcast on YouTube.

Especially if you're planning your first live broadcast, personally invite a handful of friends, family members, co-workers, or loyal customers to attend so you're guaranteed an audience from the moment the live broadcast begins. Over time, you'll discover it's easier to build a large audience for live broadcasts once you have a loyal YouTube following and begin hosting regularly scheduled live broadcasts—once per week or once per month, for example.

Hosting a live broadcast gives you certain freedoms not offered by recorded video content, including a longer length format and the ability to interact with your audience in real time. Plan the content of your live broadcasts so it capitalizes on these benefits.

Consider Live Interaction with the Audience

Depending on which service you'll use to host your live broadcasts, there will likely be opportunities for your audience members to interact with the hosts. This might be via a live, text-based chat room that's hosted in conjunction with the broadcast. In this case, the host can read questions or messages from audience members in real time, and respond to those questions or comments.

If interaction is being done using this method, consider assigning someone from your company who is off-camera to moderate the chat room, and select which questions or comments the host will address and in what order. This person is called a moderator, and when using YouTube Live can also remove or flag comments, plus put users in a "time-out" or block them altogether from the broadcast.

Having a separate moderator allows the host to focus on their broadcast, yet still include interaction from the audience without this process becoming a distraction or slowing down the flow.

Another option that may be available is the ability to "guest" one viewer at a time. This feature allows the host to select one audience member and have that person use their own computer or mobile device's camera and microphone to become part of the live broadcast. The rest of the audience will see is a split screen with the host on one side of the screen and the guest on the other. The host can bring on and disconnect the guest at their leisure and see a listing of viewers who have voluntarily added themselves to the guest que to participate.

If you opt to involve your audience members during a broadcast, remember that everything is live and anything could happen. The hosts should be prepared for this, and be able to calmly steer the flow of the broadcast, without going off-topic. Since there's no way to edit out content during a live broadcast, be prepared for a question or comment that's inappropriate or unrelated to the topic at hand. Determine in advance how you'll politely and professionally deal with unexpected occurrences or distractions, especially when audience members are involved.

Interacting live with your audience makes your viewers feel more involved, plus it gives them the opportunity to interact with your host(s) and get their questions answered or their concerns addressed in real-time. Chances are, if one of your viewers has a question, at least a handful of other viewers will have that same question, and it might not be something you thought to address on your own.

Be prepared to answer questions and address concerns in the most accurate and concise way possible. Address the person asking each question by name, and thank them for their participation. Make each person feel like a valuable contributor to the broadcast, but be mindful that you have an entire audience watching, so don't overly personalize your answers.

Add Pre-Produced Content to Live Broadcasts

For the most part, making your audience watch stagnant "talking heads" for more than a few minutes will get very boring, regardless of the topics you're discussing. Built into the broadcasting tools offered by YouTube Live and other services is the ability to add pre-produced production elements to the broadcast, such as text-based titles, a PowerPoint digital slide presentation (with animations), or pre-recorded video clips. You're also able to broadcast live screen sharing, so people can see what's on your computer's screen in real time. This works well for software demonstrations, for example.

As you're pre-planning your live broadcasts, consider what additional elements you can use to make your programming more visually engaging and interesting, especially if you're only using one pre-positioned camera (or webcam) that's continuously focused on your host(s). Of course, you should practice using these additional production elements before your live broadcast.

Promote Your Live Broadcasts in Advance

Even if your YouTube subscribers and viewers want you to host a live broadcast, it's essential that you tell them about it well in advance. You'll need to choose the most convenient date and time for your audience to participate, then start promoting the live broadcast at least a week or two in advance.

In addition to promoting the live broadcast within your YouTube videos and their respective descriptions, and in the About section and/or the channel artwork related to your YouTube channel, also rely on social media to help you get the word out about each live broadcast.

SCHEDULING CONSIDERATIONS

It's true that if you record the live broadcast and publish it on your You-Tube channel, anyone can later watch the broadcast, any time, on an on-demand basis. However, especially if you're offering a valuable incentive for people who watch the broadcast live, be sure to schedule it on a date and time that best caters to your target audience, keeping time zone considerations in mind.

If you're trying to reach businesspeople while they're at work, scheduling your broadcast to be held on a weekday, during business hours, clearly makes sense. However, if you're trying to reach viewers during their leisure time, when they typically access YouTube, consider scheduling your broadcast for a weekday evening, but not during peak dinner hours, or when your viewers may be out running errands or at the gym, for example.

Based on your target audience, if you can't come up with one good day and time to host a live broadcast, consider hosting the same broadcast live, but two or three times on a specific date, to accommodate multiple time zones. Always cater to the needs and scheduling constraints of your target audience.

In a nutshell, share the following details when promoting a live broadcast:

- What the broadcast is all about
- Who should watch it
- How each viewer will benefit by watching (i.e., why someone should watch it)
- When the broadcast will take place (provide the date and time, as well as the time zone, since you may be appealing to a national or worldwide audience)
- How someone can access the broadcast
- How someone can submit their question if you'll be soliciting questions in advance

Focus on who the broadcast will appeal to and what it will offer to attendees. Promote the benefits and incentives you're offering to attendees and explain how someone can watch (and potentially participate) in a live broadcast.

INTRODUCTION TO YOUTUBE LIVE

Since the focus of this book is on how to create a YouTube channel and then produce compelling and high-quality content for your audience, our emphasis will be on YouTube Live, although as you now know, many other live broadcasting options are available.

Choose a live broadcasting service that offers the tools you need to host the highest-quality and most professional-looking broadcast possible, while catering to the wants and needs of your audience. Again, if the primary audience for your live broadcast will be your YouTube channel's subscribers and viewers, it makes sense to broadcast using YouTube Live, which is tied directly to your YouTube channel.

YouTube Live allows you to stream (broadcast) live, directly from your YouTube channel. It provides a quick, free, and easy way to connect and communicate with your audience. As a broadcaster, YouTube Live offers a dashboard that includes tools that help you monitor your audience and view analytics in real time and host a text-based chat in conjunction with the live broadcast that allows viewers to connect with the host and hold conversations with each other.

By default, as soon as a YouTube Live broadcast comes to an end, the recorded broadcast is automatically published on your YouTube channel. As the channel operator, you have the option of first editing this content and adding post-production elements to it, if you desire.

Any YouTube channel operator can host a YouTube Live broadcast from their internet-connected computer, using tools offered by the YouTube service. If you're hosting a live *event* from your computer, there is no specialized software to download and install. However, to host a live *stream*, you'll need to download and install encoder streaming software onto your PC or Mac. To learn more about the difference between a live stream and a live event, and discover how to acquire the free encoded software that may be required, visit: https://support.google.com/youtube/answer/2907883.

At the time YouTube Live was introduced, it was also available via the official YouTube mobile app, allowing channel operators to host live broadcasts from a smartphone or tablet. However, initially, this mobile device functionality was offered only in certain geographic areas, with the promise it would be made available everywhere "within a few months." Thus, by the time you read this book, YouTube Live will likely be available from mobile devices, regardless of where you'll be broadcasting from.

One benefit to promoting a YouTube Live broadcast is that you can instruct people to simply visit your YouTube channel page, then click on the live broadcast option to view the broadcast at the appropriate time. Within their web browser, they can also enter your unique YouTube channel URL, followed by "/live," so they'd type: *www.youtube.com/[channelname]/live* for direct access to the live broadcast.

YouTube's Creator Academy offers specialized training videos and tutorials for using YouTube Live. To access this free content, visit: https://creatoracademy.youtube.com/page/course/livestream.

How to Activate YouTube Live on Your YouTube Channel

Before you're able to begin broadcasting live via your YouTube channel, the YouTube Live option must be activated. This needs to be done only once, from the Creator Studio

---

WATCH OTHER LIVE BROADCASTS FIRST

Before attempting to host your own live broadcasts, watch other live broadcasts using the service you plan to use to host your broadcasts. Pay attention to the length and flow of the live broadcast, how the host(s) interact with their viewers, and how a call of action is conveyed at various points during the broadcast. Focus also on the production elements used and overall quality of the broadcast. Figure out what works, what you could potentially do better, and what mistakes to avoid, based on your own target audience. Do your research and proper planning, and be sure to rehearse before each live broadcast. Then, if things do go wrong, be prepared to improvise.

dashboard (www.youtube.com/live_dashboard). From the "Go live. Any time. For any reason." screen, click on the "Get Started" button. To proceed, your YouTube channel needs to be verified and in good standing.

In the future, once the YouTube Live feature has been turned on, you can simply access the Creator Studio dashboard (www.youtube.com/live_dashboard), launch your encoder software, and click on the specified button to begin broadcasting. When you're done broadcasting, end the broadcast from the encoder software.

After a broadcast is over, the recorded video can be managed on your YouTube channel just like any recorded video content. Access the Creator Studio for your channel, select the "Video Manager" option, then choose the video file associated with the live broadcast. For example, you can make the video private or edit it a bit before making it available to your channel's viewers and subscribers on an on-demand basis.

Chapter 17

Using Product Placement in Videos as a Promotional Tool

One of the biggest challenges you'll have managing your YouTube channel is promoting your content on an ongoing basis and attracting an ever-growing audience. This can be a time-consuming and potentially costly endeavor, depending on which approaches you take. More grass-roots efforts, like using social media and public relations as promotional tools is free but takes time. Using paid online advertising is much faster but can get costly.

However, many companies have achieved success when it comes to creating an audience for their content by reaching out to established online influencers—people who are extremely active on social media, online personalities, bloggers, and YouTubers—and encouraging them to share details about their company, product/service, or YouTube content, in exchange for free products or payment.

"Influencer marketing" can take many forms and has become an extremely popular way for companies to tap the popularity of social media and YouTube, and reach vast audiences, without having to build their own viewers, subscribers, and/or followers. In fact, many independent companies have been launched that specialize in influencer marketing and match companies with online influencers who target to the same audience.

IDENTIFY ONLINE INFLUENCERS

As you're building your social media following and YouTube channel, it's easy to analyze your existing followers, viewers, and subscribers using free analytics tools and other fee-based, third-party resources to learn how many online friends, followers, viewers, or subscribers each has. Identify people following your company's social media accounts or

HOW TO CONTACT INFLUENCERS

Once you pinpoint potential influencers you want to work with, visit their YouTube channel page and click on the About button or read the descriptions of their videos. Within this content, you'll typically find a message that states, "For business inquires, email [insert email address]." Send the influencer an email outlining what you have in mind and what you're willing to offer in exchange for their assistance.

Another option after identifying a potential influencer is to determine if they have their own website with a "Contact Me" option, or if you're able to contact them using a direct (private) message through one of their social media accounts.

Just like professional actors, singers, dancers, and performers, more and more successful YouTubers and online personalities have agents, managers, and publicists. If you determine this is the case once you've identified someone you want to work with, you'll need to contact their representation to discuss any business opportunities.

In recent years, a handful of marketing agencies have launched that specialize exclusively in influencer marketing. These companies typically have established relationships with popular online personalities and YouTubers, and will help clients (companies like yours) pinpoint, contact, and work with well-established online influencers.

who are subscribed to your YouTube channel and who are highly active on social media. Identify people who have the biggest following. These are people to identify as influencers.

Using a bit of creativity and negotiation, reach out to these influencers and request that they share your YouTube videos, or post messages on their social media accounts that promote or endorse your company and/or its products/services. By doing this, you're generating word-of-mouth promotion using people who already have a large and dedicated following of people who fit into your target audience.

In exchange for these influencers helping you to promote your company, products/services, and/or YouTube content, offer them a reward, free products, or a financial incentive, based on the size of their following and what the influencer does to help you. Because most online influencers have their own loyal following, when they recommend or endorse something, a large percentage of people who follow them will pay attention.

If you want to take influencer marketing a step further, use a tool like Social Blade (www.socialblade.com) to find and identify well-established YouTubers, online personalities, bloggers, and others who are active on social media, and who are already successfully reaching a vast group of people who perfectly fit your target audience. Contact these influencers to discuss ways of working together to promote your company, products/services, and/or your YouTube channel.

WHAT INFLUENCERS CAN DO FOR YOUR COMPANY

Working with an online influencer or established YouTuber could potentially help your company in several ways. It can help you quickly enhance your reputation, build awareness for your brand, reach a broader audience, and generate traffic to your own YouTube channel, for example. What you ask an influencer to do could be as simple as watching several of your YouTube videos and clicking the "Share" button so their audience quickly learns about your channel. You could also devise more elaborate ways to work with these people, such as:

- Produce collaboration videos with them that you publish on your respective YouTube channels.
- Pay the influencer to mention your products using their social media accounts. This could include them publishing a link to your YouTube channel page or recommending one or more of your individual videos.
- Pay the influencer to showcase, demonstrate, discuss, and endorse your products in their online content. This is referred to as product placement.
- Sponsor one or more of the YouTuber's videos in exchange for a promotional announcement at the beginning or end of their video. This may or may not

include the YouTuber showing off your product. It could simply include the YouTuber saying something like, ". . . and special thanks to [insert your company name] for sponsoring this week's video. You should check out their website or YouTube channel to learn more about them."

How much you wind up having to pay an online influencer will vary greatly based on several factors, including the size of the audience they're reaching and what they agree to do to help you promote your company or content. For many of the more successful YouTubers, creating content for their channel is a full-time and lucrative job, and they're able to consistently achieve tens of thousands, hundreds of thousands, or even millions of views for each new video they produce and publish on their channel.

Companies have discovered that working with established YouTubers and online influencers can be extremely beneficial for several reasons. These people have large and very loyal followings. When an established YouTuber mentions or showcases a product/ service, they're making an endorsement, and that's much more powerful in the mind of a consumer than if a company used a traditional advertisement to convey a similar message, since you're taking advantage of the YouTuber's reputation and influence.

Plus, whatever you spend working with an online personality or YouTuber will likely be considerably less than running a traditional paid advertising campaign. As a company, you're also able to tap into the established audience of the online personality/ YouTuber, without having to establish that audience yourself. Thus, you're able to reach people in your target audience much faster, in a way that allows you to control the message.

WORK WITH AN AGENCY TO HELP YOU

Choosing which online personalities or YouTubers to work with, approaching and negotiating with them, then devising ways to work with them in a cost-effective way can be time-consuming. To shorten the learning curve and achieve faster results, consider working with an established marketing company that specializes in influencer marketing, or has established relationships with social media influencers and knows how to work with them to achieve the desired results for your company.

To find these agencies, use any search engine and enter the phrase, "Influencer Marketing," or research listings from YouTube's own Creators Services Directory (https://servicesdirectory.withyoutube.com). Influencer Marketing Hub (https:// influencermarketinghub.com) also offers online-based articles, tools, and resources to help you create, manage, and become successful with your influencer marketing efforts.

The following is a small sampling of influencer marketing companies:

- *Find Your Influence:* www.findyourinfluence.com/influencermarketing.aspx
- *Hello Society:* www.hellosociety.com
- *Mediakix:* www.mediakix.com
- *Rhythm Influence:* www.rhythminfluence.com
- *Viral Nation:* www.viralnation.com

If your primary focus is to work with YouTubers and promote your company's YouTube channel, it makes sense to work with an agency that not only understands how YouTube works and what motivates YouTubers, but that's owned by Google (which also owns and operates YouTube).

FameBit by YouTube (https://famebit.com) is an online-based agency that's sole purpose is to match established YouTubers with companies looking to leverage online influencers to help them promote and build their brand.

According to FameBit's website, content creators are this generation's storytellers, and they're able to tell stories about companies, brands, products, or services, for example, in a way nobody else can, while appealing to an audience that relies on the internet (not mainstream media) as their primary source of news and information. One thing many YouTubers with a vast audience have is a strong relationship with their dedicated viewers and subscribers. Their audience not only trusts them but looks to them for advice about products and services, as well as lifestyle-related issues.

FameBit believes finding the right content creators to work with is essential for a company. While some of its clients have a budget of $10,000 or more to spend on a campaign, others have just a few hundred dollars, but can still leverage the experience of FameBit when it comes to work finding and working with established online influencers.

First, your company would work with FameBit to develop a campaign concept and budget. The company then distributes your proposal to online influencers (YouTubers) who reach the same target audience. Individual content creators then contact you to share their ideas and discuss ways they can use their own content, reputation, and following to help you achieve your company's goals based on your budget. Once you agree to work with a specific content creator, you have final approval over their content that relates to your company, before it's shared with their audience in the time frame you choose.

As of mid-2017, FameBit has been instrumental in teaming up content creators and companies to create videos that have collectively earned more than 812 million views and three billion minutes of watch time.

How much you pay content creators and YouTubers to help you create and manage your campaign is negotiated between your company and the content creator. FameBit is paid a 10 percent service fee based on the total amount you spend per campaign.

LEARN ABOUT INFLUENCER MARKETING BY WATCHING VIDEOS

The founders of FameBit have created a free YouTube video that explains the ins and outs of influencer marketing. To view this informational video, visit: www.youtube.com/watch?v=B6N27uyiSto. YouTube's Creator Academy also offers an instructional video about influencer marketing, which you can find at: https://creatoracademy.youtube.com/page/lesson/best-practices. To find other instructional videos and tutorials, visit YouTube (www.youtube.com), and in the Search field, enter the term "influencer marketing" or "influencer marketing tips and tricks" to find hundreds of related videos, many of which are targeted to small-business operators and entrepreneurs.

However, if you want FameBit's experts to work hand-in-hand with your company to develop, launch, and manage your campaign, in addition to negotiating and working with your selected content creator(s), FameBit receives a 30 percent service fee based on the cost of the overall campaign. These service fees are paid after you've approved content for publishing online.

FINAL THOUGHTS . . .

Millions of business operators, just like you, have discovered creative ways to use YouTube to help them find new customers, better cater to existing customers, build their brand, and enhance their reputation. Even if you don't have a large budget, if you're willing to invest some time, you can still use original video content as powerful and highly targeted sales, promotional, advertising, marketing, and customer service tools.

One key to your success will be to tap your own creativity and the creativity of people on your team, to develop attention-getting, quality content that your viewers will appreciate and find valuable. Be sure to study what other YouTubers, online personalities, and business are doing, and figure out what will work best for your company.

Develop realistic goals, establish a detailed plan, and focus your content so it targets your audience. Then, once you create and publish content you're proud of, don't forget to continuously promote it so you're able to build a growing and loyal audience.

Other important concepts to remember are that YouTube is constantly evolving, the online habits of consumers are always changing, and technology (including the internet, as well as the cameras and equipment used for creating and editing digital video content) is becoming more advanced each day. Thus, it's necessary to stay on top of these evolutions and technological advancements and use them to your advantage when creating and promoting your YouTube channel and its content.

Within your time and budget constraints, determine what's possible, then use the tools and resources at your disposal to continuously create the highest-quality and best content you can in a way that caters to the wants, needs, and viewing habits of your target audience.

Consider YouTube and your video content creation to be a long-term endeavor. Unless you're willing to pay top dollar to promote your content through paid advertising, building an audience for your content and seeing the positive results it can generate could take weeks, months, or potentially years, depending on what goals you're trying to achieve. Be realistic when setting your goals, work consistently to achieve them, and be patient.

You'll no doubt discover that the internet, and YouTube specifically, offer tremendous potential, especially if you properly use the tools at your disposal, work hard, be consistent, and have realistic expectations. What's the next step? Visit YouTube (www.youtube.com), discover what's possible, then start doing further research about your target audience, while brainstorming ideas for compelling content.

Resources

CAMERA TRIPOD AND STEADICAM COMPANIES

- *Gitzo:* www.manwww.manfrotton.us/gitzofrotton.us/gitzo
- *Glidecam Industries:* www.glidecam.com
- *JAG35:* www.jag35.com
- *Joby:* www.joby.com
- *Libec:* www.libecsales.com
- *Manfrotto:* www.manfrotto.us
- *Redrock Micro:* http://store.redrockmicro.com
- *Slik:* https://slikusa.com
- *Tiffen Company:* www.tiffen.com
- *Vanguard:* www.vanguardworld.com

CLOUD-BASED SERVICES FOR STORING VIDEO CONTENT

- *Adobe Creative Cloud:* www.adobe.com/creativecloud.html
- *Apple iCloud Drive:* www.apple.com/icloud
- *Box:* www.box.com
- *Dropbox:* www.dropbox.com
- *Microsoft OneDrive:* www.onedrive.com

COMPUTER WEB BROWSERS

- *Firefox (PC/Mac):* www.mozilla.org/en-US/firefox/new
- *Google Chrome (PC/Mac):* www.google.com/chrome/
- *Microsoft Edge (PC):* www.microsoft.com/en-us/windows/microsoft-edge
- *Safari (Mac):* www.apple.com/safari

FREELANCER DIRECTORIES AND CASTING WEBSITES

- *Backstage:* www.backstage.com/casting
- *Model Mayham:* www.modelmayhem.com/casting/search_casting
- *Monster:* http://hiring.monster.com
- *ProductionHUB:* www.productionhub.com/casting-notices
- *SAG-AFTRA:* www.sagaftra.org/casting-notices
- *Upwork:* www.upwork.com

INFLUENCER MARKETING COMPANIES

- *FameBit by YouTube:* https://famebit.com
- *Find Your Influence:* www.findyourinfluence.com/influencermarketing.aspx
- *Hello Society:* www.hellosociety.com
- *Mediakix:* www.mediakix.com
- *Rhythm Influence:* www.rhythminfluence.com
- *Viral Nation:* www.viralnation.com

KEYWORD/SEARCH ADVERTISING PLATFORMS

- *Bing:* https://advertise.bingads.microsoft.com
- *Facebook:* www.facebook.com/business/products/ads
- *Google and YouTube:* www.google.com/intl/en/ads
- *Instagram:* https://business.instagram.com/advertising
- *Twitter:* https://ads.twitter.com
- *Yahoo!* https://advertising.yahoo.com

KEYWORD/SEARCH TERM GENERATION TOOLS

- *Google AdWords:* https://adwords.google.com/KeywordPlanner
- *Keyword Tool:* http://keywordtool.io/youtube
- *MOZ:* https://moz.com/mozpro/lander/keyword-research
- *Semrush:* https://landing.semrush.com/keyword-research-tool-3/usa.html

- *SEOBook:* http://tools.seobook.com/keyword-list/generator.php
- *WordStream:* www.wordstream.com/ad-text-generator

LIGHTING EQUIPMENT COMPANIES

- *Cowboy Studio:* www.cowboystudio.com/category_s/226.htm
- *K 5600 Lighting:* www.k5600.com
- *Kino Flo Lighting Systems:* www.kinoflo.com
- *Lowel:* www.lowel.com
- *Westcott:* http://fjwestcott.com
- *Studio 1 Productions:* www.studio1productions.com
- *UsedLighting.com:* www.usedlighting.com

MERCHANDISE MANUFACTURING AND DROPSHIP COMPANIES

- *CafePress:* www.cafepress.com
- *District Lines:* www.districtlines.com/youtube
- *Shortrunposters.com:* www.shortrunposters.com
- *Sticker Mule (Stickers and Buttons):* www.stickermule.com
- *TeeChip Custom T-Shirts:* https://teechip.com
- *UberPrints Custom T-Shirts:* www.uberprints.com
- *Zazzle:* www.zazzle.com

MUSIC LIBRARIES

- *AudioBlocks:* www.audioblocks.com
- *Getty Images Music:* www.gettyimages.com/music
- *Killer Tracks:* www.killertracks.com
- *Music for Productions:* www.musicforproductions.com
- *Premium Beat:* www.premiumbeat.com/production-music
- *Shutterstock Music:* www.shutterstock.com/music
- *Stockmusic.net:* www.stockmusic.net

ONLINE MARKETING AGENCIES AND ANALYTICS SERVICES

- *Adobe Advertising Cloud:* www.adobe.com/advertising-cloud.html
- *ChannelMeter:* www.channelmeter.com/analytics
- *Creative Market:* https://creativemarket.com/search?q=YouTube

- *Statfire:* www.statfire.com
- *Traackr.com:* www.traackr.com
- *VidStatsX:* http://vidstatsx.com

RESEARCH AND YOUTUBE EDUCATION-RELATED LINKS

- *Animoto:* https://animoto.com/blog/business/video-marketing-cheat-sheet-infographic
- *Google Business Solutions:* www.google.com/services
- *Library of Congress' Copyright Website:* www.copyright.gov or www.loc.gov/teachers/copyrightmystery
- *MWP (My Video Presenters Ltd.):* https://mwpdigitalmedia.com/blog/10-statistics-that-show-video-is-the-future-of-marketing
- *Social Blade:* www.socialblade.com
- *Social Pro Daily:* www.adweek.com/category/social-pro-daily
- *think with Google:* www.thinkwithgoogle.com/consumer-insights/video-trends-where-audience-watching
- *Video School Online:* www.youtube.com/user/VideoSchoolOnline

SOCIAL MEDIA AND LIVE BROADCASTING SERVICES

- *Facebook:* www.facebook.com
- *Facebook Business Pages:* www.facebook.com/business/products/pages
- *GoToMeeting:* www.gotomeeting.com
- *Instagram:* www.instagram.com
- *LinkedIn:* www.linkedin.com
- *Live.me:* www.live.me (www.twitch.tv)
- *LiveStream:* www.livestream.com
- *Periscope:* www.periscope.tv
- *Pinterest:* www.pinterest.com
- *Reddit:* www.reddit.com
- *Snapchat:* www.snapchat.com
- *Tumblr:* www.tumblr.com
- *Twitter:* www.twitter.com
- *YouNow:* www.younow.com

VIDEO-EDITING SOFTWARE AND VIDEO EQUIPMENT COMPANIES

- *Adobe's Premier Pro CC:* www.adobe.com/products/premiere.html

- *Adorama:* www.adorama.com/catalog.tpl?op=category&cat1=Used
- *Apple's iMovie:* www.apple.com/imovie
- *B&H Photo-Video:* www.bhphotovideo.com
- *Camtasia2:* www.techsmith.com/video-editor.html
- *Ezvid Video Editor:* www.ezvid.com
- *Final Cut Pro X:* www.apple.com/finalcutpro
- *Freemake Video Converter from Freemake.com:* www.freemake.com/free_video_converter
- *Full Compass:* www.fullcompass.com
- *GoPro:* www.gopro.com
- *Mevo camera:* https://getmevo.com
- *Movavi Video File Converter:* www.movavi.com/videoconverter
- *NewPro Video:* http://newprovideo.com
- *OneQuality.com:* www.onequality.com
- *OpenShot Video Editor:* www.openshot.org
- *WeVideo.com:* www.wevideo.com
- *Windows Movie Maker 12:* http://ccm.net/download/download-124-windows-movie-maker-12
- *Wondershare Filmora Video Editor:* www.wondershare.net/ad/video-editor-win

VOICE-OVER TALENT AGENCIES

- *Agent 99 Voice Talent:* www.agent99voicetalent.com
- *Internet Jock:* www.internetjock.com
- *Mood Media:* http://us.moodmedia.com/messaging-samples/voiceover-web-audio
- *Voice Talent:* www.voicetalent.com
- *Voice Talent Now:* http://store.voicetalentnow.com

YOUTUBE-RELATED LINKS

- *Google Account Management:* https://myaccount.google.com
- *YouTube:* www.youtube.com
- *YouTube Advertising:* www.youtube.com/yt/advertise
- *YouTube Channel Verification:* www.youtube.com/my_videos_upload_verify
- *YouTube Channels:* www.youtube.com/channels
- *YouTube Community Guidelines:* www.youtube.com/t/community_guidelines
- *YouTube Copyright Guidelines:* www.youtube.com/t/howto_copyright
- *YouTube Creative Commons Guidelines:* www.youtube.com/t/creative_commons
- *YouTube Creator Academy:* https://creatoracademy.youtube.com/page/education

- *YouTube Creator Hub:* www.youtube.com/yt/creators
- *YouTube Creator Services Directory:* https://servicesdirectory.withyoutube.com
- *YouTube Live Dashboard:* www.youtube.com/live_dashboard
- *YouTube Music Library:* www.youtube.com/audiolibrary/music
- *YouTube's Trending Video:* www.youtube.com/feed/trending

YOUTUBER TOUR PROMOTERS

- *DigiTour:* www.thedigitour.com
- *MAGCON:* www.magcontour.com
- *VidCon:* http://vidcon.com

About the Author

Jason R. Rich (http://JasonRich.com) is the author of more than 55 books, covering a wide range of topics, including ecommerce, online marketing, digital photography, social media, interactive entertainment, and crowd funding, as well as the Apple iPhone and iPad.

He's also a frequent contributor to numerous national magazines, major daily newspapers, and popular websites, and serves as a marketing/public relations consultant to businesses.

Some of his recently published books include: *Working in the Cloud* (Que), *Start Your Own Etsy Business* (Entrepreneur Press), *Start Your Own Travel Hosting Business* (Entrepreneur Press), *My Digital Entertainment for Seniors* (Que), *My Digital Travel for Seniors* (Que), and *iPad and iPhone Tips and Tricks, 7th Edition* (Que). You can follow Jason R. Rich on Twitter (@JasonRich7) or Instagram (@JasonRich7).

Index

A

about YouTube, x–xi, xii

action cameras, 103–104

Adobe Premiere Pro CC, 124–125, 132–133

advertising, 24, 173–174, 197–198, 211–215

AdWords, 213–215

AdWords Express, 214

analytics tools, 22, 48, 78, 185, 192–193, 205–208

animation, 31, 126, 140

Annotations, 167. *See also* Cards

Apple's Final Cut Pro X, 125, 133–134

Apple's iMovie, 129, 132–133

audience interaction, 20, 68, 171, 190–191, 195–201, 242–243

audience loyalty, 19, 20, 39, 195, 197

audiences. *See also* target audiences
   analytics tools and, 22, 48
   demographics, 2, 29–30, 191–192

growing, 148–149, 193, 197–200

reaching, x–xi, 15–24

target vs. actual, 192–193

viewers vs. subscribers, 191

augmented reality content, 42

Auto Fix button, 168

Avid video editing and production tools, 134–135

B

backdrops, 90, 111

background music, 45, 92–94, 139–140

backing up your work, 106, 136

batteries, 101–102

behind-the-scene videos, 20–21

blue screen use, 119

Blurring Effects tools, 169–170

brainstorming video ideas, 49–50, 143–146

branding, 73, 75–76, 120

broadcasting live. *See* live broadcasting

instructional videos, 17–18, 19–20, 40

interacting with audiences, 20, 68, 171, 190–191, 195–201, 242–243

interactive elements, 166–167

K

keyword relevance, 46, 70, 147, 159, 197, 208–209, 216

keyword tools, 209

keyword-based advertising, 198, 213–215

L

length of videos, 35, 45, 48, 77, 151

lifestyle videos, 41

lighting, 88–90, 111–114, 238

lighting adjustment tools, 168–169

liking videos, 68

LinkedIn, 233

live action video options, 42–43

live broadcasting, 238–247

    about, 23

    advantages, 238

    calls to action in, 241–242

    cameras for, 238–239

    high-speed internet for, 240

    hosting services for, 239–240

    lighting setup for, 238

    live interaction with audience in, 242–243

    planning, 241

    pre-broadcast considerations, 240–245

    pre-produced content in, 243

    promoting, 241, 244–245

    scheduling considerations, 244

    sound considerations, 238

    watching other live broadcasts, 246

    YouTube Live for, 43, 239, 245–247

locations, 111–112

loyalty, 19, 20, 39, 195, 197

M

marketing experts, 215–216

Marshall, Perry, 219–221

Mathews, Dustin, 149–152

measuring success, 203–204, 205–208

merchandise sales, 186–187

messaging, 6, 37, 116

metadata, 159–160

Mevo camera, 105, 239

microphones, 86, 90–91, 98–101, 102, 103, 113–114, 238

mobile friendly content, 4–5

mobile video editing, 125

monetizing YouTube, 173–187

music and sound effects, 45, 92–94, 126, 129–130, 139–140

N

niche audiences. *See* target audiences

O

objectives for your channel, 10, 30–31, 33–34, 39–41, 60–61, 141–142, 187, 200

online influencers, 250–254

online personalities, xi, 3, 4, 15–17, 23–24, 148–149, 186, 249–254

online synergy, 6–7

opinion-sharing videos, 17–18

organizing content, 41, 49, 76, 143–145, 199–200

out of sequence shoots, 115

P

paid advertising, 24

paid online-based ads, 174

paid product placement, 186

partnerships, 236

pay-per-click (PPC) advertising, 213

perceived value of content, 142–143

Photoshop Premiere Elements, 133

Pinterest, 233

Playlist Live events, 187

playlists, 199–200

point-and-shoot cameras, 98, 101